MEN'S LACROSSE

Don Zimmerman
Peter England

Human Kinetics

Library of Congress Cataloging-in-Publication Data

Zimmerman, Don, 1953-
  Men's lacrosse / Don Zimmerman and Peter England.
    pages cm
  Includes bibliographical references.
  1. Lacrosse. I. Title.
  GV989.Z55 2013
  796.34'7--dc23

                    2013001685

ISBN-10: 1-4504-1119-3 (print)
ISBN-13: 978-1-4504-1119-6 (print)

The web addresses cited in this text were current as of February 2013, unless otherwise noted.

Acquisitions Editor: Justin Klug; **Developmental Editor:** Laura Floch; **Assistant Editor:** Elizabeth Evans; **Copyeditor:** Pat Connolly; **Graphic Designer:** Nancy Rasmus; **Graphic Artist:** Tara Welsch; **Cover Designer:** Keith Blomberg; **Photograph (cover):** UMBC Athletics; **Photographs (interior):** © Human Kinetics; **Visual Production Assistant:** Joyce Brumfield; **Photo Production Manager:** Jason Allen; **Art Manager:** Kelly Hendren; **Associate Art Manager:** Alan L. Wilborn; **Illustrations:** © Human Kinetics; **Printer:** Versa Press

We thank the UMBC Stadium Complex in Catonsville, Maryland, for assistance in providing the location for the photo shoot for this book.

Human Kinetics books are available at special discounts for bulk purchase. Special editions or book excerpts can also be created to specification. For details, contact the Special Sales Manager at Human Kinetics.

Printed in the United States of America   10 9 8 7 6 5 4 3 2 1

The paper in this book is certified under a sustainable forestry program.

Human Kinetics
Website: www.HumanKinetics.com

United States: Human Kinetics
P.O. Box 5076
Champaign, IL 61825-5076
800-747-4457
e-mail: humank@hkusa.com

Canada: Human Kinetics
475 Devonshire Road Unit 100
Windsor, ON N8Y 2L5
800-465-7301 (in Canada only)
e-mail: info@hkcanada.com

Europe: Human Kinetics
107 Bradford Road
Stanningley
Leeds LS28 6AT, United Kingdom
+44 (0) 113 255 5665
e-mail: hk@hkeurope.com

Australia: Human Kinetics
57A Price Avenue
Lower Mitcham, South Australia 5062
08 8372 0999
e-mail: info@hkaustralia.com

New Zealand: Human Kinetics
P.O. Box 80
Torrens Park, South Australia 5062
0800 222 062
e-mail: info@hknewzealand.com

E5470

I would like to dedicate this book to my family and to all the players and coaches whom I have had the honor and privilege to work with during my involvement with the great game of lacrosse. Thanks to my co-author and friend, Peter England, for having the vision and dedication to put into words our collaborative thoughts and ideas.

Don Zimmerman

To my parents for all the obvious reasons: Everything I am, I am because of their efforts.

To my daughter, Mary, for attending countless lacrosse scouting games with me, for sharing the 2005 NCAA Lacrosse Championship experience, and for being a constant in my life. To my son, William, for playing lacrosse for all the right reasons—for the love of the game, for the brotherhood, and because you are a warrior at heart.

Peter England

CONTENTS

PART I

INDIVIDUAL SKILLS AND TECHNIQUES

PART II

TEAM PLAY

DRILL FINDER

Drill title	Page #	Number of players	Catching and passing	Decision-making	Face-off skills	Goal-keeper skills	Team attack	Team defense
CHAPTER 3 Player Stick Skills								
Balance Drill	29	1	X					
Feel Drill	30	2	X					
Control Drill	31	2	X					
Two-Step Throwing Drill	37	1	X					
Soft Hands Drill	41	2	X					
Two-Step Catching Drill	42	1	X					
Two-Step Cradling Drill	45	1	X					
Scooping Drill	49	1	X					
CHAPTER 4 Dodging, Feeding, and Shooting								
Five-Cone Dodging Drill	56	1		X			X	
Five-Cone Feeding Drill	66	2		X			X	
Two-Cone Shooting Drill	71	2		X			X	
Five-Cone Shooting on the Run Drill	74	1		X			X	

ACKNOWLEDGMENTS

Thanks to Taylor Marino for assistance with chapter 6 (Face-Offs) and to Rocco Vicchio for assistance with chapter 7 (Goalkeeping). We thank the members of the UMBC men's lacrosse team who modeled for the photographs for this book. Thanks to Mary England for typing and transcribing numerous interview sessions with the authors.

INTRODUCTION

Men's Lacrosse is written for men's lacrosse players and coaches from the junior high through college levels. It is designed to appeal to the novice player and coach as well as the more experienced player who wants to improve his overall game.

Chapter 1 introduces the game and includes the basics of the field, personal equipment, specific player positions, and penalties. Chapter 2 describes what makes a complete lacrosse player. Chapter 3 is an important chapter on the game's stick fundamentals and represents the heart of the book. Chapters 4 and 5 address the offensive skills of dodging, feeding, shooting, cutting, picking, and ball exchange. Chapters 6 and 7 represent the two specialty skills of lacrosse: the face-off and goalkeeping. Chapters 8 and 9 address defensive skills such as proper athletic stance, footwork, body and stick checking, and defending dodgers, cutters, picks, ball exchanges, and plays on the crease. Chapters 10 and 11 deal with team offense and team defense, respectively. Chapters 12 and 13 explain the intricacies of both transition offense and transition defense.

Men's Lacrosse is organized in this manner to honor the traditions of lacrosse's rich past and to reflect the tremendous growth of the sport in the last 15 to 20 years. Many things have changed in this sport. The equipment has produced a game that is both faster and safer. More than anything else, the evolution of the lacrosse stick has created changes in the game. The plastic sticks have produced greater overall stick work, easier replacement of damaged sticks, and lighter yet stronger sticks. In addition, these sticks have deeper pockets that allow novice players to pick up the stick fundamentals in a shorter period of time.

Athletes in general seem to be getting stronger, faster, and quicker; and this applies to the world of lacrosse. However, many things remain the same. Solid stick fundamentals are still the key to success in this sport. Many times lacrosse boils down to a player-on-player matchup, and individual offensive and defensive skills dictate the outcome. Overall offensive and defensive strategies have evolved, but many constants are still evident in the game. In a game that shares much with soccer, basketball, football, and hockey, a player must understand these general principles in order to play the game better. This book describes and explains those individual and team fundamentals that make up the great sport of lacrosse.

Grantland Rice, the famous American sportswriter, once wrote, "Once in a while they argue about the fastest game—hockey or basketball; then about the roughest game—boxing or football or water polo. But when it comes to the top combination the answer is lacrosse, the all-star combination of speed and body contact. It requires more skill than any other game that I know." *Men's Lacrosse* is a tribute to lacrosse's rich past and its golden future.

KEY TO DIAGRAMS

Player with the ball

Offensive player

Defensive player

Goal

Offense player path

Ball path

Defense player path

PART I

INDIVIDUAL SKILLS AND TECHNIQUES

Part I of *Men's Lacrosse* provides a solid background so that novice players will advance to overall team play. Chapter 1 introduces the sport of lacrosse and addresses the basics of the game: the field, ball, equipment, and both technical and personal fouls. Chapter 2 focuses on the whole-person approach and the mental, behavioral, and physical attributes of a complete lacrosse player. Chapter 3 looks at the proper grip and wrist position, the two primary stick positions, and the four fundamental stick skills: throwing, catching, cradling, and scooping. Chapter 4 examines the on-ball offensive skills of dodging, feeding, and shooting. Chapter 5 concentrates on off-ball offensive skills such as cutting, setting and using picks, ball exchange, and proper off-ball movement. Chapter 6 covers the special skills of a face-off specialist and the support of his wing players. Chapter 7 tackles the subject of goalkeeping. Both face-off specialists and goalkeepers have a large impact on the outcome of a game. Chapter 8 addresses on-ball defensive skills with proper body and stick positioning. Chapter 9 reviews defending cuts, picks, and ball exchange.

CHAPTER ONE

THE SPORT OF LACROSSE

Lacrosse originated among the Native Americans of North America. According to lacrosse historians Weyand and Roberts, "Some type of lacrosse was played by at least 48 tribes scattered throughout southern Canada and all parts of the United States except the extreme southwest" (1965). Native Americans played the game for recreation, military training, and religious purposes. They also played it to settle disputes. From its ancient roots, lacrosse has evolved into one of the most popular team sports in the United States. The following events helped the sport reach this level of popularity:

- Technological advances that led to wooden sticks being replaced by plastic stick heads in the early 1970s and a variety of interchangeable composite handles
- Implementation of the NCAA Tournament in 1971, allowing the collegiate champion to be determined by a playoff system instead of a coaches' poll
- Introduction of a Final Four format in 1986, showcasing the best collegiate talent in the country
- Spread of NCAA championships to nontraditional powers such as North Carolina, Syracuse, and Princeton during the 1980s and 1990s
- Explosive growth of the college game and Major League Lacrosse due to media exposure by ESPN and the Internet
- Increased participation in the game worldwide—with 25 full members and 19 associate members participating in the Federation of International Lacrosse

The popularity of lacrosse is evident throughout the sports landscape, and it has grown at all levels of the game. In 2011, there were over 390,000 male players participating in lacrosse at the youth and high school level. In 2011, 230,000 boys were playing youth lacrosse. Since 2001, the annual growth rate of youth lacrosse has been 11.3 percent. In 2011, 162,000 boys were playing high school lacrosse at an annual growth rate of 8.0 percent. Forty states have organized high school lacrosse programs, and 21 states have formally sanctioned or recognized lacrosse as a team sport. The National Federation of High Schools reports that there are 2,192 high schools sponsoring lacrosse programs and that boys' lacrosse has the highest growth rate of any sport since 2006 (57.1 percent) (U.S. Lacrosse 2011).

To appreciate the "fastest game on two feet," you first have to understand the layout of the field, the equipment needed to ensure safe play, and the set of rules that regulate the flow of the game.

Lacrosse Basics: Field, Goals, and Ball

The lacrosse field is in the shape of a rectangle 110 yards long and 60 yards wide (see figure 1.1). The field is roughly the size of a football or soccer field. The boundary lines are called sidelines and end lines. The field is divided in half by a 4-inch-wide centerline. A 4-inch square is placed at the midpoint of the centerline. The lacrosse face-off occurs at this midpoint. On either side of the midpoint of the centerline are wing lines that run parallel to the sideline. The wing lines are 20 yards from the midpoint of the centerline, and they are 20 yards in total length—they extend 10 yards on either side of the centerline. The territory between the wing lines and the sidelines is called the wing area.

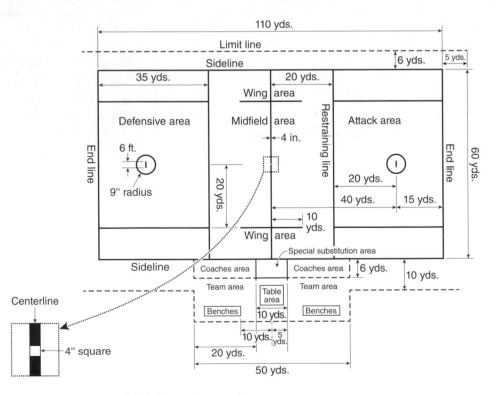

FIGURE 1.1 Lacrosse field dimensions and areas.

At each end of the field is a 6-by-6-foot goal. These goals are 80 yards apart and 15 yards from their respective end lines. A 40-by-35-yard box surrounds each goal, and this territory is called the attack area. There is 15 yards of playing territory behind each goal. This feature is similar to ice hockey, but there is much more playing area behind a lacrosse goal than behind a hockey net. A circular line with a 3-yard radius surrounds each goal; this line marks the goal crease. The territory within the goal crease is called the goal crease area. The goal is centered at the midpoint of the goal crease, facing the centerline. The goal consists of two vertical pipes joined at the top by a horizontal crossbar. The vertical pipes are 6 feet apart (measured from the inside edge of the pipes), and the bottom of the horizontal crossbar is 6 feet from the playing surface. The goal has a weighted triangular base, and a net is attached to the back of the goal. The goal line is marked between the two vertical pipes. The rear edge of the goal line represents the imaginary plane of the goal mouth. A goal is scored when the ball completely passes through this imaginary plane.

A lacrosse ball, as shown in figure 1.2, is a solid rubber ball. It is 7 3/4 to 8 inches in circumference and weighs 5 to 5 1/2 ounces. It is similar in size to a tennis ball and the weight and hardness of a baseball.

To meet official standards, the ball must bounce 43 to 51 inches (109 to 130 cm) off a concrete floor when dropped from a height of 6 feet (183 cm). The lacrosse ball comes in many colors, including the traditional white.

FIGURE 1.2   Lacrosse ball (left) compared to tennis ball.

Equipment

Lacrosse equipment is designed to protect the player in all aspects of the game. Most of the equipment is light and flexible and does not impede the movement of the player. Required equipment includes a helmet (with face mask and chin strap), a mouthpiece, shoulder pads, arm pads, gloves, and some type of footgear.

Helmet

Lacrosse helmets are similar to football helmets but are lighter in weight. Manufacturers include Cascade, Brine-Warrior, and Easton. The Cascade helmet was originally made for white-water rafting. It was adapted to lacrosse with the addition of a visor and face mask. Helmets come in various sizes and styles, but they are all designed to protect the head from the stick and to prevent concussions. A player's helmet needs to be the right size and fit. Most helmets have a padding system that allows pads to be added for a more custom fit. A four-point chin strap secures the helmet to the player's chin. Players must also use a mouth guard to protect the upper jaw. For example, Defender makes a customized mouth guard. Having a properly fitted mouth guard maximizes protection and also makes communication easier. The helmet must not be used to make contact. Spearing is a personal foul.

Shoulder Pads

Shoulder pads are much lighter than football shoulder pads because players don't tackle in lacrosse. Shoulder impact occurs in lacrosse, but it's not the same as in football. In football, players experience shoulder impact on every play. In lacrosse, players make this type of contact only when necessary and when an opportunity presents itself. Shoulder pads are worn to protect the collarbone or clavicle. College players often prefer a lighter, less bulky type of shoulder pad. Many shoulder pads are available that can be customized by removing the shoulder cuff.

Arm Pads

Players wear arm pads or elbow pads to protect their arms from stick checks. Attackmen wear the most padding because they have to absorb the most stick checks. Attackmen wear arm pads to protect the upper arm in between the shoulder and the elbow. Midfielders wear less protective padding because their play involves a combination of both offensive and defensive skills. Some players, especially defensemen, will substitute elbow pads for arm pads.

Gloves

Gloves are mandatory for all players. Lacrosse gloves are designed for protection, comfort, and feel of the stick. Numerous styles are offered by manufacturers such as STX, Under Armour, and Warrior-Brine. The goalkeeper's glove is different because it provides more protection around the thumbs. The most common injury for a goalie is a broken thumb.

Also, by rule, players can't cut out the fingers or palms of the glove in order to get a better feel for the stick (there can be no direct skin contact on the handle of the stick).

Footgear

Many brands of footgear are available. When playing on traditional Astroturf, most players wear a flat-bottom shoe such as a cross-trainer, turf shoe, or sneaker. At the college level, very few schools have the old-style Astroturf fields. For natural grass surfaces, players can wear screw-in football cleats or molded-bottom footgear. Today, most players wear molded-bottom shoes for both natural grass and contemporary turf fields. Players also have a choice between a heavier shoe (like a football shoe) or a lighter shoe (like a soccer shoe).

Stick

The lacrosse stick is the primary piece of personal equipment—it is what separates lacrosse from other sports. Historically, lacrosse sticks were constructed from wood and were handmade by Native Americans. In the 1970s, companies created synthetic plastic stick heads with a separate wood or metallic handle. The plastic lacrosse stick, as shown in figure 1.3, revolutionized the game of lacrosse. This stick provided many improvements. The stick head and shaft were lighter in weight and thereby easier to handle. The plastic stick was uniform in design and better balanced than the wooden sticks. The plastic stick could be repaired faster because of the interchangeable stick heads and shafts. The netting of the stick head was made with traditional leather or synthetic mesh. Players could form the pocket of the stick faster, allowing

FIGURE 1.3 Lacrosse sticks: goalkeeper's (left), defensive (middle), attack (right).

a novice to pick up the fundamentals of throwing and catching quicker than with a wooden stick with a rubber cap. The contemporary lacrosse stick is made up of a stick head and a stick handle.

Current stick heads come in two basic shapes and sizes. The inside measurement of a field player's stick head is 6 by 10 inches at its widest point. The inside measurement of a goalie's stick head is 10 by 12 inches at its widest point. Various manufacturers such as STX, Under Amour, Brine-Warrior, and Harlow provide a wide assortment of models. Some stick heads are more flexible than others. Some stick heads are of a traditional shape, while others have an offset style. The offset style is designed to carry the ball more securely. The stick handle is the other major component of the lacrosse stick. Today's lacrosse stick comes in several different lengths depending on the length of the handle:

- The attack or midfield stick (short stick) is 40 to 42 inches in total length.
- The defensive stick (long stick) is 52 to 72 inches long.
- The goalkeeper's stick is 40 to 72 inches long.

Handles are made of various metal composites to provide strength and lightness. The choice of stick head and handle is all a matter of individual preference.

Goalie Equipment

Goalies are required to wear a throat protector and a chest pad. Goalies are not required to wear shoulder or arm pads. They may substitute elbow pads. Most goalkeepers wear sweatpants to protect their legs from shots rather than wear athletic shorts, but this is a matter of personal preference. Most goalies think that less is better. They want to be able to move freely both inside the goal (to stop a shot) and outside the goal (to be an additional outlet when their team is moving the ball from the defensive end to the offensive end of the field, which is called clearing).

Optional Equipment

Optional equipment includes rib pads, elbow pads, an athletic supporter, and a cup. A cup is highly recommended for any player who may be standing in harm's way (i.e., in front of a goal) when a shot is taken. Obviously, this includes a goalie. It also includes any defenseman or crease attackman who spends the majority of his time near the crease.

Players

Lacrosse is a game played by two teams of 10 players each. Each team is made up of 3 attackmen, 3 midfielders, 3 defensemen, and 1 goalie. Collectively, the 3 attackmen are called the "close attack," and the 3 defensemen are called the "close defense." The close attack spends the bulk of their time in the offensive half of the field, playing near their opponent's goal and trying to score goals. The 3 midfielders operate at both ends of the field, playing both offense and defense. The close defense spends the bulk of their time in the defensive half of the field, playing near their own goal and trying to prevent goals. The goalie operates mostly in or near his goal crease area, stopping shots, leading clears (i.e., plays for clearing the ball from the defensive end), and quarterbacking the team defense. The goalie is not required to stay within the goal crease area, but he does have special privileges within its boundaries.

Substitutes play a major role in the game of lacrosse. Lacrosse is a physically demanding sport, and most players need a break from the action to hydrate with fluids and to take a breather. In lacrosse, substitutions can occur on the fly (like in hockey) or after play has been suspended by an official's whistle. When exchanging on the fly, players move through the special substitution area located on the bench side of the field. The special substitution area is 20 yards in length, situated in front of the scorer's table and bisected by the centerline. Substitution is essential for midfielders because they are responsible for running up and down the length of the field. The midfielder position also involves more specialization. Most teams have multiple specialized offensive and defensive midfield units. The rules of lacrosse restrict each team to four defensive length sticks on the field at any one time. For most teams, three of their defensive sticks are used by the close defense, and the fourth defensive stick is used by a defensive midfielder (also called the long-stick midfielder).

Play of the Game

College lacrosse games are 60 minutes in length and are divided into four quarters. High school games generally have 12-minute quarters. A halftime intermission takes place between the second and third quarters. If a game is tied after regulation play, the teams will play four-minute intervals until someone scores a goal.

To start the beginning of each quarter or after a goal has been scored, the teams position themselves in a face-off alignment (see figure 1.4). The face-off is similar to the one in hockey, but in lacrosse, it doesn't initially involve all the field players. The face-off revolves around the actions of the midfielders. The three midfielders position themselves in the middle of the field (midfield area). One midfielder aligns himself behind a wing line, and another midfielder positions himself behind the wing line on the opposite side of the field. The face-off midfielder stands at the midpoint of the centerline with his stick in the right-hand position. The official places the ball on a four-inch square at the midpoint of the centerline. The face-off midfielder positions himself on his defensive half of the centerline, and he faces his opponent's goal. The official commands "Down." The opposing face-off midfielders simultaneously crouch down and put their sticks on the ground in the following manner:

- The stick is parallel and adjacent to the centerline.
- The stick head is perpendicular to the playing surface.
- The back of the stick head is facing the opponent's goal.

The two opposing face-off midfielders have their sticks "back to back" but not touching; the ball rests on the ground between the opposing stick heads. The

FIGURE 1.4 Face-off alignment.

official commands "Set," and the face-off midfielders must remain motionless. The official blows the whistle, and the opposing face-off midfielders compete for possession of the ball. On the same whistle, all the opposing wing midfielders are released from their wing areas and also contend for the ball. During this battle for possession of the ball, the close attack and the close defense and goalie must stay behind their restraining lines until one of the following conditions occur:

- The official signals that a player has gained possession of the ball.
- The ball crosses either restraining line.
- The ball goes out of bounds.

After the face-off, the objective of each team is to gain possession of the ball and move it toward their opponent's goal. Players advance the ball by passing it to a teammate or carrying it by cradling. Many times during the game, the ball will fall to the ground, and players on each team will try to scoop the ball into their stick to gain possession. These are known as ground balls and are considered vital to a team's success. The ball can be kicked or batted by the stick, but it cannot be touched with the gloved hand except under certain circumstances. Ultimately, the objective of lacrosse is to score a goal. A goal is scored when a loose ball completely passes through the imaginary plane of the opponent's goal.

Rules

Lacrosse has several rules that are unique to the game of lacrosse, including rules related to a shot going out of bounds, to checking within five yards of a loose ball, and to activity in the goal crease area. Another one of these unique rules is the offside rule. As mentioned previously, the lacrosse field is divided in half by the centerline. The offensive half of the field extends from the centerline to the end line behind the opponent's goal. The defensive half runs from the centerline to the end line behind your own goal. At any given moment, each team must have four players in their defensive half and three players in their offensive half of the field. This usually means that the goalie and the close defense stay within the defensive half of the field, and the close attack remains in the offensive half. However, attackmen and defensemen can cross the centerline as long as another teammate remains onside for them, satisfying the number requirement. The purpose of the offside rule is to open things up and encourage more player and ball movement around each goal.

Another unique feature of lacrosse is the rule for when a shot goes out of bounds. In all team sports, if a ball goes out of bounds, the team that touched it last loses possession. This rule applies to lacrosse except when a player takes a shot. In this case, possession is given to the player closest to the ball at the point that it crosses the boundary line (end line or sideline). The purpose of this rule is to encourage teams to shoot on goal without fear of losing possession because of an errant or deflected shot. The third unique rule is the five-yard rule. Whenever a ball is loose on the ground, anyone within a five-yard radius of the ball can legally stick-check or body-check an opponent. The body check cannot be from the rear, at or below the waist, or above the shoulders.

If a ball is in flight and within five yards of a player, then anyone can stick check that opponent. In addition, several unique rules apply to the goal crease area:

- The goalkeeper can bat the ball with his hands while in his own goal crease area.
- No offensive player may step into the opponent's goal crease area.
- No defensive player may enter his own goal crease area with possession of the ball.
- Opponents cannot make any contact with the goalie while he is in his own goal crease area.

Fouls and Penalties

The game of lacrosse involves physical contact and collisions. All team sports have officials to referee the action and control the flow of the game. In lacrosse, certain actions are not permitted and are classified as technical, personal, or expulsion fouls. If a player amasses a total of five minutes of penalty time, he is removed from the game. The penalty for a foul typically ranges from a loss of possession to spending 30 to 60 seconds off the playing field and in a penalty box. As in ice hockey, the penalty box is bisected by the centerline. The offending team must keep a player in the penalty box until the timekeeper releases him or the fouled team scores a goal. If the player commits a severe foul (unsportsmanlike conduct), then he will be required to serve the full time of the foul. Like ice hockey, lacrosse uses a "slow whistle" technique. If a player with possession of the ball is fouled anywhere on the field, the official will throw a flag and allow play to continue. Play continues until the ball goes out of bounds, the defensive team gains possession, or a goal is scored.

Technical fouls are minor fouls. If neither team has possession of the ball or if the offending team has possession of the ball, then the fouled team is awarded possession. If the fouled team has possession, then the offending team must serve a 30-second penalty. Table 1.1 lists the technical fouls in lacrosse.

Personal fouls are major fouls. The penalty can be 1 to 3 minutes in the penalty box (1 minute is the norm). Table 1.2 lists personal fouls.

Lacrosse is a sport born from the Native American tribes of North America. At all levels of the game, the sport has evolved and grown, especially in the United States. This chapter has covered the basics of the game of lacrosse, including the field, the goal, and the ball. It also covered the equipment, the player positions, the general play of the game, and the face-off. Lastly, the various technical and personal fouls were explained. These rules are enforced by referees to ensure the safety and continuous flow of the game.

Table 1.1 Technical Fouls in Lacrosse

Withholding the ball from play	You can't lie on the ball on the ground; in addition, you can't trap the ball on the ground with your stick for a time period longer than is necessary to control and pick up the ball in one continuous motion.
Warding off	You can't use your free arm or hand to hold, push, or control the direction of movement of the stick or body of an opponent applying a check. You can absorb an opponent's check with your free hand; however, at the moment of stick-to-arm contact, your arm must remain motionless.
Pushing	A *push* is defined as exerting pressure after contact; this cannot be a shove, thrust, or blow. If an opponent has possession of the ball or is within 5 yards of a loose ball, then you can push him from the front or side but not from the rear. You can execute a legal push or hold using either closed hand, forearm, or shoulder while both of your hands are on the stick. To execute a legal push or hold from the side, your helmet and stick must be in front of the opponent's shoulder.
Holding	A *hold* is defined as impeding the movement of an opponent or his stick. If an opponent has possession of the ball or is within 5 yards of a loose ball, you may control him from the front or side. If an opponent has possession of the ball, then you can control him from the rear with your body as long as you exert "equal pressure" (you may match your opponent's force but not shove him). You can't hold an opponent by using the exposed handle between your gloved hands (called a cross-check hold).
Interference	If an opponent has possession of the ball or is within 5 yards of a loose ball or ball in flight, then you can interfere with the opponent's free movement on the field. In other circumstances, such interference may be called a foul.
Offside	To avoid an offside call, a team must always have four players in their defensive half of the field and three players in their offensive half of the field.
Illegal offensive screen	An offensive player can set a legal screen or pick as long as he is motionless at contact. If the player is moving, he will be called for an illegal screen.
Stalling	It is the responsibility of the team in possession of the ball to try and create a scoring opportunity
Touching the ball	You can touch the ball with your gloved hand as long as the hand is closed and remains on the handle.
Illegal action with a stick	Throwing a stick or playing without a stick is considered an illegal action.
Crease violations	Offensive players are not permitted to step in the crease including the crease circle; any interference with the goalkeeper of a technical nature while the ball is in his possession outside of the crease; any crease violation by an attacking player while the ball is in the crease; any crease violation or interference with the goalkeeper while he and the ball are in the crease.

Illegal procedure	Any action on the part of players or substitutes of a technical nature that is not in conformity with the rules and regulations governing the play of the game.
Substitution violations	Substitutions may take place without the necessity of waiting for suspension of play by an official under the following conditions: Substitute must be properly equipped; player may not enter substitution area until his substitution is imminent; player leaving the field must exit via the substitution area; substitute must wait until such player is off the field of play; substitute must always yield his position in the substitution area to any player exiting the field.
Delay of game	Any actions, either team or individual, that alter the normal pace of the play of the game.

TABLE 1.2 Personal Fouls in Lacrosse

Slashing	You can't swing your stick with deliberate viciousness or reckless abandon at an opponent with or without the ball. Also, you can't use your stick to strike an opponent above the shoulder, on the chest, on the back, or on the shoulders except when done in the act of shooting, passing, or scooping.
Cross-checking	You can't use the exposed handle of your stick between your two gloved hands to stick-check an opponent by thrusting it toward him.
Illegal body checking	You can't body-check an opponent from the rear, at or below the waist, or above the shoulder.
Tripping	You can't obstruct an opponent at or below the waist with your stick or body.
Unnecessary roughness	Any deliberate and excessively violent stick or body contact on a hold, push, or screen may be ruled unnecessary roughness.
Unsportsmanlike conduct	A foul may be called for any action considered unsportsmanlike by the official (e.g., threatening or profane language or gestures; baiting or taunting an opponent; arguing with an official; deliberately using your open hand or fingers to play the ball).
Illegal crosse or equipment	This consists of using an illegal pocket in your stick, such as a pocket that is too deep. To test for this, you can place a ball in the pocket of your stick and bring the stick head up to eye level; if the top of the ball can be seen below the bottom of the sidewall, then the pocket is too deep.
Expulsion foul	This is called for fighting or flagrant behavior.

CHAPTER TWO

PLAYER CHARACTERISTICS

The complete lacrosse player is made up of a combination of physical and psychological components. The psychological components include intelligence and passion. In addition, traits such as integrity, discipline, and confidence are crucial attributes of a successful player's personality. Integrity reflects the player's character, discipline reflects his commitment, and confidence comes from his hard work. Lacrosse IQ separates the best players from the good players, while passion and effort are variables that any coach finds desirable. The physical characteristics of coordination, balance, and overall athleticism are vital in any team field sport. Besides individual skills, players also need to develop team skills. These team skills include unselfishness, understanding your role, coachability, consistency, the ability to handle adversity, and a competitive spirit and desire to win. In addition, certain team skills are required in order to understand the nature of the game.

Integrity

Personal integrity is important in any walk of life. Integrity includes honesty, sincerity, and responsibility for one's actions. People with integrity do the right thing based on sound moral values. Coaches are always looking for players with integrity. What you say should be honest but not hurtful to your coach or teammates. For example, if a teammate asks for your opinion about his lacrosse skills, you want to be truthful and constructive with your remarks. Because your teammate trusted you enough to ask for your opinion, you should be willing to help his game, sharing your knowledge with him. Doing the right thing isn't always easy or popular, but it's the core of integrity. Character has been described as doing the right thing when no one else is around. As John Wooden said, "Ability may get you to the top, but it takes character to keep you there." On an individual level, if you are competing with a teammate for a starting spot and the coaching staff chooses your teammate over you, the right thing to do is sincerely encourage your teammate during practices and games and be prepared to step in to the spot if needed. On a team level, integrity is linked to leadership. If one person can step forward, do the right thing, and lead in a positive direction, then there is a good chance that the team will follow. You need to be responsible and accountable for your own actions. Don't be quick to point a finger of blame at your teammates. Be sure to do what you say and "walk the talk." Remember, when you are a member of a team, you are not responsible solely for yourself. You represent your teammates as well as yourself, so your personal integrity has an effect on teammates and the entire program. In addition, as a member of a team, you must be able to get along with others, and integrity helps you display acceptance and tolerance of others.

Discipline

Discipline has an individual and team component. Players need individual discipline in order to develop self-control through persistence and hard work. Individual discipline leads to behavior that produces mental or physical improvements. It helps you develop the ability to motivate yourself under stressful conditions. Individual discipline means that you train hard and keep your body in top physical shape. As you progress through the sport, proper nutrition, sleep, and rest become a factor. Through discipline, you take on this attitude: "I am going to do the things that help me reach my potential and help this team reach its potential." Some individual sacrifices are involved here, but you should keep in mind that it's a privilege to be able to play this game and it's certainly a privilege to be a member of a team. Team discipline involves requiring all team members to obey certain rules and regulations and using concrete consequences to correct unwanted behavior. If your team has certain team rules and regulations, you have to play by those rules. If you don't play by those rules, whether it be on the field or off the field, then you are not only hurting yourself but also hurting your teammates. The bottom line is that discipline creates an atmosphere that promotes making good decisions. You have to make good decisions on and off the field. Lacrosse is an avenue through which young people can learn how to make good decisions. And they can carry that knowledge with them throughout their lives—long after they hang up their sticks.

Confidence

Successful athletes usually have confidence in their own ability to get the job done. An optimistic attitude goes a long way on an athletic field. Lou Holtz once said, "Ability is what you are capable of doing. Motivation determines what you do. Attitude determines how well you do it." Confidence has to be earned, and this is done through hard work and extra practice. With a lacrosse ball and stick, players have the ability to go out on their own and practice outside of the scheduled practices. Dedicated players have the passion and desire to do the extra work. If one player earns confidence, this is often contagious. And if numerous players have gained confidence through hard work and dedication—and they display that confidence out on the field—this will spread and have a positive effect on the entire team. The synergy of team confidence is the result of passion and desire.

Passion

Successful athletes exhibit a passion, desire, and love for their sport. These athletes typically have a strong drive for self-improvement. They make a personal commitment to themselves and to their team, and they exhibit personal pride in their efforts. Vince Lombardi said, "The difference between a successful person and others is not a lack of strength, not a lack of knowledge, but rather a lack of will." Successful athletes exert maximum effort on the field. As Dave Urick, Georgetown lacrosse coach, has said, "You don't have to be a great player to hustle on the field, but all great players hustle."

When a player has passion, he is willing to work even harder off the field in activities such as weightlifting, stretching, and cardiovascular conditioning. Lacrosse, like many sports, requires a year-round commitment to improving one's skills and abilities. One way to improve is to play other sports throughout the year. By playing other sports, you will experience two positive side effects. First, you will gain a better understanding of what competition is—no matter what the sport. Second, because lacrosse is a "hybrid" sport, many elements from other sports (such as football, basketball, soccer, and hockey) are transferable to lacrosse. The most transferable skill from other sports is field sense—being at the right spot at the right time. This skill is related to improving your lacrosse intelligence.

Intelligence

Lacrosse players need to be intelligent, sharp, and savvy. They need to know and understand the game. The better you understand the game (i.e., the higher your lacrosse IQ), the better you will become at anticipating the next play. In any sport, athletes who can anticipate the next play have a distinct advantage. The ability to anticipate increases an athlete's chances of being at the right spot at the right time. That comes from studying, experiencing, and playing the game. In addition to practicing and playing the game, you should go out and watch college games. Watch those athletes playing at a higher level of competition. Identify players whom you would like to imitate or traits that you would like to adopt into your own game. In game situations, you should use your lacrosse IQ to be mentally focused, watchful, and attentive to the action. You need to be creative, imaginative, and open minded. You must be capable of calm and rational thought and have the ability to make many quick decisions during the course of a game.

Athleticism

The physical side of lacrosse is very important. Athletic skills such as quickness, speed, and agility can help make any player successful. Numerous training drills are designed to improve these three athletic skills. In particular, the element of speed is important. Like many other sports, as you progress to higher levels of competition, the speed of the game increases. From junior leagues to the MLL, speed rules. The tools that will help improve athleticism include weight training, running, flexibility training, and overall nutrition. Physical strength is improved with core work, weight training, and muscle-building exercises. At the collegiate level, year-round weight training is a given. Lacrosse is a game of ball movement and running, so physical endurance and stamina are critical components for players. Running should include running for speed and running for distance (to improve cardiovascular endurance). To help players improve flexibility, yoga is being incorporated into a lot of collegiate programs. Lastly, proper nutrition is very important for staying healthy and keeping the body functioning.

Size

In lacrosse, physical size can be an advantage, but it is not as important as in other sports such as football or basketball. Many of the best lacrosse players have average height and weight. However, with everything else being equal, a bigger player will have some advantage over a smaller player. For example, if you are a tall crease attackman, you will be a bigger target, and your teammates will be able to throw passes to spots where only you can get the ball (i.e., where other players cannot reach). If you are a tall defenseman, you will have greater range when covering passing lanes, such as skip lanes. You will also have a greater reach for applying a poke check or over-the-head check. If you are a taller player, you may have a longer stride that enables you to cover more ground, but the biggest advantage of size is having a greater reach. As a lacrosse player, you must be honest in your self-evaluation and then gear your game to your strengths. If you are small, you can focus on being quick and perhaps being a smarter player. If you are big, you should learn to use your body to your advantage. Every player has both strengths and weaknesses. You must take advantage of and build on your strengths while working to improve your weaknesses. In the game of lacrosse, there is plenty of room for players of all sizes, even at the highest levels of competition.

Coordination and Balance

Coordination is the skillful and balanced movement of various parts of the body at the same time. In many sports, you have to coordinate a piece of equipment with your body. In soccer, you have your feet and the ball. In lacrosse, you throw in an added factor: the lacrosse stick. Eye–hand coordination is very important for all positions. Goalkeepers must have very quick hands and feet because they have to react to 90 mph shots at the college level. Reaction time for a goalie must be quicker than the reaction time for a field player. A face-off specialist must have really quick hands and must be able to maneuver from a low position. This player must have a very low center of gravity and must stay balanced. Balance is a key component of any athletic endeavor. The basic athletic stance is the starting point in all sports. In this stance, the player positions his feet shoulder-width apart, flexes his knees, drops his butt, and keeps his head and chest up to create a lower center of gravity. He wants to have his body weight evenly distributed so he can move smoothly and efficiently in any direction. The best examples of a proper athletic stance are often displayed by a shortstop, a linebacker, or a collegiate wrestler.

Team Skills

A lacrosse player needs to be unselfish. He needs to understand that he is part of a larger, cohesive unit. The player must maintain the "team first" attitude rather than focus on his own desire for personal recognition and glory. An unselfish player complements his teammates. He knows their strengths and weaknesses, and he adjusts HIS game accordingly. For example, if you have the ball and your teammate has his stick in his weak hand, you need to be aware of that and adjust the speed of the feed so your teammate has a better chance to catch it. Conversely, if your teammate has his stick in his strong hand and you know that he can handle just about any feed (in terms of accuracy and speed), then you can throw the feed with authority. An unselfish player tries to make his teammates look good. For example, you make a teammate look good by throwing him a good sharp accurate pass, not a "buddy pass." You make a teammate look good by supporting him on defense in case he gets beat by the ball carrier. An unselfish player makes it easy for his teammates but makes it tough for his opponents.

A lacrosse player needs to understand his role on the team. Some players should step forward to be leaders, and others need to be willing to follow. Leadership is action, not position. If one person can step forward and lead in a positive direction, there is a good chance that the team will follow. And if a team is fortunate enough to have a bunch of leaders, that team is more likely to be successful in stressful situations. At the high school and college level, senior leadership is vital because the younger players expect the seniors to show them the way. Sometimes a leader is someone who is willing to "step out of the box" and do things that are uncomfortable, challenging his peers. That's a very difficult thing, and leaders do it in a positive way. There's no room for negativity when it comes to leadership. Not everybody is a leader. If you're not in a position to be a leader, then be a follower. Not everyone will play a starring role on his team, but each person will have a specific function. Every player needs to understand, accept, and excel at his specific role. Even leaders have to be good followers because they need to follow the coaches' wishes and then transfer that information down the chain of command.

A lacrosse player needs to be coachable. He must be willing to learn new ideas and philosophies and adjust to new techniques and strategies. One enduring trait of successful teams is their willingness to do the "little things" to win. A little thing could be something as simple and fundamental as properly gripping the lacrosse stick. Players need to be attentive to these small details that turn good teams into better teams—and turn better teams into champions. As Chuck Noll said, "Champions are champions not because they do anything extraordinary but because they do ordinary things better than anyone else."

A lacrosse player needs to be consistent. He must be consistent in his approach whether he finds himself in positive or adverse conditions. In lacrosse, you have to be a good practice player before you can be a good game player. You should come to practice ready to work hard every day. This leads to self-improvement and also helps make the team better. You need to play with poise, calmness, and confidence. Consistent attitude and effort lead to consistent performance.

In addition, you must be able to handle adversity. Adversity is inevitable in any team sport. The game of lacrosse can be mentally and emotionally challenging. You and your teammates must have the ability to persevere not only physically but also emotionally. Champions have the capacity to meet challenges, and they never give up in their resolve to overcome obstacles. Remember what Norman Vincent Peale wrote: "The tests of life are not meant to break you, but to make you." This determination not only applies to the game of lacrosse but also to the game of life. In applying this perseverance, you will gain tremendous rewards that will have a lasting, positive influence for the rest of your life.

A lacrosse player needs to have a competitive spirit and a desire to win (but not win at all costs). Lacrosse is a very competitive sport. At the high school and college levels, more and more programs are fielding very competitive teams. However, lacrosse players also need to exhibit sportsmanship. A player needs to play by the rules, be a humble loser, and be a gracious winner. Players should never humiliate an opponent. They must have respect for the sanctity of the game. Lacrosse is a very spiritual game. This is what sets lacrosse apart from other sports. The game and its history are bigger than any one individual.

Besides team skills that relate to a player's personal characteristics, lacrosse requires players to develop team skills that are based on the nature of the game. Some of these lacrosse-specific team skills are described in the following sections.

Understanding Ball Possession

In lacrosse, ball possession is very important, and turnovers are costly. The number of turnovers that occur in lacrosse is comparable to the number in basketball—more turnovers than occur in football (where each turnover is critical to the outcome of the game) but not as many as in soccer and hockey (where numerous turnovers occur throughout the game). Offensively, some lacrosse teams play conservatively; these teams value ball possession and play a settled 6v6 style, looking for an optimum shot. Other teams play aggressively, use an up-tempo style by pushing the transition, and look for a shot that puts pressure on the defense. Defensively, some teams play conservatively and wait for their opponent to make a mistake, while other teams play aggressively and try to create their own turnovers. Each style of offense and defense has its own risk and reward.

Understanding Ball Movement

Lacrosse is a game of ball movement. The ball moves faster in the air than any player can cradle or carry the ball. Offensively, players need to be multidimensional, keeping two hands on the stick and always ready to catch, cradle, and throw. A player must master the basic stick fundamentals so that he can always be a triple threat to dodge, pass, or shoot. Offense is about the "next play" and releasing the ball to a teammate. Defensively, a player needs to adjust his body position while the ball is in the air. Good defense requires defenders to constantly adjust their position to the movement of the ball.

Properly Using Space

Offenses try to create space between teammates so that defenders can't play two offensive players at the same time. Offenses want to maneuver the ball by passing, feeding, or dodging until they get in position to take a high-percentage shot, preferably without any defensive pressure near the "paint" (the crease area in front of the goal). Defenses want to minimize high-percentage shots by taking away the middle of the field or taking away the shooter's strong hand.

Having Good Timing

In lacrosse, the element of timing is important on any play involving two or more players. Offensive activities that require timing include feeding and cutting, setting and using picks, and running any set offensive play. Defenders must have good timing when sliding to the ball carrier or when recognizing and reacting to a pick above or behind the goal.

Understanding Geometry

Lacrosse players need to understand the lines and angles of the game. Much of lacrosse is based on the straight-line principle where the end points are the ball and the center of the opposing goal mouth. On offense, the ball carrier wants to make a direct dodge to the goal, staying "on the line" and getting the defender "off the line." The off-ball attacker wants to get his defender "on the line" so he can't get in a V-up position that enables him to watch both the attacker and the ball at the same time. On defense, the on-ball defender wants to shadow or overplay the ball carrier to keep him away from the middle of the field or prevent him from using his strong hand. The off-ball defender wants to get "off the line" so he can achieve a V-up position. Shooting, dodging, and goaltending revolve around angles. Dodging behind the goal is based on the attacker using the optimum angle around the crease to attack the goal. Shooting is based on the distance from the goal, the velocity of the shot, and the angle of the shot on the cage. Goaltending is based on taking away as much of the goal mouth as possible with proper body and stick positioning.

Recognizing a Numbers Advantage

Lacrosse—like soccer, hockey, and basketball—is a game of numbers. Whenever possible, offenses want low numbers so they can exploit a man-up advantage or force the defense to cover more space. Whenever possible, defenses want high numbers so they can minimize any man-up offensive advantage or have more personnel to defend less space.

Using Effective Communication

Successful teams have players with effective communication skills. The ability to listen is paramount. Players need to communicate their intentions (not what is obvious). They should communicate early—a player shouldn't wait to surprise his teammate. A player's language needs to be concise and descriptive. For lacrosse, communication can cover all aspects of play. For example, in a loose-ball situation, you can use a "Ball release" command if you are scooping, or you can use "Help left" or "Help right" as a support command. In a settled offensive situation, you can call out a set play, call for the ball if you are an open cutter, or yell "Double" if your teammate is being double-teamed. In an unsettled situation, the close attack would identify their positions and use either a "draw" call (force the defender to play you) or an "early" call (give the ball up). Furthermore, an off-ball attacker can either call "One more" (you have a shot, but I have a better shot) or "Right away" (the defender is sliding fast to you). On defense, players who are talking, moving, and animated will distract and intimidate an offense. In a settled defensive situation, slides, picks, and ball adjustments are critical. The bench, the goalie, or an inside defender will call out slide assignments: whether to slide or stay, whether to slide early or late, who has the first slide, who has the second slide, and so on. The off-ball defender must recognize and identify a pick ("Pick left" or "Pick right") and tell the on-ball defender to "Get through" the pick or "Switch." The off-ball defenders will call out support ("Help left" or "Help right") and call out any cutters to teammates. The goalie will yell "Check" on any feeds to the crease, yell "Clear the crease" if the ball is loose on the crease, and yell "Break" once he has gained possession of the ball and is ready to start the clear. In an unsettled situation, the defense calls out numbers so no attacker is left open. On a fast break, the goalie yells "Fire," and the close defense calls out their position, preparing to slide as a unit.

Providing Support

In lacrosse, teammates must always look to support each other. Offensively, teammates need to provide an outlet on either side of the ball carrier in case of defensive pressure. Defensively, teammates must support the on-ball defender with sliding help. Many defenses are based on the assumption that the ball carrier will beat his defender; thus, the defenders are constantly aware of providing support to either make the ball carrier give up the ball before he is within prime shooting range or to force the ball carrier away from the middle of the field.

Creating Deception

Lacrosse involves a lot of deception. Both attackers and defenders try to disguise their intentions with stick and body fakes. Lacrosse can be a game of chess or a game of cat and mouse with each team trying to pursue and exploit any advantage.

Position-Specific Skills

Lacrosse revolves around the interaction and team play of three field positions that are involved in the possession and movement of the ball: attackmen, midfielders, and defensemen. Attackmen are responsible for attacking their opponent's goal and scoring points. Midfielders are responsible for attacking their opponent's goal, defending their own goal, and moving the ball up and down the field. Defensemen are responsible for defending their goal and minimizing shooting opportunities. Each one of these positions requires specific skills, but players in all positions must have the ability to handle a lacrosse stick and use their athletic skills to their best advantage.

Attackmen

In the past, attackmen were chosen because they had the best stick skills on the team. Today's attackmen have quickness, the ability to make changes of direction, and strong stick skills with both hands. Fast changes of direction require footwork, agility, and quickness. An attackman will absorb more checking than other players; when an attackman operates behind the goal, the defensemen know that he can't shoot the ball, so they tend to be more aggressive with him. When an attackman drives to the goal, he has to endure a lot of physical abuse. Every field player in lacrosse plays both offense and defense. When the offense loses possession, the best attackmen become relentless riders. They don't pout when they lose the ball. They focus and are very determined about getting the ball back.

Midfielders

Midfielders are the workhorses of lacrosse. Midfielders need to have more overall skills than other players do. They must have a desire to work at both ends of the field and in between the restraining lines. Midfielders need to understand both offensive and defensive skills, so they have more on their plate as far as preparation. Midfielders must also have endurance. They are the most physically challenged of the field players because they must run up and down the field (and there are 80 yards between goals).

Defensemen

In the past, defensemen were often the slowest players on the team, but in today's game, many defensemen are the best athletes on the team. More teams now emphasize the transition game, and defensemen play an important role in this because they might be the first field player to handle the ball as they spark the offense. Defensemen must react to changes of direction and match the speed of their opponent. Defensemen need to be aggressive, but they must use a controlled aggression. They must have a heightened sense of teamwork because they need to react quickly and be able to cover for their teammates. Defense is about anticipating, reacting, sliding, and covering for teammates.

The complete lacrosse player is a composite of many different elements. He has a wide range of cognitive, creative, and judgmental skills. He exhibits the characteristics of integrity, discipline, and confidence. He has a strong passion for his sport—which is reflected in his effort, determination, and commitment—and he possesses a high level of lacrosse intelligence. Athletic skills such as quickness, speed, and agility are a must. However, size is not a crucial factor in the game; many very skilled players have average size. Lacrosse players must have many of the team skills that are needed in other competitive sports, such as unselfishness, leadership, coachability, consistency, and competitive spirit. They must also comprehend many team skills that are based on the nature of the game, including the importance of ball movement, angles, and deception. Finally, a lacrosse player must master certain skills based on the field position that he plays.

CHAPTER THREE

PLAYER STICK SKILLS

Lacrosse is a game of running and ball movement. To successfully move the ball, players must learn various fundamental stick skills. Everything starts with the grip. A proper grip involves using a "pinch" technique in which grip tension is firm but relaxed and the wrist is properly cocked. Next, the player must learn the two basic stick positions: the two-handed horizontal position and the upright triple-threat position. From the two basic stick positions, the player can proceed to working on the fundamental stick skills—throwing, catching, cradling, and scooping. Ball movement is a two-step process: throwing and catching. Throwing and catching are the essence of playing lacrosse. If you have the ball and want to maintain possession of the ball, you need to cradle or carry the ball. If neither team has possession of the ball, you want to scoop the ball off the ground and into the pocket of your stick to create possession.

Grip

Although it may seem very basic, your grip position has a critical impact on important skills such as shooting, passing, cradling, and scooping. An incorrect grip can reduce accuracy on passes and shots; thus, it can ultimately lead to increased turnovers. In this section, you'll learn how to properly hold the stick handle or shaft, including how firmly to hold the handle and where to position your hands. A proper grip sets you up to master the basic stick fundamentals.

Lacrosse skills start with how you hold the handle of the "crosse", or stick. The lacrosse grip is very similar to the grip used in both golf and baseball. The grip is the foundation of the golf swing. You grip a golf club with your fingers and use the pad of your hand as the base.

The grip is also the bedrock of the baseball swing. Hall of famer Stan Musial wrote, "The first thing I ask a young hitter to do is to grip the bat and then swing it. Nine times out of 10, the problem is right there. Most youngsters think you grip the bat with your hands. You don't! You grip it with your fingers." Just as the grip is the foundation of the golf and baseball swing, it is also the foundation of the fundamentals of lacrosse.

Use the following procedures to check your grip.

Upright Stick Position

To check your grip in the upright position, you use two hand positions: open and closed.

The first step is to hold the handle with your top hand only.

In the open hand position, you want to "pinch" the stick handle between your thumb and index finger (see figure 3.1a). You use this open grip so that the stick pocket is facing straight out, the handle is perpendicular to the ground, and the stick itself is off to the side of your body (not in front of your body). In the closed hand position, you want to close your grip but only use your fingers to do so (see figure 3.1b). With your thumb on the side of the stick handle, bring your other three fingers onto the handle.

"Pinch" the handle with your thumb and index finger.

Stick pocket forward and handle perpendicular to ground.

Hold the stick on the side of your body.

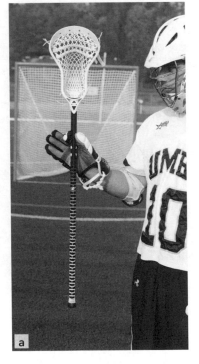

Slowly add other three fingers to the handle.

"Close" the grip with your fingers, not your palm.

FIGURE 3.1 Player checking the grip for the upright stick position: (a) open hand and (b) closed hand.

Lower Stick Position

To check your grip in the lower stick position, lower the stick to the ground at a 45-degree angle, and allow the handle to roll up toward your left armpit without compromising your grip.

Open the palm of your hand so you can look down the handle (see figure 3.2). The handle should be across your fingers, not your palm. This will help ensure that the handle ventures across your fingers and not your palm.

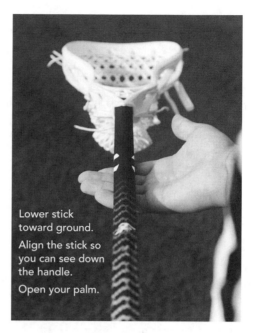

Lower stick toward ground.

Align the stick so you can see down the handle.

Open your palm.

FIGURE 3.2   Player checking the grip for the lower stick position.

Wrist Position

A proper "open" wrist position is essential to grip fundamentals. The open wrist position means that the wrist is cocked. The pinch technique gets your wrist cocked and puts your wrist directly behind the handle of the stick. The wrist is pointing away from you—and where the wrist points, the stick also points. In effect, the pinch technique gets your wrist and elbow in a straight line for maximum efficiency.

The open or cocked wrist position improves both your range and your ability to throw the ball. When your wrist is cocked, as shown in figure 3.3, you can use the whole field because you can pass the ball anywhere within a 180-degree arc. In addition, you can throw the ball at a moment's notice. When your wrist is not cocked, the head of your stick "closes" down. This limits your range and the direction you can throw, hampers your ability to make a quick pass, and causes you to have a tendency to tuck the stick for protection.

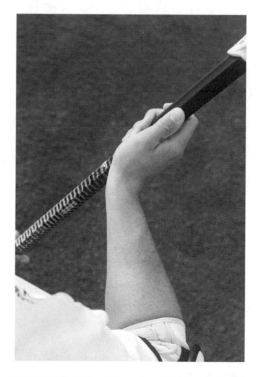

FIGURE 3.3   Player's wrist in a cocked position, which is correct.

Grip Tension

In lacrosse, you want to have "soft hands" when gripping the crosse. This means that you want a firm but relaxed grip with your fingers. You don't want to choke the handle. In exercise physiology, a tense muscle is a less efficient muscle. A lacrosse grip is similar to the grips used in golf and baseball. If you grip a golf club too tight, this creates too much tension in the upper arms. The last thing you want to do is have a real tight grip ("white knuckles"), which hampers a fluid swinging motion. A golf grip needs to be relaxed and light on the golf shaft. Legendary golfer Sam Snead, who won a record 82 PGA tour events, once said you should hold a golf club as if you were holding a baby bird—not so tight that it harms the bird, but not so light that the bird could escape.

In lacrosse, there are times when you have to adjust your grip depending on whether you are in the open field or under pressure in heavy traffic. When you're out in the open field, you want to stay loose and have a relaxed grip. Your grip may need to tighten when you are in traffic or under pressure ("under pressure, add pressure"). For example, your grip may change when you shoot because of the inertia of the shooting motion. Your grip may tighten a bit just so you can hold onto your stick. However, when you are learning to throw and catch, you should start out with the "baby bird" style.

Stick Position

Lacrosse players use two fundamental stick positions: the two-handed horizontal position and the triple-threat position. The two-handed horizontal position is executed by naturally holding your stick across the front of your body with your hands waist-width apart. The triple-threat position involves a two-step process. Step 1 is lifting the head of your stick from the horizontal position and moving it up to the area near your ear (this area is called the box). The box position is an imaginary square on the side of your helmet where most throws, catches, and cradles are executed. The second step is moving your body from a frontal, squared-up position and turning to the side so your opposite shoulder (opposite from the box) is forward. Having the opposite shoulder forward allows you to more efficiently use both your body and stick to deliver and release the ball. This position is also critical in protecting your stick.

Two-Handed Horizontal Position

From the one-handed, vertical pinch technique, you lower the crosse into a horizontal stick position across the front of your body; your hands are placed waist-width apart on the crosse, and your body is in a squared-up stance (see figure 3.4). The top hand should not be too high or too low on the handle. The optimum location for the top hand is at the fulcrum point, which is the spot on the handle where the entire stick is balanced. You want to keep your top hand on or near the fulcrum point; however, the overriding principle is that it must feel comfortable to you. You should position the bottom hand on the butt end of the stick using all fingers and not the palm. The following three drills will better illustrate the fulcrum point and proper hand positioning.

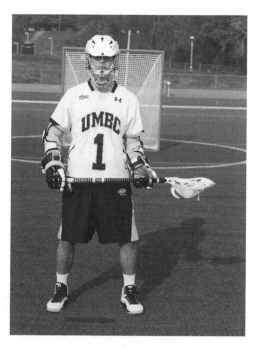

FIGURE 3.4 Two-handed horizontal position.

BALANCE DRILL

PURPOSE

To locate the fulcrum point of the lacrosse stick.

SETUP

Put the ball into the pocket of the stick with the handle parallel to the ground.

EXECUTION

Hold the stick in the fingers of your dominant hand (top hand) with the palm up. Using your nondominant hand (bottom hand) with the palm down, lightly push down on the stick handle to balance the stick on your top hand's palm. Gradually adjust the position of the stick in your top hand until the stick balances in your top hand without the need to use your bottom hand to establish the balance. Once you are able to balance the stick in your top hand, you have located the fulcrum point on the lacrosse stick.

COACHING POINTS

- Many young players believe that their hands should be positioned just below the plastic head (throat) and at the very bottom of the stick. Such a grip is too wide and will reduce feeling accuracy as well as shot power. This drill will establish the proper grip for optimal performance. Note that this should only be used for attack and midfield sticks. This will not work for a defenseman.

- If the top hand is too high on the stick, this will affect various skills. First, when throwing the ball, you'll have a tendency to push the ball. Holding the stick near the fulcrum point will allow you to snap the ball and use the maximum leverage action of the stick.

- When the top hand is too high, you may have a tendency to tuck the stick close to the body when a defender approaches. Although this will protect the ball from a turnover, you will lose the important ability to make quick and accurate passes against an aggressive defender.

- You need to be able to actually feel the ball in the stick pocket when cradling. When the top hand is too high, you lose this feeling. If the ball is knocked loose by a defender or you simply drop it, you will have a difficult time noticing unless you actually see the ball hit the ground—and if you see the ball hit the ground, you are not focused on the action in front of you! The next drill will help you learn how to feel the ball in the pocket.

FEEL DRILL

PURPOSE

To learn how the ball should feel in the stick when catching and carrying.

SETUP

Hold the stick by the throat (incorrect grip) with only your top hand, and close your eyes. Do not use your bottom hand during this drill.

EXECUTION

Have a coach or teammate drop a ball from approximately 6 inches (15 cm) into the pocket. Note the feeling of the ball when it hits the pocket and while it's lying in the pocket. Remove the ball from the pocket and return to the start position, with your top hand at the established fulcrum point. Again, have a coach or teammate drop the ball into the pocket. Note the difference in the feeling.

COACHING POINTS

- When you choke up on the stick, you can't feel the ball as well. When your top hand is on the fulcrum point, the weight of the ball in the pocket becomes more pronounced, and therefore you can feel the ball better.

- Young players often hold the stick either too high or too low. Although holding the stick low will create even more power on a shot, accuracy is drastically reduced. Always make sure the top hand is positioned correctly in order to increase accuracy and create maximum control of the ball.

CONTROL DRILL

PURPOSE

To learn the importance of placing the hands waist-width apart on the handle of the stick.

SETUP

Hold the stick with both your top hand and bottom hand together at the butt end of the handle.

EXECUTION

First, have a coach or teammate push down the head of your stick while you hold it with your hands together at the butt end of the handle, as shown in figure 3.5*a*. Try to resist the pushing motion. Normally, you can't resist the pressure, and the stick head goes down very easily. Second, shift your top hand farther up the handle and properly space your hands waist-width apart on the handle, as shown in figure 3.5*b*. Again, have a coach or teammate push down on your stick head as you resist. Normally, you can resist this push.

COACHING POINTS

Young players often think they are getting more velocity on their throws and shots by putting their hands together at the end of the stick. In reality, they are losing much more accuracy than any gain in velocity. This drill demonstrates that if you keep your hands apart on the handle, you have more control of the stick. Control equals accuracy. You can't perform any major stick fundamental without using a waist-width-apart hand position on the stick.

FIGURE 3.5 (*a*) Holding the stick with the hands together at the butt of the handle; (*b*) holding the stick with the hands waist-width apart.

Triple-Threat Position

The primary purpose of the triple-threat position is to make you a multidimensional player. In basketball, players always want to be a triple threat to pass, dribble, or shoot. In lacrosse, players always want to be a triple threat to pass, dodge, or shoot.

When throwing or catching in lacrosse, you will usually be more efficient when you have your stick positioned in the imaginary box on the side of your head and when your body is turned to the side (instead of squared up to the target). From the two-handed horizontal position (see figure 3.6a), you lift the pocket of your stick into the box position. You shift your stick handle to a 45-degree stick angle and shift your stick head (pocket) toward an imaginary box on the side of your body near your ear (see figure 3.6b). From the squared-up position, you turn your body and shift it to the side position (see figure 3.6c). You turn your upper body so your opposite or lead shoulder is pointing toward your target. If you are right-handed, then turn so your left shoulder is facing your teammate or target. Your feet adjust accordingly, remaining comfortably apart. Your stick is positioned on the side of your body; it may range from a 45-degree stick angle to almost perpendicular depending on your personal preference, individual comfort, and confidence level. When you turn your shoulders, you have to extend your arms and elbows so that the stick head is in your vision and closer to eye level. In general, you should always see the head of your stick because you want to look the ball into the pocket of your stick. This also maximizes stick protection.

When in the triple-threat position, you want to keep your stick within an imaginary cylinder around your body in order to maximize protection of your stick (see figure 3.7). You should use your helmet and upper body to protect the head of the stick. Hold your stick where you can see the stick head. You rarely want to lose

FIGURE 3.6 Player getting into the triple-threat position.

sight of your stick with your peripheral vision. This rule would be relaxed during the shooting motion. When playing, you should have your arms away from your body as often as you can and have your hands free to throw, pass, or shoot. The cylinder concept is less applicable in the open field. In the open field, you want to remain as athletic as possible by running in a squared-up manner, and you need to see the whole field. In the open field, your arms and stick can venture farther away from your body as the cylinder expands.

The "cylinder" concept is more relevant in close-quarters play. The closer you get to your defender, the less cushion he will give you, and the more you need to bring the stick closer to your body. The closer you get to your opponent's goal, the more pressure the defense will give you, and the more your arms and stick need to stay closer to your body to protect the stick. The tighter the play, the more your cylinder contracts.

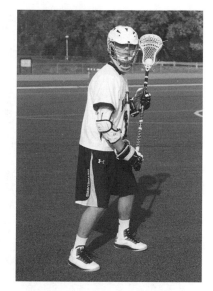

FIGURE 3.7 Player's stick within an imaginary cylinder when the player is in the triple-threat position.

Stick Fundamentals

The major stick fundamentals of lacrosse are throwing, catching, cradling, and scooping. The first fundamental that a player should learn is throwing the ball. You must be able to propel the ball to a teammate so you can establish a connection and move the ball anywhere on the field. The fundamental of catching is the other component of this connection. You need to be able to secure a ball thrown to you by a teammate. Learning how to catch and properly "give" with your stick and body is an acquired skill that takes practice and patience. Cradling the ball is a unique skill that is akin to dribbling in basketball. You are maintaining ball possession, and you are ready to throw the ball if necessary. Scooping the ball from the ground is a specialized skill that requires both technique and desire. Scooping is analogous to rebounding in basketball. It's not as glamorous as shooting, but it creates ball possessions, and this increases your chances of winning the game.

Throwing

Throwing is used for ball exchange, feeding, and shooting. Ball exchange is passing the ball to a teammate, and feeding is passing the ball to a teammate who is a threat to score. In either case, you are trying to complete a pass. On the other hand, shooting is throwing at an opponent's goal for the purpose of scoring.

When you are preparing to throw, you should get in the ready position, which is based on the triple-threat position. Place your top hand near the fulcrum point, which is typically 2 to 4 inches (5.1 to 10.2 cm) from the throat of the stick, and

use the pinch technique with the handle in your fingers. Bring the stick head or pocket up by your ear with the stick at a 45-degree stick angle; the butt end of the handle is pointing at your teammate's feet. Your arms and the stick are away from your body, and you are holding the stick within the cylinder in order to maximize stick protection. Your elbows are flexed and pointing out away from your body. It's as if you're forming a triangle between your elbows and the stick. Your bottom elbow is facing your target and is pointing toward the base of your target. From the ready position, you will shift to the loaded position for throwing. See figure 3.8 for an example of the individual ready position, the ready position for two players, and the ready position down-the-line.

FIGURE 3.8 Player in the ready position for throwing: (*a*) individual, (*b*) two players, and (*c*) down-the-line.

To get into the loaded position for throwing, you rotate your trunk, shift your body weight to your back foot, and bring the stick back in order to prepare for the throw (see figure 3.9). Trunk rotation is the first step in achieving the loaded position. Trunk rotation starts with the hips (the hips are a huge part of any athletic exercise). You turn and rotate your hips. Your hips and shoulders work together—when you turn your hips, you also turn your shoulders. This action shifts your body weight to your back foot. Everything is working and turning together in one smooth motion. Everything (e.g., hands, elbows) follows the lead of the trunk, hips, and shoulders. You are loading up, not merely bringing your stick back. When you turn your hips, your stick naturally comes back and remains off your ear. When you turn

FIGURE 3.9 Player in the loaded position for throwing.

your shoulders, you should draw the stick back instead of allowing the front elbow to come up excessively. Your front elbow will come up slightly, and the butt end of the handle will come up too. The butt end of the stick is now aimed at your teammate's knee to waist area (not the teammate's chest). If the butt end of the handle comes up parallel to the ground, the ball will begin to roll out; as a result, when you pull down with the bottom hand, you get "sky" balls (catapult movement). Before launching the throwing motion, you should execute a final little cradle to help you feel the ball.

To execute the actual throwing motion, you push off your back foot, step with your front foot, and allow your elbow to come up slightly (the rise of your elbow gives you more snap and pull action). The butt end of your handle rises to the middle of the target. You should then snap with your top hand, pull with your bottom hand, deliver and release the ball, and follow through with your shoulders and body. See figure 3.10 for an example of the throwing motion.

The need to transfer body weight from the back foot to the front foot when throwing is a universal concept in athletics. In baseball, a relief pitcher in the set position pushes off the rubber with his back foot to throw to the plate. In football, a quarterback throws off his back foot when passing the ball to a receiver. In lacrosse, you load up your body weight and push off with your back foot. You should take a comfortable and balanced step with your front foot toward your target. If you take too big a step (overextend your stride and transfer your body weight up front too fast), then nothing is left over for the throwing motion; as a result, you will "push" the ball with your stick. If your feet get too wide, then you've overcommitted. If you step too soon, the movement is disjointed, and you lose rhythm and flow.

When you are throwing, your hands need to be in sync and work together to provide the snap-pull motion. You snap with the top hand and pull with the

FIGURE 3.10 Player executing the throwing motion.

bottom hand. Your top hand is placed near the fulcrum point, and you use the pinch technique with the handle in your fingers. The pinch technique means your thumb is on the side of the stick so you can snap the stick as if you're casting a fishing pole or using a flyswatter. The snap with the top hand should involve the wrist. Your wrist goes from the cocked position to being committed or released to the target. Your top hand extends through the target when you release the ball toward the target. You finish your snap at the intended plane and direction of your target—when passing, the target would be the teammate's stick head. Wherever you snap the head of your stick or wherever the head of your stick is pointed, that is where the ball will go. If your top hand is near the throat and against the plastic stick head, you won't have nearly as much snap as you would with your hand farther down the handle near the fulcrum point; you will end up pushing the ball with your shoulders. If you use a grip with a closed wrist position and you choke the stick handle with your top hand, you will tend to release the ball too low. You can't snap well with your top hand in a closed grip position because you will not release your top hand and you will push with your shoulder. The snap is like a whipping action. You use both your wrist and shoulder to snap like a whip. If you snap the ball properly, you can hear a "whiffing" sound from the strings of the pocket.

You pull down with the bottom hand, which gives you more leverage and power. Unlike the top hand, the bottom hand is not extended out toward the target. The bottom hand drives back toward your body and toward your ribs. Your bottom hand, elbow, and arm come back into your body and ribs. The snap-pull has a shorter range of motion than a regular follow-through. The range of motion for the snap-pull action is 45 degrees to 45 degrees; in other words, on a 15- to 20-yard pass, the stick should go from 45 degrees to 45 degrees.

If you snap-pull, then you pull the stick back and recover to the ready position immediately. You want to be balanced and get back to the ready position.

TWO-STEP THROWING DRILL

PURPOSE

To learn how to snap the ball with your top hand and pull with your bottom hand in the throwing motion.

SETUP

Put a ball in your stick pocket and hold your stick at your side in a perpendicular position with only your top hand.

EXECUTION

First, step forward with your lead foot and throw the ball with only your top hand. Next, add your bottom hand to the butt end of the handle. Use both hands to execute a snap-pull throwing motion.

COACHING POINTS

The first part of the drill teaches the importance of the top-hand snap in the throwing motion. When you add the bottom hand to the stick, this completes the full snap-pull throwing motion.

Delivery of the ball and follow-through of the body and stick should be considered one continuous movement. When you step with your front foot, you follow through by stepping with your back foot. This technique enables you to maintain your balance throughout the pass or shot, and both feet adjust accordingly (the technique prevents your body from falling over and allows your momentum to follow through to a balanced position). You transfer your body weight, follow through with the back foot, and return to a balanced body position. When you throw, the force and inertia of the pass will take the stick away from you, so your top hand will slide down the handle a bit. If you are shooting, your top hand will

FIGURE 3.11 Player following through after the throw.

slide down a little farther. When you release and your top hand slides and naturally adjusts on the handle, you are properly following through (not pushing the ball) and releasing the stick toward the target (see figure 3.11). You want to follow through with your shoulders and arms so that your body is facing forward and your stick goes forward and is pointing toward your target. When you finish and release the ball, you should be facing your target. You should follow through to a balanced position.

Improving Your Throwing

You can use various methods to improve your throwing accuracy, velocity, and distance. Improving your accuracy involves making adjustments with your stick. Improving your velocity and distance is more about adjusting your body to the stick. Throwing is the first basic fundamental skill, so you should first practice the basic motion and then work on refinements that can improve your accuracy, velocity, and distance.

Throwing for Accuracy

When working on accuracy, you should aim a little high at first and then bring your aim down as you get more proficient. If you miss a teammate's stick target on a pass, you want to "miss wide" so the teammate can reach for the ball to make the catch instead of being handcuffed by the ball. Goalkeepers are taught that if they are going to miss on an outlet pass to a teammate, they should miss high and long.

Throwing for More Velocity

To increase the velocity on your throws, you should adjust your body by flexing your knees and dropping your butt. Keeping your hands waist-width apart on the handle (not both hands near the butt end), extend your arms more behind your body. When your arms are extended out and away from your body, this increases your power. When you get your hands and stick farther back, you give yourself more power.

Throwing for More Distance

You have to keep the head of your stick above parallel. If the head of the stick goes below parallel and the butt end comes up, the ball will start to roll out of the pocket. If you have to throw a long way, then the ball will catapult into the air. Therefore, while trying to throw for more distance, you need to keep your stick angle nearly the same. If you have to throw a 40-yard pass, you should angle your stick up a little higher, but your hands should stay waist-width apart. You keep the stick position the same relative to your body, but now you look up so your release angle is higher. However, you maintain the same form and technique with your stick. While maintaining your form and the angle of projection, you need to use your leg muscles to throw the ball farther. You change your body position, not your stick position. You drop your body to change the stick angle, and you use your bigger muscles. You drop your butt into a lower, more athletic position: Drop lower to throw longer.

Catching

Catching is the second half of the ball movement process. You complete this process by catching the ball when a teammate throws it to you. For example, you need to catch the ball on a ball exchange or when cutting for a feed. In a ball exchange situation, you should control the ball as it enters the pocket of your stick and prepare to move the ball or yourself. When catching off of a feed, you must secure the ball and prepare to shoot or move the ball again. The catching motion involves adjusting your body to the ball (with proper footwork), looking the ball into the pocket of the stick, giving with the ball, protecting your stick, and returning to the loaded position.

The ready position for catching, as shown in figure 3.12, is based on the triple-threat position discussed previously. Your arms are relaxed and extended from your body, and your elbows are flexed and positioned closer to your body. Catching is all about feel and cushioning the reception of the ball, so you don't need power and leverage. You want your stick on the side of your body where it's away from your body, but you should hold it within the cylinder to maximize stick protection. You will adjust your stick angle from 45 degrees to a more perpendicular stick angle. You should use the pinch technique, which cocks your wrist; the handle becomes perpendicular to the ground, and the stick pocket is fully facing the thrower (perpendicular equals full target). If you show the full face of your stick pocket, this gives the thrower the maximum surface area to use as a target. Whether you're throwing, catching, or scooping, the stick should always be off to the side of your body. You never want to have your stick directly in front of your body (in "flag pole" position). Here are some of the reasons for avoiding this position:

- *Stick position and target*—The thrower does not see the entire pocket, and you lose surface area.

FIGURE 3.12 Player in the ready position for catching: (a) front view and (b) side view.

- *Vision*—You can't see the ball into the pocket of your stick.
- *Give*—You tend to fully extend and straighten out your arms. If you do so, then you are rigid and have little flexibility to give with the ball.
- *Stick protection*—Your stick is exposed, and you are likely to get it checked by an opponent.
- *Throwing*—You have to bring your stick back and reload to throw.

To catch, you adjust your body to the pass—whether it's a good pass or an errant pass—by moving your feet and then adjusting your stick to the ball. For example, on a cross-field pass, the thrower puts the ball in the general vicinity of the catcher, and the catcher adjusts his body position to make it a perfect pass. In an open-field situation, you can either wait for the ball to arrive or step toward the ball and catch it. In general, whether it's a perfect pass or an errant pass, you want to step to the ball. In a pressure situation, you should step to an open area. You want to use the triple threat position to put your defender on your back and use your body to shield him from your stick. If you stay squared up, the defender can easily check your stick. Also remember that the stick head should be up by your eyes. That way, as you watch the flight of the ball, you can focus on the ball, and as you receive it, you can look the ball into your stick pocket. Think about how a receiver in football looks the ball into his hands and completes the catch. You should use your peripheral vision so you always know where your stick head is located.

As the ball approaches, you need to "give" with your body as if someone is throwing you an egg and you don't want to break it. You should give with everything—your hips, shoulders, elbows, and hands. Everything moves backward in one smooth, continuous, free-flowing motion. You turn your hips, turn your shoulders, and the arms follow. If you turn your hips and shoulders properly, you can let the ball come to you and then "give" with both elbows and both hands (see figure 3.13). You want to have "soft hands", which means that both

FIGURE 3.13 Player giving with the ball.

your hands and grip are relaxed. If you give with only the top hand, then the bottom hand and the butt end of the handle will come up; this causes the stick to become parallel, and the ball will fall out of the pocket.

Your body and stick need to work in harmony. The stick is an extension of the body, so the body is doing the turning and bringing the stick back while your soft hands just finish off the action. Your hips turn, your shoulders turn, and your stick follows. You give with the stick as if you are drawing back an arrow on a bow. You give by pulling back on the handle with your shoulder. This enables the stick to stay perpendicular to the ground. The turn of the hip and shoulder sets up both stick protection and the loaded position. When you turn your shoulders properly, the stick naturally comes back near your ear so that you are protecting the stick with your body. As you receive the ball, you turn your shoulders into the loaded position (see figure 3.14).

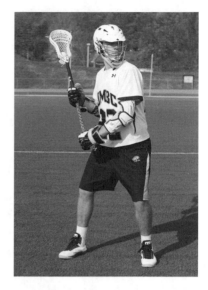

FIGURE 3.14 Player in the loaded position after receiving the ball.

As you catch the ball, you should shift your body weight to your back foot, and your stick and hands should be back. You should execute a little feel cradle so you know where the ball is in your pocket (feel cradle will be described later in this chapter). You will then be ready to throw the ball forward. It's similar to a person having a snowball up by his ear and being ready to throw it at his intended target.

SOFT HANDS DRILL

PURPOSE

To learn how to properly "give" with your top hand when catching the ball.

SETUP

No stick is used in this drill. Have a coach or teammate toss you a ball so it lands off to your side and near your head so you can catch it.

EXECUTION

Catch the ball with your strong hand. Give with the ball as if you are catching an egg and don't want to break it. Your hand will move back to cushion the impact of the ball.

COACHING POINTS

You need to learn how to properly cushion the arrival of the ball into the stick pocket. For many young players, their first instinct is to "attack" the ball with their stick. The egg toss analogy teaches the proper touch. By using soft hands, you learn that the catching motion is more of a giving, reactive motion.

TWO-STEP CATCHING DRILL

PURPOSE

To learn how to "give" with the lacrosse stick when catching the ball.

SETUP

Hold your stick pocket out in front of you at waist level.

EXECUTION

First, have a coach or teammate gently toss you a ball; this person should toss the ball up in the air so you can catch it at waist level. Use your eyes to watch the ball into your pocket, and use your hands to feel its impact. Second, shift your body from a squared-up position to a sideways position with your opposite shoulder forward. Bring your stick pocket up near your ear. Have a coach or teammate toss the ball up above your head so it lands near your stick pocket. Again, use your eye–hand coordination to adjust and catch the ball.

COACHING POINTS

This drill teaches the importance of eye–hand coordination in the catching motion.

Cradling

Cradling refers to maintaining possession of the ball with a gentle rocking of the stick. You must use some centripetal force so the ball doesn't fall out of the pocket of your upright stick. Cradling is used to carry the ball up and down the field. The stick-cradling motion requires the proper stick arc, and it is both a smooth and controlled motion. When you execute the cradling motion with the correct stick arc, your stick rocks back and forth from the ear to the back of the head. The proper stick arc maximizes both your throwing ability and your stick protection.

Lacrosse players use two basic cradling motions. The feel cradle is used for carrying the ball and for stick protection. The control cradle is used to prepare for throwing. For both types, the player's primary goal is ball possession, but each type has a different function.

Control Cradle (Passive or Carry Cradle)

The control cradle is used to hold and carry the ball in the pocket of your stick. The feel cradle is performed more with your body, and the main focus is stick protection (rather than throwing). The tempo of a control cradle is slower because you are just protecting the ball and are not in a position to throw the ball. Control cradling should be something that is minimal. You want to cradle just enough so you know where the ball is in the pocket of your stick. If you are running and there is little defensive pressure, you should use very little cradling.

Feel Cradle (Ready Release, Active, or Ready Cradle)

The feel cradle is used to set up the release of the ball. The feel cradle is performed more with your hands, and your main focus is throwing. The smaller muscles of your forearms and wrists are more involved with the feel cradle. The tempo of the feel cradle is a little quicker because you're getting the ball into position so you can release it. The feel cradle is much more active than a feel cradle. The feel cradle is more about feeling the ball in your pocket and getting the ball in the position where you feel comfortable for the quick release. When you go to release the ball, you're really just loading up. You want the ball in the proper position in the pocket so it can be released efficiently.

FIGURE 3.15 Player in the upright cradling position.

When cradling, most players use an upright cradling position, as shown in figure 3.15. You should use the triple-threat position so that you are ready to throw and the ball is protected from the defender. Sometimes you may drop your hands down into a horizontal cradling position, as shown in figure 3.16, in order to get the ball where you want it in the pocket

The horizontal cradle is not overactive, but at least you're loaded. Some very good players like to drop their hands to really load up. This is a higher-level skill that players can develop, and it's not recommended for novice players. It's a style used by box lacrosse players.

When you cradle, your body and stick act as a single unit. The big muscles of your hips and shoulders do the work, and your arms and stick just follow. You move the stick a little, but mostly your body moves. You cradle mostly by turning your hips and shoulders. Your trunk rotates, your shoulders and hips twist, and your body rocks back and forth so you're always loaded up on your back leg.

FIGURE 3.16 Player in the horizontal cradling position.

You keep your elbows in toward your body and use minimal arm and wrist action. Some wrist action is involved, but most of the work is done by the larger muscles. See figure 3.17 for an example of the cradling motion.

FIGURE 3.17 Player executing the cradling motion.

Even if you're in the middle of a cradle, you can throw a pass without recoiling your stick. You don't want to commit your hands and "break your wrists" until you're ready to release the ball. When you use the proper stick arc, you're protecting your stick with your shoulder and back without using your arms and hands. If you cradle from your ear to your nose, you have to recoil and reload to throw, and you expose your stick. If you put your stick in a tuck position in order to protect your stick, as shown in figure 3.18, then you're neither cradling nor in a position to throw. You want to establish a stick rhythm that is smooth and fluid (a "clean" cradle). Your stick tempo should allow a controlled movement of both your body and stick. If your hands are cradling at 100 mph, then you don't have any control. Young players sometimes cradle too fast with too much arm motion. Remember to only cradle when you have the ball in your stick.

FIGURE 3.18 Player in the tuck position.

TWO-STEP CRADLING DRILL

PURPOSE

To learn to cradle the ball in the upright stick position.

SETUP

Put a ball in your stick pocket and hold your stick in a horizontal position across the front of your body.

EXECUTION

Slowly rock the stick pocket up and down in the horizontal position. The rocking motion is similar to performing a reverse curl with a barbell. Your elbows are in toward your body, and you curl the stick with a slight rocking motion from your hips to waist level and back to hips. You need to rock the stick gently and smoothly so the ball doesn't fall out of the pocket. Once you are comfortable with the rocking, cradling motion, shift your body from a squared-up position to a sideways position with the opposite shoulder forward. Raise your stick to the box position. Now slowly rock the ball back and forth in the upright position. Again, your goal is to maintain possession of the ball.

COACHING POINTS

- First, make sure your hands are waist-width apart on the stick. Mastering the rocking motion of the stick pocket may take some practice. Young players often have a tendency to overcradle by using too much speed and too much stick arc. The key is to use a slow, smooth rocking motion.

- When shifting the stick to the upright position, you should make sure that the stick is not totally perpendicular to the ground. If the stick pocket has some stick angle, you will be less likely to lose the ball.

Scooping

The last stick fundamental is scooping. Scooping is the technique used to pick up a ball that's on the ground. The players on each team would struggle to gain or regain possession of the ball by scooping the ball into the pocket of their stick. Teams that get the most ground balls normally win the game because they get more possessions. Ground balls have been compared to rebounds in basketball. Playing a ground ball is a two-step process: (1) scooping the ball into your stick and (2) protecting the ball and running to daylight to avoid defensive pressure.

Playing a ground ball is a process. You need to get through a ground ball, so your feet have to keep moving, making it a continual process. Figure 3.19 shows the angles for scooping and also makes you aware that the ball is in the middle, which is halfway between the beginning of the technique and the end of the technique. The figure shows the whole approach angle and departure angle, which is a mirror image. Think of it this way: You want to swoop in and down *and* swoop out and up. Proper technique is not a sudden drop and lift, and you shouldn't wait until the last second to get low and pick up the ball. You need to prepare early. You shouldn't pick up a ground ball and then stop and stand straight up. If you do, you will lose your momentum, and defenders will be checking you. You should swoop down, pick up the ball, and swoop up and back to your natural running position.

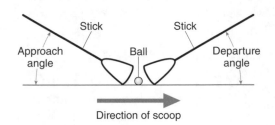

FIGURE 3.19 Scooping approach and departure angles.

General Scooping Technique

Scooping is based on adjusting your body to the ball (with footwork), using various running tempos, and putting your body weight on your back foot. Subsequently, scooping involves lowering your body position to scoop properly with your stick and raising your body position to protect your stick and release the ball.

Running Tempo Various types of running are involved in scooping. First, when you see a ground ball, you should burst to the ball with your quickness (see figure 3.20a). You use your initial burst to separate yourself from the opponent and try to gain an advantage right away. It's like the 100-yard dash in track and field—you need to get a jump on your opponent. After you burst, you must use speed and run to the ground ball (see figure 3.20b). If you're striding out when coming up to the ball, your body weight will be on your front foot. Because your body weight is leaning toward your front foot, you will usually have to chop your steps. You want to get your feet under you and get your body weight on your back foot in order to scoop.

Then, in the open field, you may or may not chop your steps, depending on your relation to the ball. You just have to get your feet in rhythm and into a balanced

FIGURE 3.20 Running tempo: *(a)* burst and *(b)* sprint to the ball.

position. If the ball is sitting out in the open field, you want to pick it up in stride and sprint down the field. If you're in a pressure situation with a lot of traffic, you may have to chop your steps. You chop your steps to get your body weight on your back foot, which enables you to be balanced and helps you get your bottom hand through the ball (see figure 3.21). You need to both time the chop properly and minimize the chopping motion. You don't want to chop too early. Chopping your steps is going to slow you down so that you can't maneuver. You chop your steps to get your feet in rhythm so that you can be more

FIGURE 3.21 Player chopping his steps as he approaches the ball.

efficient in scooping. It's like a baseball player rounding second base. The baseball player chops his steps in order to be more efficient in getting to third base before the throw from an outfielder.

Body Weight When scooping, you should get your body weight on your back leg and back foot, as shown in figure 3.22. You have to get your bottom hand down low to the ground to achieve the proper stick angle for scooping the ball. The stick needs to be as close to parallel to the ground as possible without causing you to lose efficiency. Scooping is both back foot and bottom hand dominant. If your body weight is on your back foot and your bottom hand is low to the ground, then your stick can go through the ball, and you can

FIGURE 3.22 Player keeping his body weight on the back foot when scooping.

maintain an athletic position that enables you to sprint to daylight. Your feet aren't too far apart, and you can drive your backhand through the ball.

If your body weight is on your front foot and your bottom hand is too high (top heavy), you will lose balance, control, and athleticism. You will stop moving your feet, and you won't be able to run away from defensive pressure. Your feet will be too far apart, and you'll have to "pull yourself out" of a ground ball.

Hand Position When scooping, you want to slide the bottom hand through the ball; the top hand acts as a sheath just to help control the stick, but the power comes from the bottom hand and back foot. You should use your bottom hand to drive your stick through the ball and use your top hand to continue to control the stick's positioning.

You should scoop with your dominant hand whenever possible. Some players switch hands when they scoop based on the location of the ball, but players will be more successful if they always use their naturally stronger hand to scoop the ball.

You don't want to switch hands on the stick and adjust the stick to your body. You want to keep your body between the ball and any opponents. You're shielding the ball with your body even though you don't have possession of it. When you are scooping the ball, you're adjusting your body (not the stick) to the ball because the ball is on the ground. Once you pick up the ball into your stick, you're doing the same thing—you're adjusting your body to the ball; the ball just happens to be in your stick.

Scooping Situations

In lacrosse, you will encounter two types of scooping situations: open-field ground balls and pressure ground balls. If the ball is in the open field, you should get your body more behind the ball than when a ball is in traffic. If your power comes from your back foot and bottom hand, and if you stay behind the ball, then your head will be behind the ball, and you will be able to get through the ball efficiently and maintain your balance. In the open field, your front foot will be nearer the butt end of the handle instead of the stick head. But if the ball is in traffic, you want to get your body closer to the ball. Your front foot is more toward the head of the stick, and your head is almost directly over the head of the stick ("head over head" or "eyes over the ball"). You bring your stick closer and tighter to your body, and you stay compact. You have to get over the ball so you can protect the ball with your body. You need to protect and shield the ball and the head of your stick with your body, which helps prevent an opponent from coming in and checking you without fouling you.

Another factor in your ability to successfully scoop pressure ground balls is physical strength and power. If you're the strongest, most powerful player running through traffic, your momentum will help you get the ball. You want to be as powerful as possible when going after a ground ball, so you should drive through the ground ball. The more physical strength and power you have when going to and through a ground ball, the better your chances of successfully getting the ball. When you scoop a pressure ground ball, you're anticipating your opponent checking you, so you brace yourself for physical contact.

SCOOPING DRILL

PURPOSE

To learn proper scooping technique.

SETUP

Place a ball on the ground directly in front of you within a short reach of your stick.

EXECUTION

Get your body down by dropping your butt, flexing your knees, and getting both hands to the ball. Get your bottom hand down low enough so the butt end of the stick is almost parallel with the ground. Scoop through the ball with your stick. Step with your front foot and follow through with your back foot. Bring the stick pocket back up near your ear as you turn your shoulders.

COACHING POINTS

You must get the bottom hand through the ball; the top hand acts as a sheath to control the stick. In the scooping motion, the bottom hand is dominant.

Scooping Technique: Approach As you're approaching and attacking the ball, you should start to break down and get your body into a lower position. You want to swoop down and scoop up the ball ("swoop and scoop"). Drop your butt and center of gravity by flexing your knees. Also flex your elbows. Your arms should be flexed and never fully extended. If you're a right-hander, your right elbow should be almost on top of your right knee, and your left elbow should be over your left knee. This helps keep your feet underneath you and enables you to get through the ball athletically. You should have your head down and eyes focused on the ball, but with your chin up. See figure 3.23 for an example of the approach when scooping.

FIGURE 3.23 Player approaching the ball when preparing to scoop.

For you to successfully scoop the ball, your stick angle needs to be near parallel to the ground as you are approaching the ball. Therefore, your bottom hand must be down, which means you have to flex your knees, drop your butt, extend your arms, and get your body down low to the ground. Scooping has been described as either digging dirt or shoveling snow. The lacrosse stick has a rounded edge like a snow shovel, not a pointed edge like a regular dirt shovel. When you use a pointed dirt shovel to dig dirt, the shovel angle is almost vertical as the shovel goes up and down. The phrase "digging it out" or "digging out a ground ball" connotes hustle or your cleats getting into the ground, but shoveling snow is a better analogy for scooping. If you're scooping, you must get your stick as close to parallel as possible without losing efficiency. When you're scooping snow, the angle of the snow shovel is lower than a regular dirt shovel, and your hands are lower to the ground. The scooping motion has a much less severe angle, and you are kind of skimming the snow off the surface rather than digging vertically into the surface. So you want to get your stick parallel to the ground, and you want to scoop the ball off the surface as if you were shoveling snow. When scooping the ball, you should aim your stick head 1 to 2 inches (2.5 to 5.1 cm) behind the ball.

Scooping Technique: Departure　If the ball is in the open field, you want to come out low and build back up into a sprinting speed or your natural running speed. You need to get the ground ball, stay low, and advance it by striding out. If there is no defensive pressure, you can gear down and adjust your speed accordingly. If the ball is in a pressure situation, then you need to protect your stick and escape the defensive pressure. You should get the ground ball, stay low, bring your stick close to your body for protection, and sprint to open space to avoid defensive pressure. See figure 3.24 for an example of the departure when scooping.

FIGURE 3.24　Player's departure after scooping the ball.

As you climb out of a ground ball, you should bring your head up and turn your shoulders to get your stick loaded. You should look to move the ball. As you are coming out of a ground ball, you must bring your head up and look for teammates and defensive pressure. Bring the stick back to the box position and get in a loaded position. That way, if you need to make a quick pass, you're ready to move the ball. When playing the game, you want to be a triple threat as often as you can. The best thing you can do after scooping a ground ball is look to pass the ball. If you're in a pressure situation, you will have to maneuver through the traffic and protect your stick first. When you get the opportunity, you should get your hands free and look to move the ball.

Practicing Fundamentals Using a Wall

Once you feel comfortable throwing, catching, and cradling the ball, the gold standard for practicing stick fundamentals is "working the wall." For wall work, all that is required is a ball, a stick, and a wall. Wall work is the best method for improving your fundamental stick skills, and you don't need anybody else to help you sharpen these skills. Playing catch with a friend or teammate is always more fun, but lacrosse is unique because you can improve your skills by yourself. Everybody does wall work in lacrosse. It's almost instinctual. Everybody from a novice to a national team player "hits the wall."

To do wall work, you simply bring your lacrosse stick and ball to a wall. Having a barrier behind you such as a fence can be helpful. If you make an errant pass or misjudge a catch, the ball won't go too far, and you can use your scooping technique to retrieve the ball. You stand in front of the wall and practice throwing and catching. Once you feel comfortable with this motion, you can add cradling: catch-cradle-throw. When you start out, you can stand squared up to the wall. After more practice, you should at least slightly turn your body position to a 45-degree body angle. The more you turn your body into the opposite shoulder position, the more power you will get with your throwing motion.

Here are some ways to add variety to your wall workout: You can practice throwing the ball with only your top hand on the stick, which strengthens your wrist snap; you can practice catching the ball with one hand, which accentuates your ability to "give" with the ball; you can pick out a spot on the wall and try to hit it with the ball, which improves your accuracy; or you can increase your distance from the wall and try to improve your throwing.

This chapter examined the basic stick fundamentals of lacrosse. In handling a lacrosse stick, everything starts with the proper grip, wrist position, and grip tension. Players use two primary stick positions: horizontal and upright positions. From the upright stick position, players can move on to the triple-threat position, which is the starting point for the major stick fundamentals. The four stick fundamentals are throwing, catching, cradling, and scooping. These four fundamentals are the core of lacrosse skills. Once players learn these skills, they can move on to more specific lacrosse skills.

CHAPTER FOUR

DODGING, FEEDING, AND SHOOTING

Once players feel comfortable with the four basic stick skills, they can move on to the on-ball offensive skills of dodging, feeding, and shooting. Many sports—including soccer, basketball, and hockey—involve competing for possession of a ball or puck; in such sports, the ultimate rule of play is that whoever has possession of the ball controls the game for *that* moment. In lacrosse, if you possess the ball, you can do one of three things. First, you can carry the ball downfield toward the opponent's goal and dodge opponents whenever any defensive pressure is given. If you are near the opponent's goal, you can directly attack the goal yourself by dodging. Second, you can pass or feed the ball to an open teammate who has a better opportunity to threaten the goal. As in other sports, a good assist is just as valuable as a good goal. And third, when you get within close range of the opponent's goal, you can shoot the ball to score a goal, which is the objective of the game.

Dodging

Dodging involves the feet, the hips, and the stick. Typically, a lot of emphasis is placed on the stick, but in reality, dodging starts with footwork—everything starts from the ground up. Footwork involves choppy steps for agility, bursts for quickness, and striding for speed. You also dodge with your hips, using them to execute any change of speed or change of direction. Change of speed and change of direction are offensive skills used in all areas of the game, including feeding, shooting, and cutting.

Let's take a look at an example: The defender is between you and the goal, and you want to challenge the defender; therefore, you create space and then run at the defender. You use choppy steps and use your "first move" against the defender. You use a body or stick fake and then burst for separation from your defender. You try to get the defender to commit by turning his hips; then you attack the opposite hip. Everything works in a one-piece manner. Your body and stick are working together and working in unison in a balanced manner. Your objective is to get your body and stick into a loaded position with your body weight and stick back. You want to be in a triple-threat position—a threat to dodge, feed, or shoot.

Principles of Dodging

Dodging is the essence of offensive lacrosse. Dodging can be either proactive or reactive; you can use it to generate offense, or you can use it to respond to the overplay of a defender. Dodging is combative in nature because lacrosse, like other field sports, boils down to an individual struggle between you and your opponent. Dodging is deceptive because you are attempting to disguise your intentions.

Plan of Attack

Most good dodgers have a preconceived notion of what they're going to do before initiating their dodge, but they're always ready to adjust and counter their defender's reactions.

Combativeness

Lacrosse is a combative sport. Lacrosse is all about attacking the goal. Everybody attacks the goal no matter what position they have on the field. Dodging is a one-on-one challenge. It's you versus your defender. You want to go at and challenge your defender.

Deception

Dodging involves deception, opposites, and disguising your intentions. You want the defender to think you're doing just the opposite of what you really want to do. Dodging is like the game of "tag" with a lacrosse stick. You fake or juke one way with your hips or stick, and then you go another way. You fake with your body, stick, eyes, mouth, and so on. You are deceptive with your body through change of direction and change of speed.

Dodging Mechanics

To initiate a dodge, you should pull out and create some space between you and your defender; the defender is between you and the goal. Your head and eyes should be up so you can see the field. When approaching the defensive perimeter, you want to challenge your defender in a squared-up running position (see figure 4.1).

You should challenge your defender when he is trying to stand his ground or when he is at the perimeter of the defense. You need to challenge your defender and get ready to make a good strong first move when the defender breaks down to play you. For your first move, you have to get close enough

FIGURE 4.1 Player in a squared-up running position.

to both the goal and your defender that the defender must respect you as a threat. If you're close enough, the defender must immediately react and respond to your move. If your first move is too early and you're too far from your defender, your defender will have too much time to recover or react. Ideally, you want to be a stick's length away from your defender. As a general rule, defenders want distance from their attackers, and attackers want closeness to their defenders.

When you dodge, you should use choppy steps. You dodge with your hips, and you must have your feet on the ground in order to change direction. If you use short, choppy steps, then you keep your feet close to the

FIGURE 4.2 Player executing a body fake.

ground, and your feet are ready to react and change directions. Your "first move" should be a sudden and unexpected body fake (see figure 4.2) or stick fake (see figure 4.3) to startle your defender and provoke an overreaction; then, you should burst for separation.

FIGURE 4.3 Player executing a stick fake.

If you startle your defender and he overreacts, you can take advantage of the defender's overreaction by going in the opposite direction. You want to provoke a maximum overreaction by your defender with a minimum commitment by your stick and body. If you haven't overdone the fake, you can come right back, get back on the proper line to the goal, and finish your dodge. You don't want to overdo the fake because then you and your defender will recover at the same rate. Fakes should be short, quick, and effective. The second part of this "first move" is your burst for separation, as shown in figure 4.4. The burst involves your first step and an explosion of quickness to separate you from your defender. The burst is analogous to the start of a 100-yard dash in track and field. The race is won in the starting blocks.

FIGURE 4.4 Player bursting for separation after a fake.

FIVE-CONE DODGING DRILL

PURPOSE
To learn to dodge with your hips and feet.

SETUP
Five cones are arranged in a Y pattern. The player has the ball in his stick at cone 1.

EXECUTION
The player creeps forward and strides to cone 2. At cone 2, he uses choppy steps to prepare for a change of direction and then continues to cone 3. At cone 3, the player breaks to either cone 4 or cone 5, branching from cone 3. The player attacks cone 4 or 5 with his opposite shoulder. He knifes through, which automatically brings his stick back to the loaded position.

COACHING POINTS
This drill teaches the importance of dodging with your hips and legs. It teaches how to make a change of direction with choppy steps and change of speed, which is a universal offensive skill. At the end point of the drill, you're in a loaded position, ready to either pass or shoot.

Dodging Strategy

The strategy for dodging is based on the concept that the shortest distance between two points is a straight line (when you dodge north-south, this is a straight line). In basketball, you can shoot over the defender. But in lacrosse, you can't shoot over the defender, so your goal as a dodger is to move your defender off the "line" using change of direction or change of speed. Then you can continue on the line and take the shortest distance to the goal.

When dodging, you also have to decide whether you need to set up your defender or your defender has set himself up; then you want to get the defender to react in the opposite direction of where you want to go. Remember, offense is a game of opposites. Either way, you're looking for the defender to overcommit and make a mistake in some manner, then you are going to take advantage of it by going the opposite way. In some dodges, the defender is setting up the dodge for you. The defender is attacking you, and in doing so, he creates the opportunity for you to dodge. If the defender makes a mistake, you should take advantage of that mistake and dodge around the overcommitting defender. For example, if your defender is running at you out of control, then the defender has set himself up, and you can react to his overcommitment (reactive). In other cases, you will be setting up the dodge yourself. If your defender is playing solid, squared-up defense and is holding his ground, you will need to attack him and initiate the dodge. When your defender is under control and is not making a mistake, you have to set him up and cause him to make a mistake (proactive).

Again, a north-south dodge is based on the principle that the shortest distance between two points is a straight line. The two points would be the dodger and the center of the goal. The play would be analogous to a football tailback running directly through the offensive line instead of running outside the tackles and avoiding the defense with speed or deception. If you use a north-south dodge, you run and sprint at your defender, and you use a first-move fake and burst. Your defender will open up his hips and take a deep drop step because he wants to adjust his body position and get to a better downfield angle (see figure 4.5a). The defender wants to run hip to hip with you, the attacker, so you should watch the defender's hips. Once your defender opens up his hips and drop-steps, you should attack the defender's near hip, which is the hip closest to you after he drop-steps (see figure 4.5b).

You should use a sudden change of speed or change of direction, get an overreaction from the defender, cut back against the near hip, and then go hard to the goal. If you beat your defender early with a good first move and separate from your defender, you can then go toward the goal uncontested. You won't have to worry about the defender checking you, and you will become more dangerous because you can extend your arms and free up your hands to pass, feed, or shoot. You want to beat your defender cleanly so you can focus on the next defender. If you don't put a good first move on your defender, you will have to deal with him the entire time you're pressing to the goal. You will have to protect your stick more, and you won't be able to get your arms and hands free to release the ball.

FIGURE 4.5 *(a)* The defender taking a drop step as the attacker uses a north-south dodge; *(b)* the attacker attacking the defender's hip closest to him.

If you are being approached by an opponent, you should shift your body position from a squared-up position to a sideways position similar to martial arts maneuvers. Martial arts teaches you that if you are being approached by a potential enemy, you should turn your body to a sideways position because you will have less of your body exposed to the aggressor. Remember, everything (torso, hips, shoulders, hands, and stick) is one piece and should work together. Everything is balanced and works in unison. If you rotate your trunk and turn your hips and shoulders, then your hands and stick go back naturally so that the stick is protected and your body and stick are in the loaded position. Your core muscles are torqued back for power, your body weight is on your back foot, and your stick is back so you are ready to release the ball. Your objective is to knife through the dodge by leading with your front shoulder (see figure 4.6).

FIGURE 4.6 Player knifing through a dodge with the front shoulder.

Various types of north-south dodges can be used, including bull, face, roll, and split dodges. Some north-south dodges will require you to change your hand positions on the stick, while others will not. For some north-south dodges, you will use your legs to cross over the imaginary straight line to the goal. Irrespective of the specific technique used, all north-south dodges are direct, aggressive moves against the opponent, and each dodge involves either a proactive or reactive approach.

Bull Dodge

A bull dodge, as shown in figure 4.7, is the only dodge that doesn't involve crossing over the imaginary straight line to the goal. When executed in a proactive manner, the bull dodge is the simplest of dodges. It's a simple "one move and go." You just want to sprint by the defender or use your physical strength and power to outmuscle the defender. You execute a dip-and-go move. To do this, you fake a face dodge (dip) and then perform a bull dodge. You should watch your defender's hips and get the defender off the line by using a fake face dodge. You lower your shoulder, and your stick automatically starts to come across the front of your body. You plant your off-stick

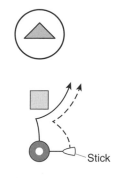

FIGURE 4.7 Bull dodge.

foot, shift your body and stick as one unit back to the line, and go. Dip-and-go is similar to the game of "tag" where you fake one way and go another. When using a reactive approach, as your defender approaches you, you will wait until the last moment, give him a fake face dodge one way, and go hard the other way.

Face Dodge

For a face dodge, as shown in figure 4.8, you cross over the straight line, and you don't change hands on your stick. You want to move your defender off the line. As you approach your defender, you should be in a loaded position with your body weight back and your stick back in a triple-threat position. When you execute a face dodge, you step over the line, but you don't want to stray too far from the line. Everything is one piece: Stick and body act as one unit. You turn your trunk, and this shifts your stick from shoulder to shoulder. Your trunk moves, but your arms and stick stay relatively still. Your shoulder comes across the front of your body, and the stick stays in the

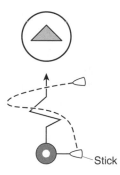

FIGURE 4.8 Face dodge.

same relative position. You should keep your stick in the same hand and return your stick to its original loaded position. If you change hands, your stick will be checkable from behind. If you make a big, sweeping stick motion during your face dodge, you will have to come all the way back to the loaded position.

In a reactive situation, your defender is running at you out of control, so you should react to his overcommitment and face dodge him. If your defender approaches you with his stick high in the air to block a pass, he may have lost his low center of gravity, which makes him easier to dodge. In a proactive situation, the successful face dodge is a two-step move: You fake a pass and then execute the face dodge. Your defender is low and in an athletic position. You set up the defender by running up to him, turning your body and stick to the side, and pretending to throw to a teammate. Part of the deception is that your defender sees you pick up the tempo of your cradle (to a control cradle tempo) as if you're going to throw to somebody. You don't want to overdo the fake. If you're in a throwing position, your defender will tend to stand up out of his athletic position and raise his stick to knock down the pass. This makes him more vulnerable to a face dodge.

Roll Dodge

For a roll dodge, as shown in figure 4.9, you cross over the straight line, similar to the face dodge, and you don't change hands on your stick. You want to move your defender off the line. As you approach the defender, you should be in a loaded position with your body weight back and with your stick back in the triple-threat position. You step over the line and get the defender to commit to one side; then you come back with a roll dodge. For a right-handed player, you turn your upper body before planting your left pivot foot. You plant your left foot and continue to roll your upper body and stick. You swing your right foot and plant your left foot back on the line. You don't want to overstep. Everything is one continuous movement as your body and stick roll back together. You use your body to protect the stick. You should keep your stick in the same hand. If you switch hands, you will have a tendency to hang the stick, which makes it more checkable. You should keep your stick perpendicular to the ground and keep it tight to your body to protect the stick. If your stick goes parallel to the ground, then it's more checkable. As you come out of the roll dodge, you want to get your stick upfield and chase your stick with your body (i.e., lead with your stick). By getting your stick upfield, you avoid hanging or dragging your stick, and you move your stick as far away from your defender as possible (separating your stick from the defender). Once you achieve stick and body separation, you adjust your body to the ball, which happens to be in your stick. When you completely roll back out of a roll dodge, you want to return to a position with your opposite shoulder forward (not square toward your target) and return to a loaded position.

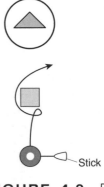

FIGURE 4.9 Roll dodge.

In a reactive situation, your defender is running at you out of control with his stick down low. In this case, you would roll dodge the defender because it protects your stick better than a face dodge. In a proactive situation, you can use a combination dodge: bull dodge into a roll dodge. You use a bull dodge to set up the roll dodge. More important, a roll dodge is a countermove. A roll dodge is not a move that you would go to initially. It's almost as if you're forced to roll. For example, if you're an attackman, you may prefer to dodge around the goal and shoot the ball, but if the defender gets way upfield on you, you can counter with an inside roll. The main advantage of a roll dodge is maximum stick protection. The disadvantage is that you take your eyes off the field and thus lose sight of both the offense and the defense. You lose sight of all the other players on the field, and this inhibits your ability to read and react. Many defenders are taught to slide when the ball carrier turns his back to them.

Split Dodge

For a split dodge, as shown in figure 4.10, you cross over the straight line, and you change hands on the stick (this is the only dodge that requires you to change hands). You want to move your defender off the line. As you approach the defender, you should be in both a loaded position and a triple-threat position. You plant your foot and shift your body weight and stick to the other side of your body. Your plant foot is the same as your stick hand. When you switch hands, your feet shouldn't cross over. To switch hands on the stick, you should use a two-step move. First, you slide your bottom hand up the shaft to just below the top hand and then move the stick in front of you with the

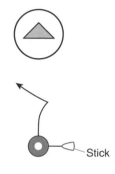

FIGURE 4.10 Split dodge.

pocket facing toward you. Second, you release the top hand, move it to the butt end position on the stick, and move the stick to the other side of your body. The stick head should go from "box to box" when you switch hands. You go hard after switching hands and move your stick upfield, adjusting your body to the ball (which is in your stick) and back to the triple-threat position.

A split dodge is a combination of a face dodge and a bull dodge. A split dodge is like a face dodge, but you switch hands on the stick. A split dodge is like a bull dodge, but you are switching hands and crossing over the straight line. When using the split dodge, one successful strategy is "setting up your strength." You put the stick in your weaker hand, make a first move, and then perform the split, pulling the stick to your stronger hand for a pass, feed, or shot.

Feeding

Lacrosse is a game of ball movement in which more than 50 percent of the goals are assisted. One unique thing about lacrosse is the relatively large area behind each goal. This area allows a lot of feeding and cutting to take place, and these skills are a key component of offensive lacrosse. Feeding is more than merely moving the ball for ball possession. Feeding is passing the ball to a teammate who has a scoring opportunity (i.e., a teammate who is a threat to catch and shoot the ball). In essence, a feed is an assist. Feeding, especially to the inside, is an aggressive calculated risk and requires smart decision making. On a feed, a poor decision could result in a turnover. Feeding is an on-ball offensive skill that is the mirror image of the off-ball skill of cutting. On a set offensive play, the feeder and cutter can be predetermined. In a freelance situation, a feeder can be any player who realizes that his teammate has a better scoring opportunity and passes him the ball.

Principles of Feeding

Feeding is used in conjunction with cutting, and the feeder must have a connection with the cutter. Feeding requires smart decisions and passes that are tailored to match the cutter's capabilities. Feeding, like dodging, involves deception, and this applies to both the feeder and the cutter.

Connection

Feeding requires the proper use of space and timing, so some type of connection needs to be made between the feeder and the cutter. The connection can be verbal or nonverbal communication. It can be visual body language such as eye-to-eye contact or nonverbal communication such as tapping your helmet or gesturing with your stick. In a freelance style offense, the agreed-on "rules of connection" are very important so that everybody is on the same page. In a set-play offense, the connection is still important, but teammates will know what to expect.

Decision Making

The feeder is responsible for the ball and must understand the importance of possession. Your team only has the opportunity to score a goal when they have ball possession. At the same time, maintaining possession also serves as great defense because the other team can't score a goal without the ball. As a feeder, you have to be a good decision maker. You can't be careless by force-feeding the ball or making a low-percentage feed to a cutter or shooter. You can't be selfish by going for the "home run" feed all the time. If the timing is not right, you have to defer on the opportunity to feed and wait for another opportunity.

Touch

A feeder needs to have a feel for his teammates' abilities. He must know their strengths and weaknesses. A good pass or feed is one that your teammate can handle. You have to tailor your feed to the ability of your cutter. You must give your teammate a chance to make the play. This concept applies not only to the location of the feed but also to the speed. It's all about touch. For example, let's say it's a sudden-death situation and you have a teammate all alone on the crease. Your teammate is a natural left-hander, but he is holding the stick in his right hand. If you feed the ball hard and your teammate can't handle the pass, then it's not a good pass. If you "feather" the ball into the crease so your teammate can handle it, you maximize the probability of a connection. You need to adjust the pass to him so he can catch it.

Deception

You don't want to disclose or give away your intentions when you are feeding. You have to disguise your intentions so you don't telegraph your feed. To get your feed through, you will often need to set up your defender by faking with your body and stick. One technique is called a dodge and step-back move: You dodge hard to the goal so your defender has to open up his hips and run hip to hip with you, then you step back and must have your hands free to feed. Another technique is "looking a defender away." This is similar to when a quarterback in football deceptively looks to one side of the field to "look off" the safety and then comes back to his real receiver. If you're looking at a potential cutter, but the cutter is not ready, you should look away and divert the defender's attention from that position. However, when you decide to feed, your eyes need to get back to the target, whether the target is the head of the stick or an open area. Only the very best players are capable of looking one way and accurately feeding the ball in another direction.

Feeding Mechanics

Imagine that a dodger, cutter, and feeder are all attacking the goal. If you are the feeder, you will typically be behind the goal; therefore, you're looking to feed the ball first, but you're still attacking the goal. Your head is up, and your eyes are scanning the field for cutters. You want to feed the ball on the run. A moving feeder is more difficult to defend than a stationary feeder. When you're moving, your defender has to keep up with you, and it is also more difficult for your defender to block your feed or get to your gloves. You can use change of speed and change of direction to separate yourself from your defender at the appropriate time and position. Your primary goal is to get your hands free. You don't want to feed through a poke check because this increases the likelihood of a turnover. If your opponent is playing a zone, then getting your hands free is not as important. Against a zone, you already have free space to operate.

When feeding, you usually want to have the stick in the box position where the cutter can see the ball. However, not all feeds will come from the box position. To avoid a defender's stick, you might have to dip your shoulder and bring your stick head lower to your side. You dip your shoulder, and your stick adjusts to your body. You don't just lower your stick position. You need to have your stick in a position where you can make an accurate pass without telegraphing the feed. You should limit cradles and make sure the ball is in the proper pocket position to feed.

You also want to have your body weight back so you can shift your weight through the feed. Your hands should be back so your stick is ready to release the ball at any given moment. If your stick is always loaded, you will be able to release the ball when the opportunity presents itself. At the moment of truth, you should look at your target and decide where you want to put the ball.

The feeding motion is similar to the throwing motion. The pace of a feed is somewhere between an exchange pass and a shot. It should be a little stronger than an exchange pass but not as hard as a shot. The feed has more urgency than a regular exchange pass because it's most likely being placed in harm's way, but it has less velocity than a shot because the intent is for the feed to be caught by the cutter. Feeding is based on putting the ball in a location where the cutter has the best opportunity to catch the ball, have his hands free, and be open for a shot on goal. The feed must be away from the defender covering the cutter. Sometimes you have to put the ball where your teammate can go get it; thus, the feed doesn't always have to go to the box position. For example, if the defender is playing the cutter up high, the open area would be down and out to the side. The feeder places the feed out to the side, and the cutter goes out and gets the ball.

So, players use two basic types of feeds: (1) feeds that are put on the stick and (2) feeds that are thrown to an area (called a spot feed).

On-the-Stick Feed

In a traditional feed, the feeder puts the ball on the stick of the cutter (see figure 4.11). If the cutter is stationary, you should put the ball right on the target (i.e., the stick). This is similar to when a football tight end does a curl pattern and the quarterback throws the ball right at his numbers. The quarterback sees the numbers and buries the ball. An example of an on-the-stick feed is a skip pass. A skip pass is made to a nonadjacent teammate with the intention of creating a shot opportunity for the catcher. A skip pass is more on a straight line, and the feeder is throwing the ball through the defense. Therefore, a skip pass is an on-the-stick feed.

FIGURE 4.11 Feeder places the ball on the stick of the cutter.

Open-Area Feed (Spot Feed)

The feeder sometimes needs to pass the ball to an open area. If the cutter is moving, you have to lead him. The exception would be if a player is cutting right at you; in that case, the cutter's stick position never really changes—the stick just gets closer to you. However, very few cuts are right at you. Most cuts are at an angle, and you have to feed the ball to a spot. Most feeds are spot feeds, and some are more imaginative than others. When you feed, you should look to a spot where you want the ball and the cutter to converge (see figure 4.12). In a spot feed, the feeder sees and puts the ball to the open area, and then it's up to the cutter to keep moving his feet so he can get to the ball. Most feeds involve timing and placement. You want to lead the cutter to an open area and let the cutter run to the ball.

Another example of a feed to an area is a lob feed. Imagine that a midfielder is staying deep, away from all of the movement inside on the crease. In this situation, you can throw the ball short so the midfielder runs under the ball, sets himself up for a quick release, and catches the ball in stride for a room-and-time shot (described

FIGURE 4.12 Feeder (*a*) sees cutter break for feed, (*b*) looks to a spot, and (*c*) leads the cutter.

later in the chapter). You're putting "air beneath the ball" so that the midfielder can run in to the ball. It's similar to an outfielder in baseball staying deep on a short fly ball with an opponent on third base. The outfielder waits, aggressively approaches the ball, and uses his momentum to catch the ball in stride. A lob feed has more trajectory than a skip pass, and you're throwing the ball over the defense. (A skip pass is a nonadjacent pass to a teammate that is not expected by the defense.) A lob feed can be used to set up a teammate for a room-and-time shot. *Room and time* means that the ball receiver has sufficient time to take a shot and has enough space from the defender to be unopposed in his shooting motion.

FIVE-CONE FEEDING DRILL

PURPOSE

To learn the basic feeding technique from behind the goal.

SETUP

Five cones are arranged in a Y pattern behind the goal. Cone 1 is placed on the end line behind the goal, and cone 3 is placed near the apex of the crease. The player has the ball at cone 1, and a teammate or coach is standing in front of the goal on the crease.

EXECUTION

The player creeps forward and strides to cone 2. At cone 2, he uses choppy steps to prepare for a change of direction at cone 3. At cone 3, he breaks to either cone 4 or cone 5 on either side of the crease. He drives hard to cone 4 or 5 in the triple-threat position, with his hands back ready to pass. When the player drives near the goal line extended, he throws a pass to the stationary coach or teammate on the crease.

COACHING POINTS

This drill teaches the importance of first using your legs when feeding. You should use change of direction (with choppy steps) and change of speed to get separation from a defender. The primary goal is to get your hands free so you can make an accurate pass to a teammate.

Feeding Strategy

Feeding and cutting are opposite sides of the same coin. Feeding and cutting are a two-man game that requires proper timing and field position. Feeders and cutters have to be on the same page and work together to be successful. Feeding and cutting are all about timing. Just like in basketball, if you have the ball and a teammate comes off a screen and is open, then you have to deliver the ball in a timely fashion. If the feed is late, this gives the opponent time to recover and disrupt the play.

Remember that you can feed from anywhere on the field. A successful feed can come from anywhere as long as there is a connection between the feeder and the cutter. Feeds can come from out in front of the goal line extended or from behind the goal. Feeds from out top are usually executed during "dodge and dump" maneuvers. You beat your man out top, then you pass off to the next open teammate or to a teammate coming off a down screen near the crease. When the ball is out front, the ball carrier has the ability to shoot, which can cause the defense to stare at the ball and therefore open up off-ball teammates. Out-front feeding is much like the strategy used by the offense in basketball.

The area behind the goal is what makes lacrosse a unique field game. Having 15 yards of playing space behind the goal makes feeding a much bigger part of the game. Because a feeder is often behind the goal, the defensive players often have their backs to the players in front of the goal. This opens up the cutting game because it's more difficult for defenders to see the ball and see their man. The feeder's prime feeding area is located behind the goal on either side of the cage but excluding the area directly behind the goal (the X-behind position). The X-behind position is located at the apex of the goal. You can feed from the X-behind position, but it's not an ideal spot. The goalie has a good chance to intercept or knock down a feed that comes from this position. If you have the ball behind the goal, you are solely a feeder because you can't score until you come up above the GLE. Once you cross the GLE, you become a threat to feed or score.

Feeding can be part of a set play, or it can be a freelance move performed to take advantage of a defensive lapse in coverage.

Set-Play Feeding

Teams will often have set offensive plays where the feeder has the ball and a cutter cuts to a certain position expecting the ball. The feeder is analogous to the quarterback, and the cutter is the pass receiver. On a set play, the quarterback doesn't wait for the receiver to finish his route before throwing the ball. The quarterback might throw the ball to a spot before the receiver even makes his cut to the sideline. The receiver doesn't wait until the ball is thrown before he makes his cuts. The receiver runs his down-and-out pattern and gets in the general area where he wants to receive the ball. When the quarterback releases the football, the receiver has to make an adjustment to the pass. In lacrosse, sometimes the cutter cuts before the ball leaves the feeder's stick, and the cutter tries to get to a predetermined area in anticipation of the feed.

Freelance Feeding

In a freelance situation, the cutter reads the feeder, makes a connection with the feeder, and cuts to an open area. In football, the set play sometimes breaks down, and the quarterback scrambles away from the defense. When the quarterback scrambles, pass receivers are taught to come back to the ball and shorten the pass. The pass receivers read the quarterback, make a connection, and make adjustments by finding the open area in the defensive coverage. In lacrosse, sometimes the cutter doesn't cut until the feeder looks at him. When the feeder's stick is in position and his hands are free, then the cutter bursts to the ball. The cutter must anticipate and wait until the ball leaves the feeder's stick before committing to a certain cut—then he must go get the ball.

Shooting

Shooting is a combination of accuracy and power. It all starts with the technique. To be a successful shooter, you have to develop the proper shooting motion and technique. Accuracy and power both come down to your technique. Accuracy is the top priority and involves fine-tuning your technique. Power is the second priority. You should never sacrifice accuracy for power. Once you develop your technique and work on accuracy, then you can work on making it more powerful. You can add power with your legs. You use your larger muscles (legs, trunk, shoulders, hips) to provide power, and you use your smaller muscles (forearms, wrists) to provide accuracy. Your legs, trunk, shoulder, and hips provide the power behind a shot; but your arms and hands are the guiding and controlling mechanism. If you want to add power to your shot, you can add in a hop-step motion. In baseball, a hop step is used by an outfielder who has room and time to step up into the catch and make a throw to home plate.

Principles of Shooting

When you shoot, you need to keep several key principles in mind. Shooting is like throwing in that you use the same motion, but your intentions are different. When throwing, you normally want to keep your stick within the cylinder in order to maximize stick protection, but with shooting, you want to extend your stick as far back as possible to increase shooting velocity. Also, shooting is about finishing. You must be able to put the ball into the net in stressful circumstances. Sometimes those circumstances require you to take an extra step to increase your shooting angle, but this also increases your chances of receiving a body or stick check by your opponent.

Intentions

Lacrosse throwing and lacrosse shooting are similar. For shooting, the same principles apply regarding body and stick position as when making a pass; however, instead of a teammate being the target, your opponent's goal is the target. When shooting, your intentions are different from when you are throwing. If you're throwing to a teammate, control is more of a factor because possession is still a key element. If you're shooting, you want to be accurate, but at the same time, you're trying to get the ball past the goalie. You're willing to give up possession of the ball in order to score a goal.

Cylinder

If at all possible, you always want to get your arms away from your body and get your hands free to shoot the ball. If it's a room-and-time shot (which is discussed in the upcoming section on shooting strategy), you can fully extend your arms and plant your feet so the cylinder is expanded. If you're shooting on the run, then you want to "bear in" toward the goal, and you can't hang your stick (your cylinder is smaller than on a room-and-time shot). If it's an inside shot, you have to bring your stick in closer to your body.

Finishing

Finishing is completing the task of shooting. In lacrosse, there are no style points for shooting. A goal is a goal. You can finish from anywhere on the field. Finishing a play could involve a point-blank shot or a 15-yarder. Finishing is more of an attitude and being able to handle pressure. For example, when you have an inside scoring opportunity, you're naturally going to tense up a bit because of the excitement of the shot, but you still need to keep your hands relaxed and confident (soft hands). You will be excited, but you can't allow the situation to paralyze you. If you physically choke the stick, you'll probably "choke" on the shot.

Shooting Mechanics

For shooting, the starting point is the triple-threat position, with your hands properly placed, waist-width apart, on the stick (see figure 4.13). The important thing is turning your opposite shoulder to the target. The momentum of your shot is going to make you turn your body. When you shoot, you will follow through toward your target and finish facing your target. It's similar to a baseball relief pitcher in the set position: He points his opposite shoulder at home plate from the set, but he faces the plate when he follows through with the pitch. If you're facing the goal, your hands and stick will be exposed to the defender, and you will likely miss the goal with your shot. For example, the majority of missed shots by right-handed players are shot wide left because the player's natural momentum pulls the ball to the left. Again, you need to keep your hands waist-width apart when shooting. Don't bring your hands together. Shooting is a combination of accuracy and power, but accuracy is more important. If your hands are waist-width apart, you can properly control your stick, and control equals accuracy. Some younger players bring their hands together because they think this gives them more power, especially with an underhand shot. However, if you bring your hands together, you lose complete control of the stick. You don't want to sacrifice accuracy for what you perceive to be power.

The shooting motion is similar to the throwing motion. You turn your torso, shoulders, and hips together in one continuous motion that naturally brings your hands and stick back into a protected position. This turning action needs to be smooth so

FIGURE 4.13 Player in the proper position when preparing to shoot.

the ball doesn't wobble in your stick. This action also puts your body and stick in the loaded position. When you turn and rotate the core muscles of your torso, this torque is loading up your body and stick. When you're properly loaded, your body is torqued, your body weight is on your back foot, and your hands and stick are back. When your stick is back, you can hide the ball from the goalie; and you can pass, shoot, or dodge (triple threat) at any given time.

Again, your stick should be in the loaded position when you are preparing to shoot. Then, if you drop your butt and flex your knees, your stick movement for the shot is similar to that for the throwing motion, except you try to extend your arms a little more and your front elbow rises more for extra leverage and power as you follow through to the target. If it's an outside shot, you may want to get your hands and stick farther back to provide more power and velocity (see figure 4.14). Because your body weight is on your back foot, you push off your back foot and step and explode through your front foot. You transfer your body weight from your back foot through your front foot. If you transfer your body weight to your front foot too early, you will lose the power from your legs (the power now comes from your arms). Your torso should rotate, and your shoulders and hips should turn your body.

Your wrists are heavily involved in the shooting motion. Your wrists snap, roll over, or roll under. Wrist snap is more of an overhand shot and is part of the

FIGURE 4.14 Player in the loaded position but with the stick back for more power.

FIGURE 4.15 Player's wrist snap during the shot.

larger snap-pull motion (see figure 4.15). Snapping your wrists at the end of your shot applies the "finishing touch" to the shot allowing the ball to go straight and maximizing accuracy.

If you roll your wrist over, the ball will have topspin and a tendency to hop. In baseball, batters roll their wrists over when they swing through the ball. If you roll your wrist under, the ball will have a tendency to backspin, skip, and pop up as if you're skipping a stone. Your hands begin waist-width apart, but your top hand slides or releases down the handle a bit, never compromising your ability to control the stick. Accuracy is more important than power, so it's natural for your top hand to slide a little—but never to a point where you're going to lose accuracy. When you shoot the ball, you can let your top hand slide down the handle and release the stick toward the target. You follow through by getting your stick and top hand through toward your target (see figure 4.16).

FIGURE 4.16 Player following through after the shot.

TWO-CONE SHOOTING DRILL

PURPOSE
To learn the shooting motion.

SETUP
Two cones are placed laterally in front of a goal. The player is positioned at one cone, and a coach or teammate is positioned at the other cone.

EXECUTION
Facing the coach or teammate, the player assumes a triple-threat position. The coach or teammate tosses the ball up in the air between himself and the player. The player runs to the ball and maintains his opposite-shoulder position. The player adjusts his body to the ball and catches the ball in his stick. The player executes a hop-step motion with his legs (to increase power) and shoots the ball at the goal.

COACHING POINTS
- This drill teaches you to turn your body and stick to get the stick into the proper loaded position. You want to maintain an opposite-shoulder body position when shooting.
- The stick position is farther back than when throwing or feeding because you are trying to get velocity on your shot.
- The hop step is added to the motion so that you can increase velocity by using your legs rather than compromising your stick position and losing the ball.

Players can execute various types of shots depending on the game situation, the shooter's location on the field, and the skills and intentions of the individual shooter. A shooter can release the ball high using an overhand shooting motion, release it from near the waist using a sidearm motion, or release it from below the waist using an underhand motion. The sidearm and underhand shooting motion are more advanced skills and will not be covered in this book. Where the ball is released by the shooter and where he intends to place the ball on the cage help describe what kind of shot the player is taking. For example, a high-to-high shot is released by the shooter from a high overhand motion, and the ball is targeted for the upper regions of the goal cage. For the purposes of this section, a shot can be high to high, high to low, or a bounce shot. A high-to-high shot is used by the shooter to beat the goalkeeper with velocity and accuracy. A high-to-low shot is used to force the goalkeeper to move his body and stick toward the ground, which requires more time and effort from the goalkeeper. A bounce shot off the ground or turf is used by the shooter to deceive the goalkeeper; the goalie must properly judge the upward trajectory of the ball. Three fundamental shooting opportunities arise in lacrosse: room-and-time shots, on-the-run shots, and inside shots.

Room-and-Time Shot

A room-and-time opportunity can present itself anywhere on the field. The main criterion is that you have time for an uncontested shot. Typically, a room-and-time shot is an outside shot, but it depends on where you are on the field and the type of defensive coverage. The farther you are away from the goal, and the more cushion and room you have, the more you can plant your feet and fully extend your arms. At times, you will need to have your stick in the cylinder, but when you have the room and time, you want to fully extend your arms away from your body and be able to plant your feet. If you have the room and time to keep the ball in your stick for two or more seconds, then you can add in a hop step. When you shoot, you should always have a slight elbow flex, bend your knees, and transfer your weight from your back foot to your front foot. The shooting trajectory can be high to high, high to low, or a bounce shot (see figure 4.17).

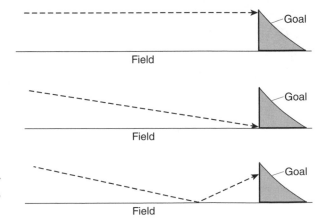

FIGURE 4.17 Shooting trajectory for a room-and-time shot: (a) high to high, (b) high to low, and (c) bounce.

Examples of when you may take a room-and-time shot include when a team-mate throws you a lob feed, when a teammate throws you a skip pass, or when you initiate a three-quarter bounce shot.

Lob Feed   If you're a midfielder out front, you may look for the lob pass. If the defense has dropped in and all of the action is closer to the goal, you don't want to come in and then have to come back out. You want to stay deep. This makes you an easier target to find. If you're inside with everybody else, you blend in. The feeder sees all the inside action, but if he looks beyond that, he can find you easier because you have separated yourself. The feeder wants to lay the ball short. You're staying deep, and you move in toward the ball. You have to read the flight of the ball and adjust to the ball because the ball has more of an arc on it. As you move in, you're setting yourself up for the catch and quick release on the shot. You have to catch the ball and release it quickly, so you need to set yourself up before you catch the ball.

Skip Pass   On offense, players typically exchange passes with the player adjacent to them in their offensive formation. Normally, the ball will move from one player to the next with some type of rhythm so the opposing defense has to constantly adjust their body positions and defensive coverage. Sometimes, instead of making the adjacent pass, the ball carrier tries to sneak a skip pass (the pass skips the adjacent teammate) to a nonadjacent teammate who is set up to take a shot on goal. You look for the skip pass first as you will normally have the adjacent pass. The skip pass has more urgency than a lob feed, but the opportunity for a room-and-time shot is still there.

Three-Quarter Bounce Shot   A three-quarter bounce shot is similar to skip-ping a stone across a pond. You have to bend your knees, drop your butt, and bring everything down lower to get the rock to skip. For a three-quarter bounce shot, you need to drop your knees, drop your butt, keep your arms away from your body, plant your back foot, transfer your body weight from your back foot, and follow your hands through to the target. Stone skipping and a three-quarter bounce shot are like an outside slap shot in hockey. The hockey player gets lower and then drives the shot to the net. For this outside shot, everything stays relative. You just lower your body (bend knees, drop hips), and your stick stays in the same relative position. Your entire body drops down, and the stick just follows. When you drop down, you mostly adjust your body, not your stick. You need to retain your balance, which is part of your technique.

When you shoot a bounce shot, your target is a spot on the field where you want the ball to bounce (not the goal). You focus on the spot where you want the ball to bounce, but you also have a mental picture and a sense of where the goal is located. You look at the goal before you shoot, but then you look down on the ground where you want to shoot the ball and follow through toward your target. If you hit the spot, then the forces of nature take over, and the ball is on target. If your stick comes through at a certain angle and the ball hits the targeted spot on the ground, the ball will have the same return angle to the goal.

Note, however, that a bounce shot will be slower on dry turf and faster on wet turf. A bounce shot on turf creates such a true bounce that it's easier for the goalie to react. Because the turf provides such a true bounce for the goalie, you see more "net-to-net" shots and fewer bounce shots on turf. A bounce shot on grass has a similar bounce to a shot on a turf field, but because of the nuances of the field (grass and bumps), it won't be the same as on turf. If you shoot the ball too hard on grass, the ball's deflection will be very erratic and unpredictable. When shooting an outside bounce shot on grass, you should take something off the shot because this will give you a smaller variation. You can make the ball and the nuances of the field work better for you. If you have a grass field, you need to know the surface and make it part of your home-field advantage. You should work on your outside shot so you learn all the nuances of your home field and get to know the bounce it gives you. For example, at Johns Hopkins, coaches had a name for the bounce shot at Homewood Field: the "Hopkins Bounce."

On-the-Run Shot

For a shot on the run, you want to knife through your dodge and get your shoulders and hips turned into an opposite-shoulder position. You get your arms away from your body and get your hands back. Your stick is back to protect it from your defender and to get it into a loaded position. When you're shooting on the run, you always want to "bear in" with your shoulder and get your body lower. Even though you're bearing in, you still need to be loaded at all times. If a defensive slide takes place or a teammate is open, you've got to be ready to pass the ball. When you're ready to unleash a shot, the goalie should see the back of your shoulder. You want to hide your stick so the goalie doesn't know when the shot is coming. Or if you use a fake, it must be a sudden, convincing fake that causes the goalie to move prematurely. You should get your whole body into the shot. You work from the ground up and shoot off your back foot. You use your shoulders, hips, and trunk. Your lower body drives your upper body through the target. You should bring your shoulder up and over and should "bury" your shot. Your shoulders follow through to your target.

FIVE-CONE SHOOTING ON THE RUN DRILL

PURPOSE

To learn how to get into the loaded position while running to shoot the ball.

SETUP

Five cones are arranged in a Y pattern out in front of the goal. The player has the ball at cone 1.

EXECUTION

The player creeps forward and strides toward cone 2. At cone 2, he uses choppy steps to prepare for a change of direction. At cone 3, he makes a dodging move and breaks to either cone 4 or cone 5. He drives hard to cone 4 or 5, gets his stick back, and shoots the ball at the cage.

COACHING POINTS

Between cone 3 and cone 4 or 5, the player needs to get into a loaded position as quickly as possible without impeding the speed of his dodge or hanging or dragging his stick. By the time he gets to cone 4 or 5, he should be loaded and able to shoot the ball. He shouldn't wait until he gets to cone 4 or 5 before he gets into a loaded position. He must get it done between the cones.

Inside Shot

An inside shot is a combination of accuracy and quickness of release. The closer you are to the goal, the less power and more accuracy you will need on your shot. Quickness of release is more important. You won't have any cushion from your defender, so you won't have a lot of time to shoot inside. You need to minimize your movements inside and use a more compact shooting technique to release the ball quickly. This is not done using the larger muscles: It's all hands, wrists, and forearms. The next part of finishing inside is releasing the ball. How quickly and efficiently you release the ball is important for a successful shot.

A shooter near the crease wants to deceive the goalie with his shot. He wants to fake ("twitch" or "flick") with his body or stick and catch the goalie by surprise. For example, he can fake with his eyes, head, and shoulders, or use a quick "pump" of his stick. A twitch is meant to "startle" the goalie. The goalie is startled by the fake and overreacts to the fake with his body or stick. The shooter fakes the goalie, waits for an overreaction by the goalie, and releases the ball into an undefended area of the goal. The fake puts a premium on the snap-pull motion. The fake involves a quicker snap-pull action than the action used when you release the ball. If you overfake, then you may get the same overreaction, but by the time you recover, the goalie has also recovered. You want to minimize your hand and stick commitment on the fake. If you go past the perpendicular position with the stick, then you've got to reload your stick. Ideally, you will use one or two fakes and release the ball. Anything beyond two fakes is counterproductive. If you fake more than two times, you will be more focused on the fakes than on putting the ball into the goal.

Here are some examples of inside shooting techniques:

- Shoot at the area from the goalie's weak-side hip to his ankle. (If you shoot at the goalie's feet, then he can kick save the ball.)
- Fake the goalie high and then shoot low.
- Fake the goalie stick side and then shoot to the opposite side.
- Fake the goalie and work from his body out to the pipes.

Note that if you're in a one-on-one situation with the goalie, you're in a position where you're expected to score a goal. Everyone expects you to score, and all the pressure is on you as the shooter. The longer the ball stays in your stick and is not in the goal, the more the pressure increases. Also, the longer you hold onto the ball, the greater the risk of a defender sliding to you, and the greater the chance that you will commit a crease violation.

Shooting Strategy

Shooting a lacrosse ball involves juggling many variables. The two most important aspects of shooting the ball are accuracy and velocity (power). As mentioned, accuracy is the first priority. Once you develop some accuracy, you can work on focusing your shot with more precision. You need to develop a shooting technique that you can rely on in a game situation and that enables you to deliver the ball to the target with confidence. On a team level, you have to follow the philosophy of the coaching staff. Some coaches want their players to "shoot to score," while other coaches want their players to "shoot for the pipes."

Accuracy and Power

In the battle between accuracy and power, accuracy is much more important. You should never sacrifice accuracy for power. If you shoot the ball from the outside, you still need to have control. It doesn't matter how hard you shoot the ball. If you don't have good control and you don't have any idea where the ball is going, then your shot won't be effective. There are times when you don't want to be exact in shooting the ball. You just want to blow the shot by the goalie. You don't need to be exact, but you want to be on target (somewhere on the net). If you have a room-and-time shot from 10 yards, then you're just "looking for net." You put the ball on net and make the goalie save it. You're challenging the goalie and trying to beat his reaction time. The bottom line is that accuracy dominates power. It's like a golfer who has some technique but has no control over his swing. Hitting a golf ball 300 yards doesn't do any good if the ball goes into the woods.

In the past, the targets or holes on practice shooting nets were in the corners. In today's shooting practice nets, the targets or holes are located 18 inches down and 18 inches away from the pipes. Nonetheless, the importance of accuracy in shooting is being more and more recognized. The current shooting nets have a better margin of error. If you aim 18 inches in and 18 inches down and your shot is off by 6 inches, your shot will be 12 inches inside the pipe and still in the net. If your personal shot has a margin for error or variation of 12 inches, you will want to bring your target in 18 inches. If your shot is 12 inches off, it will still be on target. If you aim for the corners and your shot is off by 6 inches, you will miss the goal. If you aim for the pipes and your shot is at all wide, you miss the goal. Many young shooters hit the pipes because they are aiming for the pipes. They are better shooters than they show, but their targets are wrong. Instead of aiming at the orange pipes, the players should aim 18 inches in and 18 inches down and make that their target. Now if they make that shot, it's a great shot.

Shooting Practice

When practicing shooting, you want to build up the technique first. You need to develop good habits while working on the proper technique so it becomes second nature. You should start very close to the goal and then work your way out from the goal cage.

Whatever shot you're working on, you have to develop the technique and get it so you can repeat that technique on a consistent basis. You want to develop a shooting technique so you can get into a rhythm and groove your shot. The purpose of building your technique is to ensure that your shooting motion becomes second nature. You practice your technique so that when you get into the heat of battle during a game, your shot is a natural habit and reaction. You don't think about the shot—you just execute it because of muscle memory.

When you practice your shooting technique, you should start out closer to the goal. This removes the need for power. You start off focusing just on technique, and then you work your way back and add power. You can't suddenly change your technique just to give yourself more power. Start at 10 yards and put the shot on goal. You don't have to be perfect. You will put more shots in the goal with this method and get more positive feedback. You will get more reps because more balls go into the cage and you don't have to chase them. You should work your way back in increments of 2 yards, working first on accuracy and then adding in velocity. Pregame basketball drills are similar to lacrosse shooting. Teams start off doing layup drills and then work their way back to longer shots. As you start playing in more games and at higher levels of competition, you should practice the shots that you'll see in actual game situations. Although you want to practice the shots that you expect to get in a game, you also want to be versatile so you can adapt to any circumstance.

Shooting Focus

You should first identify your target and work on delivering the ball to your target. Start out with no goalkeeper in the cage; your target is the entire net of the goal. Once you successfully deliver the ball to the "net target," you can practice shooting with a goalie inside the cage. The presence of the goalkeeper forces shooters to limit their targets to the area from the goalkeeper's body out to the pipes. As you become a more skilled shooter, not only does your target get smaller, but you also improve your ability to deliver the ball to a smaller target. The overall shooting focus is to work from the center of the goal out to the edges of the goal cage. Once your targets are toward the pipes of the cage, you must become more precise. Precision is the overall objective of shooting focus.

No Goalie in the Cage   If the goalie isn't in the cage, your focus should be on net, not pipe. The goal is inside the pipes. Pipes are not part of the 6-by-6-foot goal. The pipes are outside the 6 by 6 feet. The pipes are there just to hold up the net. The pipes are painted orange, and they attract shooters. If you hit the pipes, then you missed your shot. You need to start by putting your shot on target, which is the net. You're building confidence, and you're reinforcing the concept that putting your shot on target means the net. You want to put the shot on target and then work your way out to the pipes (instead of working in from the pipes). You should put it in the net and then fine-tune your shot as you move the target toward the outside. You never want to get too close to the pipes. You don't want to aim at the pipes and then venture inward. Also, you don't have to be perfect when you shoot. For example, young players often strive for perfection by shooting for the corners.

Goalie in the Cage   If there is a goalie in the cage, you should look at the goalie and then work off his body (not work from the pipes inward). Specifically, you should look at and aim for the goalie's hips and then work your way out from his hips. If you aim for the goalie's hips, you know you will be on target. When you shoot the ball, you have an open area between the goalie's body and the pipes. You look for an open area, but you also have a feel for the goalie's body and the pipe. You should put the ball between the goalie's body and the pipe. You want to bisect that open area between the goalie's hip and the pipe.

Shooting Precision

Your first priority is accuracy and putting your shot on target. Then you should work on trying to execute a consistent "aim small, miss small" shot. As you progress and become a more competent shooter, you start to develop accuracy in putting the ball where you want to put it. You need to develop precision with your shooting. You want to have a pinpoint target so that when you aim small, you will miss small. The target you're aiming for is 18 inches down and 18 inches inside the pipes, not directly in the corners. In golf, if you have an 8-iron and your target is the green, you should aim for the pin (the hole). If you miss, you will miss somewhere near the hole. If you aim for the green but you miss the green, your miss will be more severe. If you aim for a specific spot and you try to hit that spot, your variation will be much smaller. You need to look at the target (the net), then you should aim small to miss small. You pick out a small area and try to hit it. You focus on an exact spot in the net, and you use your precision to hit it. If you miss the exact spot, you won't miss it by much.

Shooting Team Play

The rules of lacrosse are set up to reward inaccurate shooting. If the shooter misses the goal but his teammate is closest to the end line when the ball crosses the line, then the shooting team retains possession. Thus, there is not a big penalty for inaccuracy because the shooting team gets the ball back. If the other team was awarded the ball when a shot goes out of bounds, you would see a lot more accurate shooting. If shooters knew that their team wouldn't get the ball back, they would make sure that they put the shot on goal. Professional (MLL) lacrosse includes a 45-second shot clock that limits the time for putting a shot on target. Most sports award the ball to the opposite team of whoever touched the ball last before it went out of bounds, and not many sports have a playing area behind the goal. In soccer, if you miss the goal, the ball is out of bounds immediately. In basketball, if you miss the hoop badly, then the ball is out of bounds. Hockey is the only other sport with an area behind the goal, but the puck doesn't go out of bounds—it hits the boards and bounces back in for anybody to play. This element of lacrosse has created two schools of shooting philosophy.

Shooting to Score   If you shoot, you shoot to score. If you don't think you can get the ball into the goal from where you are, you should not shoot it. You have to challenge goalies and make them demonstrate that they can save the ball. If the goalie does demonstrate that, you will then have to take more chances by putting your shot more to the outside. Your objective is to put the ball on target (i.e., on the goal in general).

Possession Shots   If you shoot, you shoot for the corners. The offensive team has the ability to get the ball back on missed shots as long as they are the closest to the ball when it goes out of bounds. If you aim for the corners and your shot is off by a foot, you'll miss the goal and regain possession. If you aim for the center of the net and you're off by a foot, then the goalie can make an easy save.

The three offensive on-ball skills are dodging, feeding, and shooting. Dodging is based on the north-south, straight-line principle. Players can use four types of north-south dodges to attack the goal: bull, face, roll, and split dodges. Feeding is assisting your teammates who are working hard to get open off ball. Shooting is something you have to go out and practice on your own. You have to put in the extra time and effort. If you think you can become a good shooter by shooting only in organized practices, you're mistaken because you only get a limited number of opportunities in these circumstances. You need to develop a consistent shooting technique. You should start close to the goal and work your way out from the cage.

CHAPTER FIVE

CUTTING, PICKS, AND BALL EXCHANGE

In addition to the on-ball offensive skills discussed in the previous chapter, lacrosse players must be able to execute off-ball skills such as cutting, picks, and ball exchange. Cutting is a multi-edged sword. It can be an aggressive, direct cut to the goal; a cut to set or use a pick; or a cut to execute a ball exchange. Picks are a major offensive weapon. Picks can be set anywhere on the field and are employed to free up an offensive player to pass, feed, shoot, or receive a pass. Ball exchange is catching a pass from a teammate and maintaining ball possession.

Cutting

Cutting has been described as dodging without the ball. With dodging (described in the previous chapter) and cutting, you're basically trying to accomplish the same thing. When you dodge and go to the goal, you are moving to an area in front of the goal, just like a cutter. You're trying to get the ball to a certain position on the field where you can take a high-percentage shot. With both skills, you're trying to free your hands from your defender, either with the ball (dodger) or without the ball (cutter). Cutting and dodging involve the same basic techniques: change of speed, change of direction, and deception. Cutting and dodging both include the first move, the burst, and the separation from the defender. For example, cutting can be similar to executing a split dodge without the ball. When performing a simple split dodge, you fake one way and dodge the other way. When cutting, you set your defender up by faking in one direction and then burst to the ball.

Cutting also involves unique principles of its own. If you separate from your defender, you can then cut to an open area or to the ball. If you're open, you may use animation or may call for the ball to gain the feeder's attention. Once the ball is in flight, you may need to adjust both your body and stick to maximize stick protection and create a loaded position for a shot. You have to cut through the feed to stay open as an offensive threat and cut to the tangents of the crease to minimize any crease violations. Cutting involves timing and field position. Cutting and feeding are two aspects of the same process, so timing is critical. When you cut, you want to cut to an open area of the field. Cutting can be part of a set offensive play, or it can be a freelance move. To get open on offense, you should cut to an open area or to the ball.

Principles of Cutting

Principles of cutting include committing to the cut, being ready to make adjustments, using body language effectively, calling for the ball, and always being a moving target. You have to commit to a cut and adjust your body and stick to the feed. You can use body language to get the feeder's attention so he knows that you are about to cut. At the last moment, you may have to call for the ball even though this might give your position away to your defender. In addition, you need to be a moving target in order to make things difficult for the opponent defending you and for the goalkeeper who has to follow your potential shot.

Committing to the Cut and Making Adjustments

Commitment is the mental aspect of cutting. If you become tentative when you cut, you will not execute properly. At some point, you have to commit to the cut. You must decide to "go for it" and see what happens. You need to have the following confident attitude: "I'm going to get open on this cut." Commitment is mental, and adjustments are physical. You make a commitment to cut to an open area (you tell yourself to turn on the green light and go), but at the same time, you must read the ball and your defender and must be ready to make any adjustments. Adjustments involve moving your legs and stick to respond to the flight of the ball.

Using Body Language

You use deception to get open and use animation when open. If you make a cut and you're open, you can be animated by using some body or stick movement. You use animated body language or stick movement to communicate with the feeder and make a connection. You can jiggle, pump, or twitch the head of your stick to the feeder. Stick animation is an attention getter, but you don't want to overdo it and be all over the place. By using animation, you are sending this signal: "Yes, I'm open. I can do it; give me the ball." You may not be an easy target for the feeder to identify, and animation sets you apart. Animation is positive body language that lets your teammate know that you are confident about receiving the feed.

Calling for the Ball

If you think you're open, you have to convey that to the feeder. If you think that you may go unnoticed by the feeder, you need to call for the ball. Your language should be decisive and demanding so it gets your teammate's attention. The main disadvantage of calling for the ball is that it gives away your position. For example, calling for the ball would be a last resort on a backside cut. However, having a chance to get the feed and make a play is always better than walking away empty handed. If all else fails, you should then call for the ball—this will help you avoid instances where you're open but you don't receive the ball.

Being a Moving Target

You want to be moving toward the ball when it's being fed to you. If you cut directly to the goal crease, you will then be standing still with no place to go. You will be a stationary target. If you cut to the tangents of the crease, this allows you to cut through the ball or feed. On a successful feed, the cutter usually ends up on the feeder's "doorstep."

Cutting Mechanics

Cutting mechanics involve many sequential components. The first step is getting your body and stick in a ready position to receive a feed. You initiate a first move in order to burst and separate from your defender. Your objective is to cut to the ball, not the goal. Once you commit to the cut, you adjust your body and stick to the flight of the ball. Then you explode through the feed, catch the feed on the run, and prepare to shoot or pass (loaded position).

Ready Position for Cutting

If you are anticipating making a cut or you are actually cutting to an open area or to the ball, you should run in a squared-up position toward the ball to take advantage of your speed, quickness, or agility. You want to give the feeder a full target and show him the complete head of your stick; in addition, you must be able to see the head of your stick in order to maximize catching ability and stick protection. On a pass from a feeder, you want to look the ball into the pocket of your stick. You need to use your peripheral vision so you can see the feeder, the ball, and your stick. If your stick is in the proper box position, your helmet will protect the stick head from your defender. If you cut and lose sight of your stick, then you're "dragging" it and exposing it to checks from behind. Ideally, you want to get your stick upfield and to the ball instead of dragging or pulling your stick. See figure 5.1 for an example of the proper ready position for cutting.

FIGURE 5.1 Player in the proper ready position for cutting.

First Move

When you are cutting, your first move is similar to dodging in that you want to fake your defender and then burst for separation. But first, you have to set up your defender. You can use change of speed, change of direction, or any other kind of deception with your body or stick. When your defender turns his hips, you burst and get the defender on your back. Your first step, or burst, gives you separation from your defender. For example, you might jog in one direction and then make a change-of-speed move to get your defender to accelerate. When your defender turns his hips, you cross over to change directions and burst past your defender. Another example of using stealth to get open is to "lull your defender to sleep." Normally, you always want to keep your feet moving on offense or defense. Your feet should be moving and making adjustments because you don't want to start moving from a dead standstill. If you're cutting, you want to keep your feet moving, anticipating when and where you need to cut, and then execute your burst. The only time you would stand still is when you are setting up your defender (lulling him to sleep). You appear to relax in an attempt to get the defender to relax too, or you divert your defender's attention elsewhere, which then frees you up. For example, you might drop your stick to your side to show a relaxed state.

Burst and Separate

Successful cutting comes down to your first step, just like when dodging. You want to make a good, hard first move and try to get that burst or explosion that allows you to separate from your defender into an open area. Defenders are taught to play between their man and the goal; therefore, if you burst and separate from your defender, you will usually be able to put your defender on your back and keep your body between you and the defender. Even if your defender is on your side or your shoulder, your body should still be between your defender and your stick. One way to create this separation between you (the cutter) and the defender is through a spot feed (see figure 5.2). The cutter breaks to a specific spot, and the feeder puts the ball in a location where the cutter

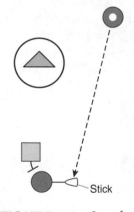

FIGURE 5.2 Spot feed.

can beat the defender to that spot. The cutter puts himself in a position where he is between his stick and the defender, and the feeder puts the ball in a spot away from the defender.

Once you get separation, you should cut to the open area. At that point, it's up to the feeder to get the ball to the cutter. Unlike dodging, you don't have the ball, so timing with your feeder is critical. If you burst to the open area but your feeder is not ready to feed the ball, then your defender can recover. For example, if you burst too soon, you will have to slow down, which makes it easier for your defender to recover.

FIVE-CONE CUTTING DRILL

PURPOSE

To learn how to cut to the feeder.

SETUP

Five cones are arranged in a Y shape out in front of the goal. The player is positioned at cone 1. A coach or teammate is behind the goal (at the apex) with a ball.

EXECUTION

The player creeps forward and strides toward cone 2. At cone 2, he uses choppy steps to prepare for a change of direction at cone 3. When the player gets to cone 3, the coach with the ball will choose a side and carry the ball in that direction. The player breaks to that side with his stick up for a feed from the coach. The player catches the ball and shoots the ball at the cage.

COACHING POINTS

- This drill teaches the importance of timing and mirroring the movements of the feeder.
- Cutting is dodging without the ball, so these two skills adhere to the same principles.

Cut to the Ball

You want to cut to the ball, not to the goal. If you cut to the goal, the feed will need to be longer, and you could step into the crease. When you cut, you should run squared up to the ball to take advantage of your speed. Once you get that initial burst and separation, you want to cut hard but also have enough control so you can adjust to the feed. You have to commit to the cut, but you must also be able to adjust your body and stick position to the flight of the ball. When you cut, it can't be at 1,000 mph and out of control. UCLA basketball coach John Wooden would tell his players, "Be quick but don't hurry." The same applies here. You need to be quick for separation, but you shouldn't hurry to complete the play. When you cut, your body and stick need to be under control. Sometimes you have to gear down to complete the play.

When the ball leaves the feeder's stick, you have to be poised and ready to make any type of adjustments to the ball with your feet (choppy steps) or your stick. Once you make any needed adjustments, you want to burst to the ball and explode through the feed. You must have a little something "left in the tank" to make the last explosive move to the ball. At this point, you turn your upper body and turn your shoulder 45 degrees, which allows you to knife through the traffic and puts you in a comfortable and relaxed position to catch the ball. You want to be able to look the ball into your stick and "give" with the ball as it enters your stick pocket (see figure 5.3). Once you catch the ball, you can continue to turn your trunk and finish turning your shoulders; you should shift your body weight back and get in a loaded position with your hands and stick back, ready to throw or shoot and protect your stick. Ideally, this motion puts you into an opposite-shoulder position where you're able to make the next play immediately (e.g., quick shot off a cut).

After you catch the ball, you should keep moving and continue to run to make sure you stay open. If you're a moving target, then it's more difficult for your defender to keep up with you and more difficult for the goalie to defend your shot. When a player cuts and scores, his momentum will often carry him right up to the feeder—where they both celebrate the goal.

FIGURE 5.3 Player cutting through a feed.

Cutting Strategy

Cutting strategy revolves around three key issues: timing, field position, and techniques for cutting near the crease. Cutting requires proper timing because it involves coordinating your actions with a feeder. An off-ball cut can come from any position on the field, and some areas are more dangerous than others. Lastly, cuts near the crease have a special character. You can cut to the tangent of the crease, cut backdoor, or cut to the middle of the crease.

Timing

Cutting and feeding are all about timing. When the feeder is ready to deliver the ball (i.e., the feeder has the ball in a preferred feeding position, and his hands are free), the cutter needs to be in a good scoring position. As the cutter, you don't want to cut into the open area too soon. If you cut too early, you will have to slow down and adjust your speed to the timing of the play. If you're "ahead of the game," you will need to slow down to get back on schedule so that you can accelerate off the run (instead of from a standstill) when it is time to cut. If you cut too soon and then slow down, this gives your defender time to recover. On the other hand, you don't want to cut into the open area too late. If the feeder is no longer in a good feeding area or his hands are no longer free from his defender, you have missed the opportunity to make a good connection with your feeder.

In the end, you and the feeder must time your movements properly in order to maximize your connection. However, there will be times when you cut properly but the feeder doesn't see you or sees you too late. That is just the nature of the game. It's similar to a play in football when a receiver makes a move and is open but the quarterback doesn't see him. The solution is that the receiver goes back to the quarterback and tells him that he was open on the play; the team can then go back to that play later in the game. The key is communication. The connection between a cutter and feeder will not always be perfect, but they can always go back and try it again.

Cutter's Field Position

Just like a feed, a cut can come from anywhere on the field. When the feeder is in the prime ball-side feeding position, you want to cut to an open area, be poised and ready for the feed, and then adjust to the ball. Your cut depends on your team's offensive strategy, your position, the positioning of your teammates and the opposing team, and the individual preferences of your feeder. You have to know where the individual feeder likes to feed the ball from and how much defensive pressure he can tolerate and still get his hands free. For example, sometimes you have to time your first move so that it occurs as the feeder approaches the prime feeding area. If you wait until the feeder is already inside the prime feeding area, by the time you get open, the feeder may no longer be there. You don't want to cut and encourage a low-percentage feed.

Cuts Near the Crease

If you are cutting near the crease, you can use specific types of cuts: tangent, backdoor, and middle-of-the-crease cuts. The crease presents certain challenges to the cutter because it is both an obstacle and an opportunity. You can't step into the crease, but an effective cut near the crease provides a great opportunity to score a goal.

Tangents   The tangent is a straight line that just touches a circle, or in this case, the perimeter of the crease circle. If you cut inside near the goal, you should angle toward the tangents of the crease. That way, if you catch the ball, you will have room to continue moving forward. Focusing on catching a ball in traffic is demanding enough. You don't need to make it more complicated by worrying about whether or not you're going to step into the crease for a technical foul and loss of possession. If you develop a good cutting angle by going toward the tangents of the crease, then a crease violation never becomes an issue. If you cut to the goal and don't score but your momentum takes you into the crease, your team loses the ball. It's bad enough to miss a feed; it's worse if you miss a feed, step into the crease, and lose possession of the ball. If you angle toward the tangents of the crease, you will tend to move toward an opposite-shoulder body position. You will automatically get your hands back in the proper position to catch and shoot. You will also be angling away from your defender and better able to protect your stick.

Backdoor Cut   A backdoor cut, as shown in figure 5.4, is a cut toward an open area on the non-ball side of the field. You are not cutting toward the ball nor the goal. You are cutting to the opposite tangent, and it is more of a stealthy, deceptive cut because you don't want to alert the defense. For a goalie, stopping a shot on a backdoor cut is more challenging because he has to travel farther across the crease to block the shot.

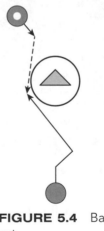

FIGURE 5.4   Backdoor cut.

   When executing a cut, the worst thing you can do is have your stick out in front of your body. This exposes your arms and stick to the defender. The exception to this would be a situation in which you want to lead with your stick so that it gets there first (before your body). For example, if you cut backside and you're wide open, you can afford to lead with your stick because of the lack of defensive pressure. If you lead with your stick, you then have to quickly adjust your body so that when you catch the ball, your shoulders are turned and you can release the ball close to the crease with your forearm and wrist. You always have to keep in mind the importance of shielding your stick.

Middle-of-the-Crease Cut   At times, you will need to cut straight down the middle of the crease—right in front of the goal—because that's the open area (inside the tangents of the crease). This is a middle-of-the-crease cut (see figure 5.5). Mentally, you want to focus on the ball and eliminate any distractions, but trying to avoid stepping into the crease is a major distraction. If you cut straight down the middle, you have to control your body and your momentum so that you don't step inside the crease. Because you have to be mindful of not stepping into the crease, you should adjust your speed and apply the brakes. If you're cutting down toward the middle of the crease, you almost have to "slip" inside the crease instead of using a hard, driving cut. Even when you slip underneath, you should adjust back to the tangent. However, if you can't return to the tangent, you need to cut "with the brakes on." The stopping point is 1 yard from the crease for a margin of error. If you're inside, you must be aware of the crease, know where the defenders are located, and adjust your body accordingly. When you're

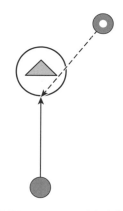

FIGURE 5.5 Middle-of-the-crease cut.

inside on the crease, you should have your body weight back so you have a little bit more power on your shot. If you catch the ball inside, the goalie will not have to move much, so you need to get rid of the ball in a hurry.

Picks

In many sports, screening is an offensive maneuver used to obstruct an opponent with your body. One offensive player gets near a teammate's defender and obstructs this defender with his body. The other offensive player gets free from his defender so he can drive in to score, shoot the ball, feed the ball, or receive a pass from another teammate.

In lacrosse, a screen can be either a post or a pick. When you set a post, you are facing the ball, and it's up to the cutter to break off of you. If you set a post, you are not actively trying to engage an opponent. You are basically a "lamp post," and your cutting teammates use you as an obstruction. When you set a pick, you are facing the opponent whom you want to pick. If you set a pick, you are actively trying to pick off your teammate's defender in order to free your teammate.

Picks in lacrosse come in two varieties: on-ball and off-ball picks. This chapter deals with off-ball offense, but in the case of an on-ball pick, the pick involves the additional element of a teammate carrying the ball and using on-ball techniques. The discussion here combines the on-ball and off-ball concepts because what makes the pick unique is the pick setter. Sometimes the player using the pick has the ball, and sometimes he doesn't. An on-ball pick is based on dodging. You set a pick near the ball carrier, and the ball carrier tries to dodge past his defender and drive unimpeded to the goal for an assist or a shot.

An off-ball pick is based on cutting. You set a pick away from the ball, and a teammate cuts off the pick for an offensive opportunity. From a defender's perspective, the on-ball defender is going to be more focused on the ball; thus, he is more likely to be picked off by a pick. On the other hand, an off-ball defender's coverage won't be as tight because he will "open up" to see his player and the ball. The defender may be more subject to a "pop" move from the crease.

Here are the general principles for executing a pick:

- *Deception*—You want to surprise the defense with a pick. The element of surprise is a big part of setting a successful pick. You don't want to telegraph a pick.

- *Communication*—Any type of communication will help set up a pick. Communication can be eye contact, body language (e.g., tap your helmet, raise your hand), or verbal (e.g., code words).

- *Mental commitment*—When using a pick, you must expect to get open. If you go through a pick in a tentative way, you give your defender more opportunity to recognize, adjust, and play you.

Pick Mechanics

Two players are involved in a pick situation: the pick setter and the pick user. The pick setter's main objective is to screen or block his teammate's defender. The pick setter must remain motionless when the pick user arrives so he isn't penalized for executing a moving pick (causing his team to lose possession of the ball). The pick user's main objective is to run his defender into the pick and take advantage of any momentary defensive confusion.

Pick Setter

The pick setter is the player who is setting the pick. Before contact, the player should be facing his target (this is the one time that the player isn't maintaining an opposite-shoulder posture). When setting a pick, you need to be able to "read" the defender's hips. You should widen yourself out as much as possible to make contact. To increase the width of your pick, you want to have an "open chest" in order to give yourself the maximum surface area or body exposure. By rule, you can adjust your body position as much as you want up until the moment of contact with the defender. At the moment of contact, there can be no movement, and you must remain stationary on contact. You want to be as athletic as possible when setting a pick. This will enable you to adjust your feet and adjust and hold your position up until the last second before contact. You need to stand tall so you can brace yourself for contact. You should hold your stick in the box position. Your stick should be at a 45-degree stick angle with the head of the stick just outside your shoulder. Your lower hand should be in front of your groin so you can protect yourself from contact. By rule, you can't drop the head of your stick down low to interfere with the free movement of a defender. See figure 5.6a for an example of a pick setter's individual position for a pick and figure 5.6b for the pick setter's position with a defender.

Pick User

The pick user is the player using the pick. If you are a pick user, you want to sprint into, through, out, or away from the pick (see figure 5.7). When you sprint, your defender must focus more on you and less on the pick. Sprinting also forces your

FIGURE 5.6 Pick setter's position for a pick: (a) individual position and (b) position with a defender.

defender to open up and run hip to hip to keep up with you. When you force your defender to open up, this provides a greater surface or body area for the pick setter to make contact with, which makes the pick more effective. As the pick user, if you jog into, through, and out of a pick, then your defender doesn't have to open up and can shuffle through the pick sideways (less body area to be picked). If you're tentative going into, through, or out of a pick, you won't be able to take advantage of any indecision or inability by the defenders. Your defender will be able to recover.

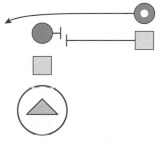

FIGURE 5.7 Pick user moving into, through, out, or away from the pick.

Pick Strategies

Picks are a two-man game that requires proper timing, angle, and field position. Offensive players involved in the pick need to understand these elements. In addition, offensive players need to understand how the defense will react to a pick. That way, the offense can counter those defensive tactics and take advantage of the situation. This section covers offensive pick strategy along with counters that the offense can use against specific defensive tactics.

Offensive Pick Strategy

As mentioned, offensive pick strategy involves three key elements: timing, angle, and field position. The timing of the two players, the angle taken by the pick user, and the proper use of field position are the three ingredients that affect the success of a pick.

Timing   Any play that involves two or more people will always require proper timing. The pick setter and the pick user need to arrive at the location of the pick at the same time so that the defender does not have time to recognize the pick and communicate with his teammates. If the two players are not equidistant from the pick location, they need to judge distances and slow down or speed up accordingly. The pick user and pick setter must work together to set up the pick user's defender. The following drill can be used to work on timing for a pick.

THREE-CONE PICK TIMING DRILL

PURPOSE
To learn how to properly time a pick.

SETUP
Three cones are spread out in a linear fashion.

EXECUTION
A coach or teammate has the ball at cone 1. Cone 2 is the midpoint and the location where the player wants to set up the pick. The player is stationed at cone 3. The coach or teammate makes his move toward cone 2, and the player also makes a move toward cone 2. The coach with the ball arrives on one side of cone 2 at the same time that the player arrives on the other side of the cone.

COACHING POINTS
At first, both parties should arrive at cone 2 at the same time and should mirror each other's movements. Later, the player should work on arriving at cone 2 a little earlier. In a game situation, the pick setter will arrive earlier. He can adjust his body and stick position up until the moment of impact with the defender.

Angle   The pick user has to work with the pick setter to achieve the proper angle and thus allow the pick to be effective. For an on-ball pick, the pick user's angle should be going to the goal. The principles of dodging remain the same. The pick user wants to dodge in a north-south direction directly to the goal. The pick setter's chest should be facing upfield, not toward the sidelines. The timing and angles of picks in lacrosse are similar to a running back setting up his blockers in football. The running back knows where to cut and knows the angles to use to set up his blockers. Some running backs are better than others in setting up their blockers.

Field Position   A pick can be set anywhere on the field. Typically, players set picks behind the goal (especially at the X-behind position), out top near the center front, or on the wing (Canadian-style pick). For example, a pick-and-roll can be set up behind the goal, and the defense will often execute a switch. The pick user steps away from the pick to free his hands. The pick setter opens up to see the ball and anticipates a double team (the pick setter doesn't want to turn his back in case of a double team). If the pick setter sets a pick and rolls to the goal, he should have his stick up ready to handle an outlet; his hands should be ready for a redirect pass or feed. An on-ball pick out top is a little different, but it follows the same principles. The main difference is that the pick user and pick setter are above the GLE and can shoot the ball.

Offensive Reaction to Defensive Pick Strategy

Defenses will attempt to neutralize the effects of an on-ball pick by either sliding through the pick and staying on their man, switching on the pick, or doubling the pick, especially if a midfielder sets a pick for an attackman. Most teams want to stay on their matchups (each defender stays on his assigned attacker). College teams will assign defenders to specific opposing offensive players based on agility, speed, strength, intelligence, and so on. However, if you set an effective pick, the defense will have to adjust and switch. In this situation, a switch is reactive in nature because the defense has no other choice. On the other hand, a switch or double can be actively used as a tactic to neutralize the pick.

Counter to Defensive Switch Some defenses like to switch on picks, and your offense can take advantage of that tendency. For example, you can use a "Sunrise" pick behind the goal. An attackman is covered by a defenseman, and a midfielder is covered by a defensive short-stick midfielder. The offense sets a pick behind the goal, anticipating that the defense will switch. Once a switch occurs, the attackman is matched up against a defensive short stick (SS), a much more favorable offensive matchup. See figure 5.8 for an example of this counter to a defensive switch.

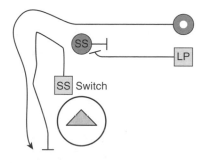

FIGURE 5.8 Counter to defensive switch: sunrise pick.

Counter to Defensive Double Some teams double the pick user at the pick, while others double the pick user from behind. Typically, the defender playing the pick setter doubles the ball from behind and executes a blind-side double, or jump. The pick user and the pick setter have separate tactics to execute in order to take full advantage of the double. The pick user needs to carry both defenders away from the goal, as shown in figure 5.9. The pick setter should get wide (not deep) from the ball carrier, as shown in figure 5.10.

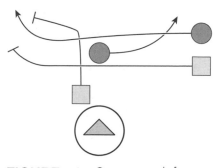

FIGURE 5.9 Counter to defensive double: Pick user carries defenders away.

If you are the pick user, you must have your head on a swivel so you can use your peripheral vision to look for both defenders and the open pick setter. You should turn and sprint away from the defensive pressure. You want to run from the two defenders at a 45-degree angle and run to daylight (an open area). You don't want to "corkscrew," which means turning into the defensive double team. You need to get your hands free so you can make a quick pass. In general, defenders are taught to stay on doubles. If both defenders stay on the double

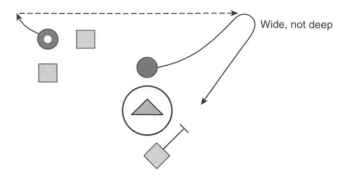

FIGURE 5.10   Counter to defensive double: Pick setter gets wide, not deep.

team, you want to carry both defenders away from the goal. The farther you carry the two defenders away from the goal, the longer it will take them to recover. If both defenders are committed to you, then you're not in a hurry to pass the ball. Be quick to escape, but don't hurry to pass. You want to continue to carry them for as long as you need to because your team will have a two-on-one advantage somewhere. If the blind-side defender leaves you, you should make a quick pass because the ball will move faster than the defender can recover, and you might still be able to take advantage of the defense's overaggressive play.

If you are the pick setter and your defender doubles the pick user, you should yell, "Double, double, double!" If you yell your teammate's name, he will have a natural tendency to turn toward the player talking to him, and he will therefore turn right into the double team. You want to be in the pick user's line of vision to facilitate any possible outlet pass. You need to adjust your position so you are in an open passing lane and can get the ball where you have an advantage. For example, you would not want to cut to the goal because the pick user might not see you. Also, if you received a pass from the pick user, you might be shortening the slide for the next defender sliding to you. Keep a "big eye" on the man (next sliding defender) and a "little eye" on the ball (pick user).

As the pick setter versus a double, you should get wide, not deep. If you run parallel to the end line and get wide, you will be more of an offensive threat. You want to position yourself to get the ball and maintain the man-up advantage. Ideally, you should split your original defender and the next sliding defender. You don't want your original defender to be able to recover to you, and you don't want to shorten the slide of the next sliding defender. The pick user is making a 15-yard pass no matter what, and you just have to make it to the optimum spot. If you run to the end line and get too deep, you're going away from the goal, and your original defender can successfully recover and beat you to the GLE. By getting too deep, you allow your original defender to "play two": The defender doubles the pick user and recovers to play the pick setter. Remember, you should never allow a defender to play two offensive players.

Ball Exchange

Ball exchange is another offensive maneuver that involves one player who has the ball and a second player who is off the ball. A ball exchange is a pass between two teammates. A pass connotes both intent and target. A pass is not a shot. Its velocity is moderated so that the catcher can handle the pass. A pass needs to be on target in order to secure a successful ball exchange. Lacrosse is a running game. If you're standing still when you throw or catch the ball, a defender will likely be able to disrupt the process with his body or stick. If you have defensive pressure, you need to cut or move in order to throw or catch the ball (you don't always have to cut for a shot). Ball exchange depends on your feet and your hands, not only to free yourself from your defender, but also to ensure a solid connection between the thrower and the catcher. Ball exchange involves principles of dodging and cutting: change of speed, change of direction, and deception.

- *Run until you throw*—You must have your hands free to throw the ball and must use your feet to escape defensive pressure, especially from defenders who have longer sticks. You should run until you release the ball in order to keep your hands free from your defender. If you are running but you stop to throw, you become a stationary target for your defender; a stationary target is always easier to play against than a moving target. If you have created some space between you and your defender and then you stop, you will allow your defender to catch up and get closer to you so he can get into your hands.

- *Run until you catch*—You must have your hands free to catch the ball and must use your feet to escape defensive pressure. To keep your hands free from your defender, you should run until you catch the ball. If you're running but you stop to catch the ball, you will experience the same problems just described for throwing.

If the thrower is running until he throws and the catcher is running until he catches, the pass will typically be a lead pass to the outside. When passing, you should always lead your teammate to the outside, away from defensive pressure. It's similar to a quarterback throwing a lead pass to a pass receiver toward the sideline and away from the defensive pressure. If the thrower misses his target, he wants to "miss wide" as opposed to handcuffing the catcher. The catcher can handle a wide pass better than one that handcuffs him. He can reach out to catch a wide pass, but a pass to his waist renders his hands ineffective.

The primary technique for getting yourself open on a ball exchange is a V-cut. A V-cut is only necessary when there is defensive pressure. You drive your defender toward the goal, and your defender must give ground. When your defender is backing up, you pull away from him—that's what gives you separation or space so your hands are free to throw or catch the ball. It's similar to when a pass receiver sprints and drives the cornerback back so he has to give ground. The pass receiver separates from the cornerback and then comes back for the ball. For the V-cut, the angle is at 45 degrees because this opens up the passing lane and shortens the pass. If you make a V-cut and come back for the ball, the defender can't get into the passing lane. For example, assume midfielder 1 has the ball at field location 5, and midfielder 2 is located at field location 3 (see figure 10.1 for details about these field positions). Both are stationary, and they have a 20-yard pass between them. Midfielder 2 makes a 45-degree V-cut to the cage and back out. What was a 20-yard pass is now a 10-yard pass from midfielder 1 to midfielder 2. See figure 5.11 for an example of this V-cut.

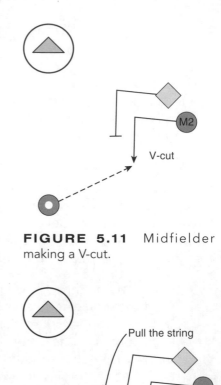

FIGURE 5.11 Midfielder making a V-cut.

On the other hand, if you use a straight cut, then the pass is longer, and the defenders can step into the passing lane. A V-cut tends to shorten the pass between teammates, and shorter passes usually have a higher percentage of completions. When you execute a V-cut, you should usually step to the ball right before you catch it. Some coaches teach players to do a 45-degree cut and then let the ball come to them. If you can't step to the ball, you need to adjust your body to the ball. In some instances, you may make a V-cut, and your defender will overplay you. In this case, you should do a reverse V-cut (see figure 5.12). You break off as if you're go-

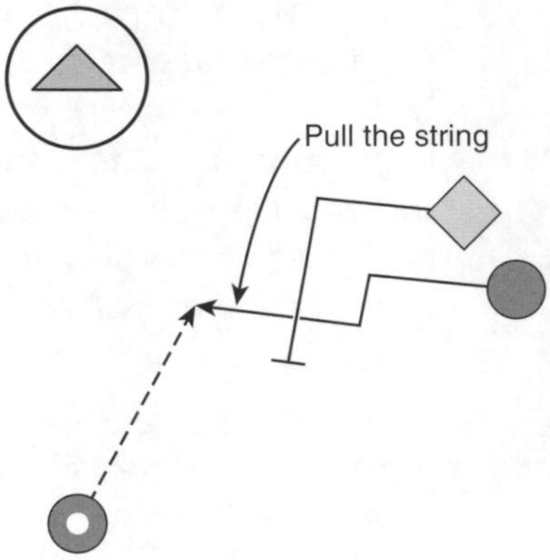

FIGURE 5.12 Reverse V-cut.

ing to get the ball, encouraging your defender to overplay you, and then you cut backdoor. The purpose of the backdoor move is to keep your defender "honest."

Off-ball offensive play involves various skills such as cutting, using a pick, ball exchange, and off-ball movement. Players may use cutting to create space, to catch a pass from a teammate, or to receive a feed for a scoring opportunity. Setting and using a pick are important skills. A pick is a major offensive weapon. Picks can be used anywhere on the field to get a player open for a pass, feed, or shot. A V-cut is the most effective tactic for achieving a successful ball exchange when a player is under defensive pressure. Off-ball movement is based on the straight-line principle. The offensive player is forcing his defender to either watch the ball or watch him.

Off-Ball Movement

By using proper off-ball movement, you can set yourself up to execute a cut, pick, or ball exchange. Off-ball movement involves using your legs to get your stick in the right position to cut, pick, or exchange the ball. Off-ball movement is one of the most difficult things to teach and learn in offensive lacrosse. Young players tend to stare at the ball on offense, and they have no idea what's going on away from the ball. Off-ball defenders are taught to "V-up" on you so that they can see you and the ball. In contrast, you want to position yourself so that your defender is in a straight line between you and the ball (see figure 5.13). You should keep your head on a swivel so you can follow this rule: "Big eye on your man, little eye on the ball." Your primary focus is reading your man, and your secondary focus is watching the ball. You read your defender by watching his eyes, head, and body movements. If your defender makes a defensive mistake, the only way you will know about it is if you watch him. If you continue to adjust your position ("occupy your man") so that the defender is in a straight line between you and the ball, this forces the defender to make a decision. He can either watch you or the ball. If the defender chooses to focus on you, he will not be an effective team defense player because he will not be able to effectively slide. If he chooses to focus on the ball, you need to be a threat to score. You want to be close enough to him so that if he makes a mistake and "ball watches," you can cut and be dangerous and open in three steps.

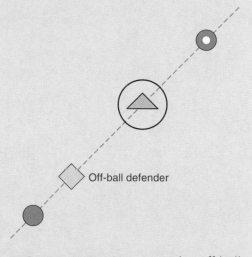

FIGURE 5.13 Lining up the off-ball defender in a straight line from the ball carrier.

However, in a man-advantage situation (e.g., 6v5) or if the opposing team is using a zone defense, the straight-line rule does not apply. In a zone defense, defenders are more focused on the ball than on a specific offensive player because each defender is really playing two attackers. If it's 6v6 and the opposing team is playing man-to-man defense, then the straight-line rule does apply.

CHAPTER SIX

FACE-OFFS

A face-off specialist needs to have both the head and the heart of a warrior. When the whistle blows, the face-off is a personal battle between two players. Mentally, a face-off specialist needs to have confidence in his abilities, concentration skills to anticipate the referee's whistle, and poise to maintain his composure if things aren't going well. Emotionally, he can never give up in his efforts to control the ball—this applies during the draw itself or the subsequent loose ball. Successful face-off specialists share one key ingredient: They take a lot of pride in what they do. Physically, they must have quickness, strength, and agility. Like many other team sports, lacrosse is a game of offensive "runs" whereby teams gain offensive momentum and score goals in bunches. Control of the face-off plays a critical role in this regard. If your team is on an offensive run, then gaining a face-off allows you to continue your momentum. If your team has just been scored on, then control of the next face-off allows you to minimize or stop the growing momentum of your opponent.

Face-Off Rules

The face-off ritual is a unique activity that starts the beginning of each quarter and also starts play after either team scores a goal. The referee places the ball at the center midpoint of the field along the 4-inch-wide centerline. Each face-off player stands on his defensive side of the field (the same side of the field as the goal he is defending). The referee commands "Down," and both players bend down and assume the face-off stance (see figure 6.1).

When you assume the face-off stance, your stick head has to be back to back with your opponent's. You must have both gloves wrapped around the shaft of the stick, and your right glove can't touch the plastic head of the stick. Both gloves must touch the ground and can't touch the centerline. Your stick is parallel to the centerline but not touching the centerline. Your stick head must be perpendicular to the ground, and both your gloves need to be in contact with the ground. The reverse side of your stick head must match up evenly with your opponent's, and no part of your stick may touch the resting ball. Your feet cannot touch your stick.

The proper stance creates a "neutral zone" whereby you must position your entire body (head, elbows, hands, knees, feet) to the left of the plastic head of your stick. It is legal to lean your body over the centerline, but you can't lean your body into the neutral zone and over the resting ball before the whistle. The

FIGURE 6.1   Face-off stance.

referee will command "Set," and each player must then remain motionless until the referee blows his whistle to start play. At the sound of the referee's whistle, each player uses his body and stick to try to gain possession of the ball.

Face-Off Setup

The face-off setup is the preparation stage before assuming the face-off stance. Every player will have his own unique stance and style. Your individual preference will be based on comfort, balance, and execution. If you are able to make effective moves and countermoves out of your individual stance, that's all that matters. Body positioning is based on getting close to the ball and close to the ground but staying athletic and balanced throughout the process.

Many players like to line up as close to the ball as possible and get their stick as close to the ball as possible. This is called crowding the ball. Typically, stronger players want to get closer to the ball, and quicker players want to get farther from the ball. Some players like to get as low to the ground as possible and thereby closer to the ball ("low man wins the face-off"); if you do this, you must be sure to stay on your feet and stay athletic. If you lose your feet, you can't react quickly enough to the ball, and you compromise your athleticism. More than anything else, your stance must be athletic the whole time: from the setup, throughout the execution of any stick techniques and stepping moves, and during any reactions by you to your opponent. Your stance must allow you to be well balanced. You want to make it difficult for your opponent to push you backward, and at the same time, you must be effective moving forward with your stick move.

For the setup, your hands should be no more than shoulder-width apart on the handle of the stick. You can use either a traditional grip or a reverse or motorcycle grip on the handle. The choice of grip is a matter of personal preference. If you use a traditional grip, your right hand is palm up with knuckles down toward the ground, and your left hand is palm down with knuckles up toward the sky (see figure 6.2a). A player who uses a laser or jump move over the ball will use a traditional grip. If you use a reverse grip, both hands are palm down with the knuckles facing toward the sky (see figure 6.2b). The strength of the reverse (motorcycle) grip is its application to the very popular clamp and plunger moves.

When gripping the stick, you want your right hand as close to the plastic head as possible. This gives you more control of the plastic stick head. Control of the stick head plays a critical role in face-off success. Your left hand should be about 12 inches (30.5 cm) from your right hand and placed more in the middle of the handle. Proper stick technique is the key to stick quickness; thus, your stick head should be just touching the ground so you have very little body weight on your hands. Your stance should allow you to not put any body weight on your hands, meaning you should be able to get in your stance and lift your hands without losing your balance.

When you are setting up, your feet should be about shoulder-width apart with your left foot somewhat staggered behind your right foot (see figure 6.3). In general, your right foot is pointing toward the ball, and your left foot is pointing downfield. If your feet are underneath your shoulders, you are better balanced and more mobile, and you can effectively execute your first step.

FIGURE 6.2 Setup grips: (a) traditional and (b) reverse or motorcycle.

FIGURE 6.3 Player in proper face-off stance.

On the contrary, if you rest your body weight on your left knee or if your left foot is too far back (like a track and field sprinter), then your ability to take your first step is minimized, your balance is compromised, and your mobility is limited. When your body weight is on your left knee, you can't step, you can't get out of your stance and chase a loose ball, and you have less balance. If you position your left leg like a sprinter to get your body lower, your feet will be too wide, and you will become less athletic in stepping or getting a ground ball. In a sprinter's stance, your body weight is more on your right foot (not your left foot), which negatively affects your balance and minimizes your ability to counter your opponent's body and stick movements. Some face-off players prefer to put more body weight on their right foot because they think this enables them to get closer to the resting ball.

Also, note that your setup should be the same on every face-off; otherwise, you may disclose your intentions to your opponent. In a sense, a player's stick move is somewhat readable because of his hand position (wrists are cocked or not cocked), elbows, foot placement (feet are pointed forward or toward the corner of the field), body posture (you crowd the ball on one move but not another), and stick head position (stick head is light or heavy on the ground; body weight on hands).

Face-Off Whistle

Just before the face-off action, the referee will back away from the two face-off specialists and signal the start of play with his referee's whistle. In a face-off, you want to anticipate the whistle, explode on the first sound, and get out quickly with your body and stick. Various stick moves and techniques can be used to gain an advantage and gain possession of the ball. The primary stick moves are the clamp, plunger, rake, top, reverse clamp or laser, and jam (more details on these can be found later in the chapter). Current players favor the clamp and plunger, although some also use the laser and jam. The popularity of each stick move has evolved over time because of the changing technology of the lacrosse stick, the changing procedural rules of play, and the preferred methods of high-profile face-off specialists at the college and professional levels.

All the moves involve maneuvering the plastic stick head with your hands in a particular manner to control the ball and to get the ball out so that you or a winger can scoop it for possession. The main objective is to move your hands and get your hands over the ball so that you can get the ball out for a ground ball. If you have too much weight on your hands, this will adversely affect your quickness and balance. Then, on the whistle, the first thing you must do is take that weight off your hands, which slows down the quickness of your stick technique. It also compromises your balance because you can be more easily moved and body-checked by your opponent.

On the whistle, your first step plays a crucial role in executing most stick moves (e.g., clamp, plunger, top). Your first step can be with either foot, but typically you will use your right foot. If you step with your right foot, you block your opponent's stick move and minimize his opportunity to create a fast break. Stepping with your right foot enables you to get into your opponent and knock him off the ball. This gives you an advantage (knocks the opponent off the ball) and takes away the opponent's advantage (fast break) with the same move. When you step, you should keep your feet under your body so you can stay balanced. By staying balanced, you can counter any body checking by your opponent, and you can react to any ball movement. If you step with your right foot, then more of your body weight is on your left foot so you can push off with your left foot and explode with your right foot (see figure 6.4). The objective is to move your feet so you can get out of your stance and get a ground ball.

FIGURE 6.4 Player prepared to step and explode with the right foot during the face-off.

Face-Off Ball Possession

During a face-off, you will sometimes execute your stick move and immediately control the ball—getting the ball out, scooping it for possession, and going. That's a "clean" face-off. Ideally, you don't want to deal with your opponent. However, in most cases, there will not be immediate possession, and both players will vigorously compete for the ball. You should use your body to move your opponent off the ball and put yourself in an advantageous body position. You need to keep your chest over the ball and keep your head down and your eyes on the ball until you have control of the ball (see figure 6.5).

Early in a face-off, you may not want to scoop the ball because your opponents are crashing in on you or you don't have the proper stick angle for scooping the ball. (Don't scoop a ball at your feet.) When you can't cleanly scoop the ball, your objective is to control the ball with your stick head (get your stick underneath your opponent's stick) or shaft and draw the ball out in the direction and distance you want. If you don't have control of the ball, you can always "goose" or kick the ball into an open area. If at all possible, you should put

FIGURE 6.5 Player using his body position to his advantage during the face-off.

the ball into an open area where you or your wings can get a more uncontested scoop. The desired ball direction can be forward, to the side, 45 degrees behind, or directly behind you. You can push the ball forward for a fast break, rake it out to the side, or draw the ball behind you.

On a face-off, your ultimate goal is to get the ball off the turf or ground and into the upright pocket of your stick so you can move the ball to a teammate. This often requires you to position the ball first, your body second, and your stick third; you then execute a scooping technique. Many stick moves involve using your stick head or shaft to draw the ball between your legs either for yourself or for a winger.

Draw and Box to Scoop

During a face-off, if you're directing the ball behind you, the best technique is to draw the ball where you want to scoop it, box out your opponent, and then scoop the ball. You don't want to turn your body (or open up) first and then push the ball out to scoop it. If your opponent is a good athlete, he could run around you and get the loose ball. You need to position your body between your opponent and the ball and keep turning and adjusting your body to screen or box out your opponent (see figure 6.6). Boxing out means your back is toward

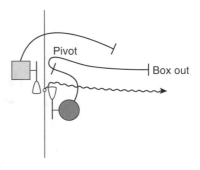

FIGURE 6.6 Boxing out.

your opponent, similar to a basketball player positioning himself for a rebound. In basketball, the player sees the shot, locates and feels for where his opponent is, and makes the turn to box him out from the rebound.

You should stay low and use your butt, hips, back, elbows, and stick to keep your opponent on your back. It comes down to staying athletic. Sometimes your feet have to get wider to counter the force from your opponent. This enables you to brace yourself. For example, if you draw the ball directly behind you, you should then block your opponent with your body (so he doesn't take off around you), push off with your hands, pivot your body, box out the opponent, and scoop the ball. If you draw the ball out at 45 degrees behind you, your body will naturally be in position to block your opponent's straight-line access to the ball, which increases your chances of scooping the ball.

Scoop to Protect and Pass

When you are ready to scoop the ball, you can use either a one-hand or two-hand technique to scoop the ball (see figure 6.7). Whenever possible, you should use both hands because this makes you more of an offensive threat. You need to pick up the ball on your first attempt. Sometimes the competition for a loose ball on a face-off is so fierce that your window of opportunity is limited. If you mishandle the first scoop, you might not get another uncontested chance.

Once you scoop the ball, you must protect the ball while also having the ability to make a quick pass. Both tasks are important. If you focus only on stick protection,

FIGURE 6.7 Scooping using *(a)* the one-hand technique or *(b)* the two-hand technique.

the opponents will swarm all over you, and you will likely get the ball checked out of your stick. Having the ability to protect and pass helps you defend your stick from a check. You must have the ability to get rid of the ball immediately. After scooping the ball, you should bring the stick to your face or protect it with your body. Once you have possession of the ball, you must be ready to make a release pass (to a winger) or run away from any pressure. You don't want to lead your wingers into the middle of the field where there is more traffic. If you have an open winger to your off-ball side and you don't have time to pivot to your strong hand, you can use a shovel pass (see figure 6.8). If you're pressed up against the sidelines, you can use a jump pass to get the ball to a teammate (see figure 6.9).

If you lose the draw, you can still win the battle for the loose ball. If your opponent is consistently beating you with his move, and your jam is not effective, you can change your strategy. You can offer no fight on the opponent's first move but then beat him to the loose ball. If you don't beat him to the ball, you can time your movement so that you are able to poke-check the opponent's bottom hand when he is in the act of scooping the ball.

Face-Off Stick Moves

Stick moves are the initial movements of the face-off specialist's body and stick to gain possession of the ball. These moves are the bread and butter of a face-off specialist's skills. The traditional stick moves were the clamp, rake, and top; but these moves have evolved into other variants such as the plunger and jam moves. A stick move is the first critical step in the sequence of executing a successful face-off.

Clamping Moves

Clamping is the most popular stick move in lacrosse. All clamps require you to stay low and clamp down on the ball with the back of your stick head. The primary clamp moves are the power clamp, quick clamp, and plunger.

FIGURE 6.8 Shovel pass.

You can use either a traditional grip or a motorcycle grip when clamping. You're trying to "pinch" the ball into the back of your stick head so that you can go back with the ball or come up and around with it for a fast break. In the setup, your wrists should be cocked so that you can use your hand quickness and strength to clamp your stick down over the ball. Having your wrists cocked allows you to build up torque so you can explode into the move. Your feet are pointing toward the resting ball, and you have more body weight on your left foot.

FIGURE 6.9   Jump pass.

Your body posture must be balanced and as low as possible without causing you to lose mobility. On the whistle, you use your wrists to rotate the back of your stick head flat to the ground and trap the resting ball into the back of your stick head. You should step with your right foot near your stick head and move your stick head to the right. Stepping with your right foot enables you to block your opponent's stick head and take away his chance to initiate a fast break. When you move your stick to the right, the back of your stick head gets more narrow as it moves into your opponent's stick head, and this maximizes your ability to get underneath his stick head.

Power Clamp

In the setup for the power clamp, you cock back the wrist of your top hand. On the whistle, you trap the ball with the back of your stick and step with your right foot. A power clamp is a top-hand-dominant clamp with more emphasis on the right hand clamping the ball into the ground. You lift up on the butt end of your stick with your left hand and apply more pressure and leverage over the ball (instead of keeping the butt end of your stick flat to the ground). See figure 6.10 for an example of the power clamp.

Quick Clamp

In the setup for the quick clamp (also called the punch or push clamp), you cock your left hand back and cock your right hand the opposite way to get more power on the move. On the whistle, you punch or push your left hand and the butt end of your stick forward into the ground. A quick clamp is more bottom-hand dominant. You keep your left hand and the butt end low to the ground and clamp the ball into the back of your stick. Ideally, you should step first with your right foot, but some players prefer to take their first step with their left foot and then reset their stance with a right step. See figure 6.11 for an example of the quick clamp.

FIGURE 6.10 Power clamp.

FIGURE 6.11 Quick clamp.

Plunger

The plunger is an extremely popular clamp move designed to start a fast break. Your setup is similar to the power or quick clamp, and you can use either a motorcycle or traditional grip. On the whistle, you use a power or quick clamp and step with your right foot. You clamp down hard with your right hand, and you lift the butt end of your stick vertically to strongly pinch or trap the ball into the back of your stick head. Your stick handle looks like a household plunger in action. You move the stick head back toward you and then forward and around your opponent. You "squeeze" the ball out front for a fast break. See figure 6.12 for an example of the plunger.

FIGURE 6.12 Plunger.

Raking Moves

Raking involves performing a raking, sweeping, or pulling motion with your stick and punching the ball with your stick head so that there is a sideways, lateral pulling action. The rake move can be done using the traditional method or a quick-punch rake.

Traditional Rake

In the past, opponents were allowed to closely line up the back of their stick pockets in proximity to the resting ball on the centerline. This made a traditional raking move an effective strategy. To execute a traditional rake, you would cock your wrists in a reverse fashion compared to a clamp move. On the whistle, you push the back of your stick head forward into your opponent's stick and "trap' the ball, pull your stick head across the front or your body from right to left, and rake the ball out with a sweeping motion of both hands. See figure 6.13 for an example of the traditional rake.

With the traditional rake move, you're trying to "rip" the ball down the centerline as fast as you can, and you're hitting it off your opponent's stick, which forces it down the line.

Currently, the traditional rake is not as prevalent because it doesn't give you any real advantage.

FIGURE 6.13   Traditional rake.

Recently rules were implemented to create more distance between the opponent's sticks. Today, neither stick may touch the 4-inch centerline which creates more of a gap between the backs of the player's stick pockets.

If you are just ripping the ball out to the side, the ball will end up going to a no-man's-land. In essence, you don't really have any control of the ball, and you're not dictating where you're putting the ball. It becomes a 50-50 ground ball.

Quick-Punch Rake

Another option is the quick-punch rake. On the whistle, you turn your stick head counterclockwise with the pocket of the stick facing the ground (opposite motion of the clamp move) and drop it to the ground behind the ball. You keep the butt end of your handle and the stick head flat to the ground and then punch or slap the ball underneath your opponent's stick with a sweeping or raking motion to the side. See figure 6.14 for an example of the quick-punch rake. Because your intention is to slap the ball, not trap the ball, your right-foot first step is not as important. The quick-punch rake is more successful against a topping move, but currently it's not as prevalent because of the dominance of clamping and plunging moves.

FIGURE 6.14 Quick-punch rake.

Topping Moves

All topping moves involve lifting your stick head or shaft over the resting ball and placing your stick between your opponent's stick and the ball. You want to neutralize your opponent's stick movements and then direct the ball out so you can scoop it. The three major topping stick moves are the top or jump move, the reverse clamp or laser move, and the jam move.

Top or Jump

In the setup for the top or jump move, your wrists are not cocked, and your hands and stick are very light on the ground because you want to go over the ball to execute your move. Your feet are pointing toward the centerline, and your posture is not crouched as much toward the ground as on a clamp. On the whistle, you lift your stick head over the resting ball and thrust the back of your stick head OR shaft forward, making contact with your opponent's stick head (e.g., stopping his clamp). You step with your right foot to minimize a fast break. Typically, you will lift your handle over the ball. You should aim your handle for the top of your opponent's stick head and knock him off the ball. You bring your stick down, controlling the ball either with the stick head or shaft, and then draw the ball between your legs. See figure 6.15 for an example of the top or jump move.

FIGURE 6.15   Top or jump move.

Reverse Clamp or Laser

In the setup for the reverse clamp or laser move, your wrists are prepared to rotate the stick counterclockwise, and your hands and stick are very light to the ground. Your feet are pointing toward the centerline. Whichever foot you prefer to take the first step with, the other foot should have more body weight on it so you can push off effectively. On the whistle, you lift your stick off the ground, turn your stick head counterclockwise so the front of the stick head is facing the ground, and step. You drop your stick head over the ball, trap the ball between the front of your stick pocket and the ground (opposite of a clamp), and draw the ball out. A variant of

this move is lifting your stick pocket over the ball but you don't clamp down on the ball. Instead, you tap the ball with your stick head and draw the ball out to the side by pulling the butt end of your stick toward the sidelines (raking). This is the signature move of Kyle Harrison, former NCAA player of the year. See figure 6.16 for an example of the reverse clamp or laser move.

FIGURE 6.16 Reverse clamp or laser move.

Jam

The setup for the jam move is similar to that for the top and laser moves. On the whistle, you lift your stick over the ball, thrust your top hand or shaft forward toward the top of your opponent's stick head, and make it a scrap or fight. Typically, you will "shaft the ball out" between your legs, which does not lend itself to an offensive fast break. The jam is primarily a defensive move. If you're struggling against your opponent, you might want to jam him and make it a 50-50 ground ball (3v3 instead of 1v1). See figure 6.17 for an example of a jam.

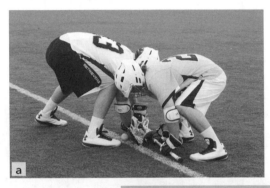

FIGURE 6.17   Jam move.

Team Face-Off Strategy

The face-off is a 3v3 game. The face-off unit includes the face-off specialist and two wingers. Typically, one winger has a short stick (SS) and is designated as the offensive winger; the other winger has a long stick (LS) and is designated as the defensive winger. However, a team can also use two short sticks or two long sticks on the face-off as long as the rule requiring only four long sticks on the field at any given time is followed. The two wingers play a critical role in the success of the unit. The primary objective of the face-off unit is to start a fast break or gain possession of a loose ball. Much of the face-off is a mind game in which each team is trying to deceive the other team.

In terms of team depth, a team needs to have three face-off specialists, a minimum of two short-stick wingers, and a minimum of two long-stick wingers. The face-off specialist must communicate to the two wingers regarding where he intends to put the ball and whether or not he wants them to shut off their opponents.

Face-Off Specialist Strategy

If you're a face-off specialist, one strategy you may use is to scoop the ball yourself. To do this, you should direct the ball away from traffic and put the ball 4 to 5 yards away from the face-off spot. If you push or pull the ball out too far, the wings will get involved in the play. When using this strategy, you want your wingers to shield and box out their opponents, making it a 1v1 game between you and your opponent.

You may also base your strategy on the position of the opposing long-stick winger. If the opposing long-stick winger is positioned at the centerline, you should draw the ball either backward or forward. If the opposing long-stick winger is positioned at the offensive end of your wing line, you should draw the ball back at 45 degrees for solo or wing pickup. If the opposing long-stick winger is positioned at the defensive end of your wing line, you should draw the ball forward at 45 degrees for solo or wing pickup and a fast break. For example, let's say your short-stick winger is positioned at the centerline with his opponent; in this case, the short-stick winger can "pull him deep" (ride out his opponent away from the action) so the face-off specialist can draw the ball behind for an easy grounder for himself (see figure 6.18).

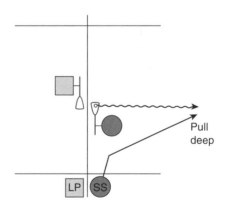

FIGURE 6.18 Face-off specialist pulling the opponent deep.

Or, another example might be if the opposing team's long-stick winger shuts off your short-stick winger and takes away the fast break *or* takes away the easy ground ball. In this case, you can position your wings at the centerline; then, if you put the ball behind you, you have a little more time to get behind the ball and scoop it yourself (see figure 6.19).

Wing Strategy

As a winger, your primary responsibility is to keep track of your man and to take away any fast breaks. On the whistle, you need to get a burst off the wing line and get your man on your back. That way, if the ball comes down the centerline, you will have an advantage. It usually takes about 3 seconds for the wings to get involved with any ball scrums.

If you are the offensive winger, you should line up near the centerline or line up where you think the ball will be directed by your teammate (see figure 6.20). Offensively, you want to either scoop a loose ball or provide an outlet for a release pass by your teammate. Defensively, if the opposing team's face-off specialist is dominating play, you will play at the defensive edge of the wing line. If you're the defensive winger, you should line up near the centerline or line up where you think the opponent's face-off specialist will direct the ball (see figure 6.21). Defensively, you want to minimize any fast break situation. Offensively, you want to scoop any loose balls or provide an outlet.

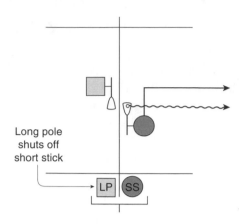

FIGURE 6.19 Face-off specialist getting behind the ball.

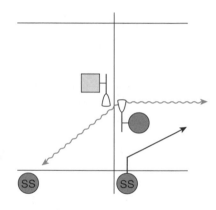

FIGURE 6.20 Ideal field position for an offensive winger.

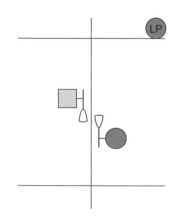

FIGURE 6.21 Ideal field position for a defensive winger.

If neither face-off specialist clearly wins the ball and gets it out, the face-off becomes a stalemate or scrum and a ground-ball war. For example, if both players are trying to clamp and neither is winning the battle, they will tend to circle in a counterclockwise motion (see figure 6.22). If a scrum occurs, the wingers should settle in and locate their man (hip to hip); they must always make sure that someone is on the defensive side of the field. The wingers, especially the long-stick winger, need to watch their men and be responsible for their men (a winger can't lose track of his man). They must play defense and take away any fast breaks. The wingers should circle the scrum at 5 yards. They need to cover as much of the field as possible. If a winger is too close to the scrum and the ball comes out, he won't be able to get to it. The wingers should "mirror" each other

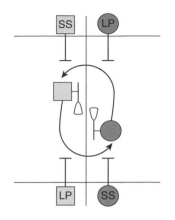

FIGURE 6.22 When the face-off specialists clamp one another, both players move in a counterclockwise motion.

around the scrum. If both wingers are on the same side of the field, the ball could pop out on the side where nobody is located; then the advantage goes to the opposing team. If there is a scrum, the face-off specialist should keep his short-stick winger on his butt. It may be more effective for the face-off specialist to get the ball to his short-stick winger than to scoop it himself. The long-stick winger wants to stay hip to hip with and neutralize the opposing short-stick winger.

Face-Off Drills

Face-offs are a personal battle. Facing off is a specialist skill that requires a lot of discipline and training. The following drills teach the fundamentals of the basic stick moves. As with any contest that requires close body contact, repetition is the key.

CHOP DRILL

PURPOSE
To learn hand and stick quickness.

SETUP
The player gets in his stance; a coach or teammate is positioned nearby.

EXECUTION
The player practices bringing the stick head back and forth over the resting ball. The teammate or coach can say "Go" and then "Stop" or can use a whistle.

COACHING POINTS
This drill helps players improve their hand quickness and make the "topping" motion more natural and second nature.

CLAMP DRILL

PURPOSE

To learn how to clamp the ball.

SETUP

The player gets in his face-off stance.

EXECUTION

The player practices clamping over the resting ball. The player can use either a power clamp or a quick clamp stick maneuver.

COACHING POINTS

- The purpose of the drill is to introduce the clamping motion.
- At first, the player doesn't move his feet. Then he can add a step with his right foot and follow with a left-foot step to reset his balance over the ball.

CLAMP AND DRAW DRILL

PURPOSE

To learn how to draw the ball between your legs.

SETUP

The player gets in his face-off stance.

EXECUTION

The player clamps the ball with his stick, steps with his right foot, and draws the ball between his legs. The player can use either a power clamp or a quick clamp stick maneuver.

COACHING POINTS

- This drill teaches players how to draw the ball out between their legs, which is a common technique with many stick moves.
- The player can add a pivot on the right foot and scoop the ball.

BACK-TO-BACK DRILL

PURPOSE

To learn how to box out.

SETUP

Two players get back to back over a resting ball; a coach or teammate is positioned nearby.

EXECUTION

The teammate or coach says "Go" or blows a whistle. Both players jockey for position over the ball, but they don't use their sticks. On the second command or whistle, both players attempt to scoop the ball.

COACHING POINTS

In this drill, the goal is to move the opponent off the ball and box him out for possession.

FOOTWORK DRILL

PURPOSE

To develop foot agility.

SETUP

The player places his stick handle on the ground; a coach or teammate is positioned nearby.

EXECUTION

On a command or whistle, the player jumps back and forth over the handle of his stick, jumps back and forth over the head of his stick, and jumps back and forth along the length of his stick.

COACHING POINTS

This drill helps players develop foot agility, which is vital in the face-off technique.

The face-off is a ritual in the game of lacrosse that involves the face-off specialist and two wingmen. It is used to start off each of the four quarters of play and to reset play after one of the teams has scored a goal. This chapter examined the particular rules and skills that pertain to face-offs. Each face-off specialist has a unique setup when addressing the ball. When the referee's whistle blows, the face-off specialist uses various stick moves—such as a clamp, plunger, top, jam, or rake—to control the movement of the ball. He tries to draw the ball out into a favorable field position, box out his opponent, and then scoop the ball. He scoops the ball to both protect the ball and to make a pass to a teammate. The two wingmen help control the ball or execute defensive skills. The face-off is one of the most unique parts of lacrosse and contributes to its heritage.

CHAPTER SEVEN

GOALKEEPING

Goalkeeping may be the most important position on the field because it often has the most influence on the outcome of a game. Good defenses with good goalies will always be competitive. Good defenses with excellent goalies are difficult to beat. Goalkeeping may also be the most difficult position to play because this position requires a unique set of mental and physical skills. Most goalkeepers march to the sound of a different drummer. In the game of lacrosse, each possession is a battle of wills, and the final outcome of the contest is determined by the trading of shots and saves. A goalie must have confidence in his ability to save every shot. In reality, the goalie won't be able to save *every* shot, but his belief and effort are what matter. The primary responsibilities of a goalkeeper are stopping shots, clearing the ball after a save or from a dead-ball situation, and quarterbacking the defense. Before discussing these responsibilities, however, let's take a look at the mental and physical qualities of a successful goalkeeper.

Goalkeeper Qualities

Goalkeepers are made up of a collection of psychological and physical attributes. Psychological traits of an effective goalkeeper include courage, mental toughness, concentration, composure, and persistence. To be a goalkeeper, you must have courage so you can overcome the fear of being hit by a high-velocity shot. You need to understand that playing goalie does involve getting hit with the ball. This "badge of courage" is shared by all goalkeepers. As you learn to make saves and improve your technique, you will be less likely to get hit by a shot. You must be mentally tough so you can cope with difficult situations and emerge without losing confidence. You have to accept the challenges and responsibilities that come with stepping in front of the nets for your team. You must be able to handle the pressures of being the last line of defense. As a goalie, you can go from a hero to a goat in a matter of seconds.

You need effective concentration skills that enable you to focus only on the ball through all of the offensive traffic. You must also be able to size up the field with your peripheral vision while concentrating on the ball. You need intelligence and the ability to make smart decisions. Another key trait is composure, which enables you to maintain control over your emotions. For example, if you give up a goal, you need to forget it and move forward. You must have a short memory, and you should not show dejection when scored on. This is not the place for "licking one's wounds" in the heat of battle. You must remain cool, calm, and collected because your teammates rely on you. You need to have persistence. Being persistent and never giving in are crucial because your next save or the final save of the day may be the one that wins the game for your team. Even a not-so-stellar performance may be rewarded with victory.

In short, goalies have two levels of performance: ordinary and extraordinary. You want to be a dependable goalkeeper. You need to be good enough to save the shots that you are supposed to stop. You want to be someone who shows up every outing—someone whom your teammates can count on to provide a steady, even performance no matter what the situation. Teams rally around a dependable goalie. In addition, you have to sometimes make the extraordinary save that you're not expected to make. You should look at all saves, even the very difficult ones, as an opportunity. Realize that the tough shots—the ones that appear to be a sure goal—are a chance to make a game-changing play. This type of save may change the momentum of the game and may be a back breaker for your opponent. Excellent goalkeepers have a knack for making tough shots look like routine saves. When a great shot is turned back with a great fundamental save, the shooter's confidence is diminished. Great shooters attempt to will the ball into the goal when they are shooting. Great goalkeepers have an even greater ability to will these shots out of the goal.

Goalkeepers must have many of the same physical qualities required of players in other positions; however, quick hands and feet are particularly essential for a goalie. Good vision is important for ball movement and to follow the flight of a shot from the opponent's stick to your stick. You need to have excellent reflexes. Goalkeeper is the position that requires the best reaction skills. General drills such as jumping rope, foot agilities, juggling, and anything that improves eye–hand coordination will be helpful for a goalie.

Stopping the Ball

For your opponent, the ultimate objective is to score a goal against your team. As a goalie, you want to give yourself a chance to save every shot by getting your eyes, stick, and body ready for the shot. You don't want to be in a shot ready position for too long (ideally, no longer than 30 seconds at a time) because you only have "so much in the tank." Before the shot, you should watch the head of the player's stick, not his body movements. Your eyes are focused, your stick is ready, and your body is relaxed. Shots come from various directions and are thrown with various velocities and degrees of accuracy. You want to maintain a disciplined body and stick position and force shooters to make good shots in order to beat you. When the opponent shoots, you need to react and attack the ball with both your stick and your body. If you are in a frozen or nonathletic posture, then you're merely in a defending or blocking position. The goalkeeper can use his stick and body to stop the ball from going past the imaginary plane of the goal. You may catch it, deflect it, or trap it to the ground. As long as the ball doesn't go into the goal, you've done your job.

Body Positioning for Goalkeepers

When preparing to stop the ball, a goalie's stance is similar to a football linebacker, a collegiate wrestler, or a baseball infielder. You should start to get ready from the ground up. Your stance needs to be both athletic and comfortable. The purpose of a proper athletic stance is to maximize balance and keep weight distribution even. You want your body weight on the balls of your feet. You can't be too far back on your heels or too far forward on your toes. By having your body weight pressed more toward the insides of the balls of your feet, you will be able to burst and explode better. In a traditional stance (see figure 7.1a), your feet are directly under your shoulders. In a modern stance (see figure 7.1b), your feet are spread wider than your shoulders. The choice of stance is purely a matter of personal preference.

When trying to fine-tune your stance, you should err toward the inside (too narrow a stance) rather than the outside (too wide a stance). If your stance is too wide, you won't be able to move quickly or efficiently, and you will depend only on your upper body. Whatever stance you use, you must be able to step and follow with your feet toward the shot.

Your feet can be squared up to the shooter or staggered with one foot more forward than the other.

FIGURE 7.1 *(a)* Traditional stance and *(b)* modern stance for goalies.

FIGURE 7.2 Goalie foot placement: *(a)* pointing outward and *(b)* straight forward.

Goalies typically use two types of foot placements: pointing outward at about 45 degrees (see figure 7.2*a*) or straight forward (see figure 7.2*b*). Some goalies use a pigeon-toed stance so they can more efficiently push off with their back foot and have more lateral movement. Foot placement should be based on comfort and personal preference.

To help you react, you want your butt down and your knees flexed. Otherwise, you will have to perform the flex after the shot is taken, and this slows down your reaction time for making the save. Your chest and head should be up, and you should lean slightly forward, which allows your head and chest to counterbalance your butt. Your hands and elbows should stay in front of your chest. This maximizes your ability to efficiently move the stick pocket in a propeller motion to meet the shot. You want your elbows flexed and pointing down, your hands up, and both elbows and hands relaxed and away from your body. If your bottom hand is held in too close to your body, this can result in the shot passing by and making you resemble a matador waving his red cape at a passing bull. You want your hands, feet, and face toward the ball whenever possible. And, when the shot is imminent, your body needs to be still and relaxed, and your feet must be set. See figure 7.3 for a front and side view of the goalie's body position.

Stick Technique for Goalkeepers

Most goalies hold the stick pocket in the box position at a 45-degree angle (see figure 7.4). Your bottom hand should be farther out from your body than your top hand so that the stick is slightly tilted back toward you. You want your stick pocket to be fully exposed to the shooter. For stick height, you may have the stick pocket at the level

FIGURE 7.3 Goalie body position: *(a)* front view and *(b)* side view.

of your head, shoulder, or chest. Some traditional styles require goalkeepers to lower the stick pocket for outside shooters. However, with modern styles, you will have your stick pocket high all the time. You hold the stick with both hands in the "pinch" technique using your thumb and index finger (as discussed in chapter 3); the other three fingers should gently rest on the side of the handle.

In addition, proper grip is vital in stopping shots. If you choke the handle with your top hand, you won't have the full surface of your stick pocket facing the shooter. You should have a very light and relaxed grip. You don't want to grip the top of the handle too tightly because this will cause everything to start tightening up.

FIGURE 7.4 Proper stick position for a goalie.

Shot-Stopping Strategy

The most important element of shot stopping is making sure that you lead with your stick and follow with your body (see figure 7.5). You should lead with your stick by driving your top hand to the ball; then, you should step with your ball-side

FIGURE 7.5 Goalie stopping a shot by *(a)* leading with the stick and *(b)* following with the body.

foot and drive through the ball.

The key is to get your top hand to the shot by using either a traditional sweeping motion or a modern propeller motion with your stick. The primary difference is how you want to reach a high shot to your off side. If you are a right-handed goalie and you hold your stick at a 10 o'clock position, then a high off-side shot is just off your left ear. In a traditional sweeping technique, the stick would first go low and then up in a counterclockwise motion to reach the off-side shot (see figure 7.6). In a modern propeller technique, the stick would go high across the face in a clockwise motion to reach the same shot (see figure 7.7). In today's game, the vast

FIGURE 7.6 Traditional sweeping technique for a goalie.

FIGURE 7.7 Modern propeller technique for a goalie.

majority of goalkeepers use a propeller technique to reach the offside, high shot.

You should always look the shot all the way into your stick pocket. You want to stop the ball, not catch the ball. If your stick is slightly tilted back and your elbows are flexed, you should be able to absorb and cushion the shot and minimize rebounds. You need to minimize rebounds because many rebounds lead to goals; plus, you want to control the ball and initiate the offense with a clear. Some coaches emphasize that goalies should catch the ball. However, the most important thing is to stop the ball first—and catch it if possible.

You should always step toward the shot with your ball-side foot. When you step, you are driving to the ball with your opposite hip, which keeps you low in an athletic position. Your first move is not stepping with your ball-side foot. If you pick up your ball-side foot and step toward the ball, you will raise your body position. Your ball-side step is to maintain your balance.

The quicker you accelerate toward the shot, the quicker you will be in a position to save the ball. In general, you should step and drive toward the point where the ball crosses the crease. You want to come out and intercept the angle of the shot. Step directly toward the shooter (do not step sideways). Some goalies do prefer to step sideways, but this method is not recommended. You should follow through with your trailing leg using either a two-step move or a three-step move. When using a two-step move, you first step with your ball-side foot and then follow up with your far-side foot to regain balance. When using a three-step move, you first step with your ball-side foot, then step with your far-side foot, and follow up with your ball-side foot to regain balance and position. You need to drive both elbows and hands toward the ball. Both hands work together to get to the ball. Your body acts as a secondary line of defense behind the stick.

Goalkeepers must have a repertoire of strategies for facing various types of shots. Each situation will require a different strategy. Some strategies depend on the field position of the shooter, whether the ball is coming from behind the goal or from in front of the goal. Other strategies involve using specific techniques to stop the ball on shots that are not high-to-high shots. These shots include a low shot, a bounce shot, or an inside shot.

Midfield Zone: Ball Above the GLE

The goal line extended (GLE) is an imaginary line that extends out to the sideline on each side of the goal line from the crease area. When the ball is located between the midline and the GLE, it's in the midfield zone and is considered to be "above" the GLE. If the ball carrier is above the GLE, he is a triple threat to dodge, feed, or shoot. When the ball crosses the midline, the ball is not within shooting distance. As the opponent is coming toward the defensive box, you (the goalie) should take that opportunity to talk to your defense and direct your team. Once the ball starts to approach scoring distance, you must focus on the ball.

You never want your body or stick outside the pipes of the goal. Your feet and stick should always be inside the pipes. Never give up the inside pipe against a shooter. Goalies can travel either a high or low arc when following ball movement

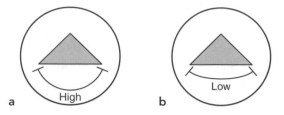

FIGURE 7.8 Goalie's *(a)* high arc or *(b)* low arc when following the ball movement.

(see figure 7.8). If the ball is out front, you should take a comfortable step off the goal line and play a high arc, which cuts down the angle of the shot. If you go too far out on your high arc, this may put you out of position when the opponent uses quick ball movement. If you use a lower arc, your move to the far pipe will be shorter on a cross-crease pass or a backside shot. You must always follow the ball from stick to stick. Seeing the ball is critical, so you can't be distracted by anything that's going on around you. You should maintain a high stick position. It's easier to go from high to low with your stick. Use small foot movements across the arc, and don't cross your feet. You have to "creep" along the arc, as shown in figure 7.9. By using small movements, you keep your feet close to the ground. Keeping your feet on the field will help you reestablish your balance and position and help you step and react to any shots. If you take wider steps, your feet will be off the ground for longer periods. If a shot is taken when you're in the middle of a long step, you won't be able to react and make a save.

Ball Behind the GLE

When the ball is located between the end line and the GLE, it's in the attack zone and is considered to be "below" the GLE. If the ball carrier is below the GLE, he is a double threat to feed or dodge but not to shoot.

In this situation, goalkeepers use either a traditional approach (see figure 7.10a) or an ice hockey approach (see figure 7.10b) when positioning themselves in the goal. If you use the traditional style, your body is facing the ball behind the goal. In a hockey style, your body is facing the front of the cage. You turn your head to follow the ball movements behind the goal. Your ball-side foot is up against the near-side pipe.

For your crease positioning, you will use one of three styles—playing in the middle of the crease (see figure 7.11a); favoring the near pipe, which minimizes the near-side shot (see figure 7.11b); or favoring the far pipe, which minimizes the backside shot (see figure 7.11c). Your stick is up, and you are playing an arc based on the chosen style. Your arc may be a little deeper than your out-front arc. If the opponent dodges around the goal, you must get to the near pipe and hold the pipe. If the opponent makes a feed to a cutter, you must pivot (turn around) and must always see the flight of the ball. When you turn, you should always take away the inside pipe on the flight of the ball and turn to the angle of the feed. You must maintain a high stick position and concentrate on stopping the high shot, thus forcing the low shot (cutters usually shoot high).

FIGURE 7.9 Goalie creeping along the goal mouth.

FIGURE 7.10   Goalie position in the goal: *(a)* traditional approach and *(b)* ice hockey approach.

Low Shots

A low shot in lacrosse is like a ground ball in baseball. In baseball, when a ground ball comes to an infielder, the infielder steps to it, drops his glove to the ground, and stays low. His arms are loose and away from his body, and he is ready to react. If the ball is hit so hard that the infielder doesn't have time to get his arms away from his body, or if the baseball takes a weird bounce, the infielder must play the ball in tight. Goalies are like infielders: You keep your stick to the ground, stay low and relaxed, and "gobble" up the ball (see figure 7.12). If the shot is a "worm burner" on a grass field, you must get the stick low and be able to fight back up on an unexpected bounce. You need to stay over the shot so that everything is over the ball. You don't want to lift up and come out of your stance. You should stay low and pounce on or smother the shot as if you're putting out a fire.

Bounce Shots

For bounce shots, you must be ready to go down, but you must also be ready to come back up and have the presence and ability to react. Your movement needs to be controlled rather than released. You can't release your weight low on a low bounce. If you let your body weight drop beyond your knees, you will become top heavy and will be unable to react. You want to control your body weight so you can maintain your balance, keep your good position, and still be able to fire up. You also have to read the angle of the shot because you know that the ball is going to come back up. You should drop your hips (not your arms) and prepare to come back up with your body, as shown in figure 7.13. Everything stays relative. Also note that if it's an especially high bouncer on turf, you should go out to meet the bounce shot; then your shoulder and upper body can get a piece of the ball.

FIGURE 7.11 Goalie crease positioning: *(a)* middle of the crease, *(b)* favoring the near pipe, and *(c)* favoring the far pipe.

FIGURE 7.12 Goalie reacting to a low shot.

FIGURE 7.13 Goalie reacting to a bounce shot.

One-on-One Shots

As a goalie, you can use various strategies to deal with a one-on-one situation against a shooter. You can drop your stick and bait the attacker to shoot up (see figure 7.14a). You can take a pipe and bait the attacker to shoot to the open area (see figure 7.14b). You can also hold your position, see the ball, and cover your opponent's stick with your stick (see figure 7.14c). In a one-on-one situation, the bottom line is that you must do whatever works.

FIGURE 7.14 Goalie reacting to a one-on-one shot: *(a)* dropping his stick and baiting the shooter high, *(b)* holding a pipe and baiting to the other pipe, or *(c)* holding his ground.

Clearing

Clearing means clearing the ball out of your defensive half of the field. The opposing team can turn the ball over with a bad pass, a misjudged catch, or a goalie-saved shot. Anybody on defense, including the goalie, can gain possession of the ball and clear the ball out with ball and player movement. Typically, a clear is initiated by a goalkeeper after making a save.

For the goalkeeper, the most important thing is to complete the shot-stopping technique and make the save first. When you have full possession of the ball, you should then initiate the offense by clearing the ball from the defensive end of the field to the offensive end.

After you make a save, your teammates will be running upfield and toward the wings. Your job is to distribute the ball. You need to make intelligent decisions with the ball. If you make a mistake here, it can cost you a goal. If you lose possession of the ball, the opposing team will have a distinct numbers advantage and can convert a scoring opportunity, which can be a back breaker. You have a progression of "looks" when determining where you want to pass the ball. Your first look can be to the on-ball defender who might be breaking upfield. Your second look is to the other two upfield defenders. Your third look is to either close defenseman on either wing.

If everybody is covered, then you have 4 seconds from the moment of possession to exit the crease with the ball. Most goalies will circle behind the goal and exit behind the crease. You must stay alert to any opponent chasing you or trying to jump you as you exit the crease. Once you identify your target, you should turn your hips and shoulders toward it and throw an outlet pass. You need to be athletic in throwing the ball; you have now become a field player. The sequence is "fire" to the shot, make the save, and then make an accurate outlet pass. After making the save, if you keep your feet still and don't turn to the opposite-shoulder position, you will make a weaker pass.

Quarterback of the Defense

As the goalie, you are the quarterback of the defense. You are also the "eyes" of the defense. You are in position to watch both the ball and the player movements of the opposing team. You can encourage the on-ball defender to play smart, aggressive defense. You can also direct the flow of the off-ball defenders to support the on-ball defenseman. Just like a quarterback in football, the goalie receives a lot of attention. The attention is positive when things are going well and not as positive when things aren't going well.

You must lead by what you say and what you do. As the goalie, you must be a field general and communicate with your teammates.

Goalies often make the following calls to direct the defense:

- *Ball locations*—The goalie will call out "Left front," "Center front," "Right front," and so on.
- *Hold calls*—The goalie may tell the defender covering the ball to get into the ball carrier's gloves and to use his body to drive him away from the goal.
- *Pick calls*—The goalie can anticipate and alert his defenders to potential picks.
- *Check calls*—When the feeder releases the ball, the goalie can make an early "Check" call. An early check call gives the inside defenders plenty of time to check their opponent. The goalie wants to anticipate the check call but should wait until the ball leaves the feeder's stick. The goalie doesn't want an interference penalty.
- *Slides*—The goalie determines who is sliding ("Who's hot?") and when the slide is going to occur ("Red"). "Hot" means which defender is going to slide to the ball carrier and "red," or a similar type call, signals the slide. Some teams prefer to have on-field defenders or coaches on the sideline determine the sliding responsibilities and have the goalie concentrate on the ball.

Goalies also lead through their actions. Most goalies lead by example with effort, hustle, enthusiasm, and hard work. As a goalie, your relationship with your defense is critical. You should encourage and praise your teammates' efforts. Never blame any particular teammate for a goal. Any goal is scored on the entire defense, not just one player. You can help maintain the overall morale of the defense by making the opponent earn every goal and by not giving up any easy goals. Specifically, you don't want to give up any goals to the near-side pipe, on shots from very far out, or on feeds directly over the goal. You also don't want to give up goals at the beginning or end of quarters. In the former case, you allow your opponent to gain some momentum, and in the latter case, your team can't retaliate.

Goalkeeping Drills

Goalkeeping, like facing off, is a specialty skill. You need lots of discipline and training to be a goalkeeper, primarily because it requires many unique skills. In the end, repetition is the key to playing in the goal. Practice doesn't make you perfect in the goal, just closer to reaching your potential. The following drills will help you reach your potential.

TWITCH DRILL

PURPOSE

To learn to maintain your stick position.

SETUP

The goalie is in the cage, and a coach or teammate has the ball.

EXECUTION

The coach or teammate "twitches" (fakes) with his stick, forcing the goalie to hold his position, and then shoots. When the coach or teammate shoots, the goalie moves to the shot.

COACHING POINTS

A goalie must not be faked, especially on the first stick move by the shooter.

TOP HAND DRILL

PURPOSE

To learn to meet the ball with your top hand.

SETUP

The player has a basketball only and is positioned opposite a solid wall.

EXECUTION

The player throws the basketball against a wall using just his top hand and catches the ball when it rebounds back. The motion is similar to dribbling a basketball on the court but you're doing it vertically versus horizontally.

COACHING POINTS

This drill teaches the importance of getting your top hand to the ball.

TOP-HAND DOMINANT DRILL

PURPOSE

To learn the importance of the top-hand movement to the ball.

SETUP

The goalie gets in a ready stance and holds the stick with only his top hand (gripping the stick with the thumb and index finger); a coach is positioned nearby, facing the goalie with the ball in his stick.

EXECUTION

The goalie says, "Ready." As the coach shoots the ball, the goalie puts both hands on the stick handle and saves the shot.

COACHING POINTS

If you take away the bottom hand in the drill, this accentuates the top hand. This drill teaches that the top hand is the most important hand in getting to the ball.

TENNIS BALL DRILL

PURPOSE

To learn how to get to the ball with your top hand.

SETUP

The goalie is in his ready stance but without his stick; a coach is positioned nearby.

EXECUTION

The coach throws a tennis ball to the goalie. The goalie steps, looks the ball into his top hand, and catches the ball.

COACHING POINTS

This drill teaches the sequence of stepping, looking the ball into your top hand, and catching.

LUNGE DRILL

PURPOSE

To learn to fire up to a shot.

SETUP

The goalie performs this drill by himself.

EXECUTION

The goalie takes an exaggerated step, which brings his body low. The goalie straightens up, then takes another step, and so on.

COACHING POINTS

This drill helps the player understand that as he goes down, he still must be able to fire back up. The drill is an excellent conditioning drill, especially for the thighs.

A goalkeeper needs to have certain physical characteristics such as excellent vision, good reflexes, and quick hands and feet. More important, a goalkeeper must have mental and emotional traits such as courage, toughness, concentration, composure, and persistence. The three most important functions of a goalie are shot stopping, clearing the ball, and acting as the quarterback of the defense. Shot stopping requires proper body positioning and stick technique; the goalie must lead with the stick while stepping toward the shot with his body. Shooters use a variety of shots that a goalie must be familiar with and be comfortable stopping with his stick and body. Shot stopping also depends on field location. Techniques are tailored to whether the ball is in the midfield zone or the attack zone. Goalkeepers are responsible for clearing the ball from the defensive end of the field. Usually, the goalie initiates the clear by stopping the shot and making an outlet pass to a teammate running upfield. Lastly, goalkeepers are the quarterbacks of the defense. They are the eyes and voice of the team defense, anticipating the opposing team's movements and communicating the defense's countermoves.

CHAPTER EIGHT

ON-BALL DEFENSE

On-ball defense refers to the matchup of a single defender playing against an opponent who has the ball or is about to receive the ball. Typically, as an on-ball defender, you will deal with two main scenarios. In the first situation, your man does not have a lot of distance from you. In the second, your man (or a teammate's man) has distance from you and is running toward you or the goal; in other words, the offensive player has a running start. General on-ball defensive concepts include determining a proper cushion, assuming a breakdown position at stick's length, defending on the "snap count," and shadowing your man. On-ball defensive strategies are designed primarily to address three situations. Basic on-ball strategy is designed to contain the man who is carrying the ball. A second strategy involves containing a ball carrier who is dodging. The third strategy includes techniques for countering a ball carrier who is bearing into the goal for a shot. On-ball defense will vary based on field location. On-ball defense is more challenging in the midfield zone because the ball carrier is a triple threat. However, on-ball defense in the attack zone has its own challenges. This chapter covers tactics and strategies for playing on-ball defense in these various situations.

General On-Ball Defensive Concepts

On-ball defensive concepts include providing the proper cushion, assuming a breakdown position at stick's length, defending on the "snap count" (forcing the ball carrier to go where you want him to go), and using the shadow technique.

Cushion

Cushion refers to how much room or space you give your opponent. The amount of cushion should be determined by your speed and ability to get to your opponent and by where your opponent is located in relation to the ball and to the goal (distance). If you have speed, you can give your opponent more cushion and help out more inside on team defense. If you're slow, you won't be able to "cheat" as much off your opponent. If your opponent is far from the goal and is not dangerous, you will have less urgency. For example, if your opponent has the ball 30 yards from the goal, you should not go out to chase him at 30 yards. In this case, you can go out to a distance of about 22 to 25 yards from the goal; however, you don't want to be rushing out to a ball carrier while he is running at you. The key is to position yourself so you can force the ball carrier in the direction you want him to go. You should then stand your ground in a breakdown stance but keep your feet moving. That way, you will be able to run alongside him while matching his speed. When the ball carrier becomes more of a danger to shoot, you must be running alongside him, step for step, so that you are able to neutralize his shot if necessary.

Breakdown at Stick's Length Away

If the ball is thrown to your opponent on the perimeter, you need to arrive at the ball in a breakdown stance, ready to play defense when the opponent catches the ball. When you pick up your man on the perimeter, you should adjust your field position on the flight of the ball. If your opponent is in a dangerous spot, you must break down immediately and be ready to play.

You need to close down the distance between you and your opponent efficiently and with minimal risks. The breakdown position places a premium on being low in body, stick, and vision. You want your body position and your center of gravity to be lower than your opponent. Your stick should be low, targeting your opponent's bottom hand. Your eyes should focus low on your opponent's midsection.

Defense on the Snap Count

The offensive player's biggest advantage is the "snap count." Unlike football, lacrosse doesn't include an actual snap count, but the offensive player has a similar advantage because he knows when and where he is going to attack the goal. For on-ball defense, the bottom line is that you should always assume the worst. You should always assume that the ball carrier may use deception to set you up for a dodge and may shoot the ball for a score at any time. You may not be able to determine the ball carrier's intentions (catch and pass OR catch, dodge, and shoot), but you can anticipate his actions. The ball carrier can go in either direction—right or left. You want to force the ball carrier to go in the direction that you want him to go, either to his weak hand or down the alley. You do this by overplaying one side or by using the field to your advantage. The purpose of your positioning is to discourage the opponent from taking a strong-hand or good-angle shot.

Squared Up Versus Shadow

In the past, on-ball defenders were taught to play the ball carrier in a squared-up position. With this technique, you match your opponent's body and stick position, and you want to see the front of your opponent's jersey. You're not necessarily forcing your opponent into a slide.

On-ball defenders are now taught to shadow or overplay their man and force him into a specific direction (e.g., away from his strong hand or away from the middle of the field), anticipating that a teammate will slide from the crease or from an adjacent position. In today's game, slides are coming early. With the shadow technique, you're basically just forcing the attacker toward the area where the sliding defender is going to be. Most teams then "release" the first defender. For example, if your team defense is taking away the middle of the field, you should force your opponent down the side of the goal and shadow him into the crease or adjacent slide. You wouldn't necessarily see the front of your man's jersey. You either release back to the crease or double-team the opponent from behind.

On-Ball Defensive Strategies

When you are the on-ball defender, you can use one of three strategies depending on the level of threat that your man presents to you: basic, dodge containment, and shot prevention. Sometimes your man is just carrying the ball, sometimes he wants to dodge, and sometimes he wants to create and make his own shot. If your man is just carrying the ball, you should use the basic on-ball defensive tactics. Although the threat may be low, you still have to give some resistance and apply some defensive pressure on the ball carrier. If the ball carrier does not give up the ball and decides to attack the goal in a north-south dodge, you must drop-step, move your body downfield in a hip-to-hip position, and get into a stick-on-stick position. In the dodge containment strategy, you are like a football cornerback giving ground on a wide receiver and then closing down the distance when he becomes a threat to complete the play. If the ball carrier still does not give up the ball, bears into the goal, and attempts to create a shot, you must use your body and stick to drive him away from the goal. In the shot prevention strategy, you are like a football interior lineman blocking a defensive end from the quarterback.

Basic On-Ball Defense: Defending the Ball Carrier

Not all ball carriers are trying to dodge or shoot. Many times a ball carrier is merely transferring the ball to another teammate. Your opponent is moving the ball so that the defense has to adjust, and the opponent might be looking for a desired matchup. In this case, the level of threat is the lowest—the ball carrier is not attacking the goal. Regardless of the level of threat to you, you have to give some resistance and apply some defensive pressure on the ball carrier. You are not necessarily preventing your man from receiving or throwing an adjacent pass. You need to pick him up so that he doesn't have an unimpeded path to the goal and cannot march straight toward the goal. Basic on-ball defense involves picking up or addressing the ball carrier, playing low-risk body and stick position, and releasing him when he passes the ball—always staying alert for a give-and-go maneuver. You want to disrupt the flow of the offence by making it difficult for your opponent to receive the ball easily.

Approaching the Ball: Closing Down the Distance

When addressing or picking up your individual opponent who has the ball or is just receiving a pass, you need to use proper body position, stick position, and vision.

When approaching the ball, you should use strides to close down the distance between you and the opponent. When you get closer to the ball carrier, use choppy steps so you can be under control in a breakdown position, ready to react to an imminent dodge. The breakdown stance enables you to play active one-on-one defense, maintaining the proper body and stick position with your body weight evenly distributed and with a low center of gravity. Your feet are shoulder-width apart, your knees are bent, and your butt is down. Your feet are comfortably apart. Your arms are relaxed and flexed at the elbow, and your hands are loose and away from your body. Your head and chest are up. In general, you want your head lower than your opponent's, although at times this might not be possible (e.g., when a 6-3 defender is guarding a 5-8 attacker). If your head is lower than your opponent's and if your body is flexed, you will have a lower center of gravity; thus, you will be in an optimal athletic position. Your body weight should be on the balls of your feet, not the heels or toes. By being balanced and maintaining a proper breakdown stance, you will be able to react to any change of speed or change of direction. See figure 8.1 for an example of a defender in a good breakdown stance.

Off the ball, you want your stick to be in a "port" position. In this position, the stick is at your side and at a 45-degree angle, as shown in figure 8.2. The port position is similar to the box position, but it's primarily an extended position used to block passes, not to catch or throw.

FIGURE 8.1 Defender in a breakdown stance.

FIGURE 8.2 Defender's stick in a port position.

As you're approaching your opponent, your stick should shift from a port to a poke position. Your bottom hand is on the butt end of your stick handle and is positioned off your hip (not near your midsection). Your stick angle is parallel to the ground and your stick is out in front of you, away from your body. Your stick head is pointing toward your opponent's bottom hand on his stick or his navel. A poke position is targeted at your opponent's bottom hand. (The poke check will be covered in more detail later in this chapter.) Your stick pocket should be down. If necessary, you can check down on your opponent and "follow your pocket." You're more likely to foul if you have your stick up near your opponent's helmet. You don't want to chase the head of your opponent's stick because you will be more likely to stand up and raise your center of gravity, overextend your body position, or check his helmet resulting in a one-minute penalty.

As you're closing down the distance, you should focus on your opponent's bottom hand and jersey number. Your eyes should be focused low on your opponent's midsection, jersey number, and bottom hand (not on the head of his stick). Keep this in mind: "Where his numbers go, he goes." Offensive players fake with their helmet, eyes, shoulders, and especially the plastic head of their stick. If you focus high on your opponent, you're more likely to be faked by these elements. As you are approaching the ball, you must be aware of the "fatal step" on defense: If you're closing the distance between you and the ball carrier, but he unexpectedly drives aggressively at you to dodge, then you have to stop closing the gap. You must put on the brakes while keeping your feet moving. You must have your body and stick under control and must be ready to drop-step downfield to counter the dodge.

At times, you may be under more pressure to adjust to a ball carrier who has lots of distance from you and is running toward you. Specifically, your man may have a running start against you, or you may be sliding to another offensive player with the ball. In the first scenario, you may have more options for going out and defending him on your terms. Your goal is to be running with him in the same direction and matching his speed to the goal. In the second scenario (sliding to a teammate's opponent), there may be more urgency for you to get there and neutralize the shot.

When defending a player with the ball, you should not allow your opponent to get a running start on you. You can't expect to play an opponent if he gets a running start. For example, in a 40-yard race, if one runner starts from a standstill and the other runner gets a running start, the runner with the running start would

Running Starts

If you are playing on-ball defense and your opponent has a running start, this can be a challenging situation. If the ball carrier gets some space from you and decides to drive hard to the goal, you can't let him get a "head of steam" and attack you while you're standing still. You must go out and position yourself where you can confront him, run with him, and get your momentum with him so you can match his speed. The restraining line is 20 yards from the goal. You want to run with your opponent so that when he hits the restraining line, you have a 2-yard cushion, and you're ready to actively defend him. You make your stand at the restraining line, but you shouldn't wait at the restraining line and let the ball carrier get a head of steam.

have an advantage. The runner who started from a standstill would have trouble keeping up with the opponent. He would have more success if both runners were going the same speed when they hit the starting line. When you are playing on-ball defense, if the ball handler tries to get a running start against your position, you need to go out and play him.

Picking Up a Teammate's Man

If your teammate loses body positioning on the ball carrier, you may have to slide to the ball carrier. You might also have to do this if the ball carrier is uncovered because of a fast break. Your priority is to neutralize the shooter by getting a piece of his glove and thereby preventing a high-quality shot (not taking the man out with your body). You should lead with your stick and follow with your body. You must use a proper slide angle when picking up the ball carrier; you should slide to where you expect your opponent to get to (not where he is now). You need to reach the opponent before he reaches the spot where he wants to shoot the ball. Your stick position changes from a port to a poke position. If you close down in a port position, this gives the shooter more time with his hands free. Focus on his gloves and numbers (not on the head of his stick), and poke-check his gloves. You must arrive under control in a proper breakdown position ("Be quick but don't hurry"). If you're out of control, the opponent will beat two defenders. If necessary, put your shoulders to your opponent's chest, hitting low and driving him out. If the ball carrier passes the ball before you reach him, you should turn back to the inside and help out with team defense.

Running With the Ball Carrier

After you have satisfactorily closed the distance on your opponent, you should be a stick's length away, and your eyes should be on his waist. Your objective is to neutralize your opponent as a potential threat. Note that if your opponent is running around the offensive perimeter, then he is not a threat. If he carries the ball in an east-west direction at a moderate speed, you can shuffle by moving laterally without crossing your feet. If he sprints, you should react by switching from a shuffle to a hip-to-hip position, as shown in figure 8.3. Your objective is to run with the ball carrier, keep up with his pace, play solid body and stick position, and force him to give up the ball to an opponent who is not in a position to create more offense.

FIGURE 8.3 Defender in a hip-to-hip position on the opponent.

Release

Your opponent will pass the ball to a teammate but he is still an offensive threat, so you drop off to take away the give-and-go. On defense, you always assume the worst, so you are always anticipate a classic "give-and-go" offensive maneuver. Teams either use the traditional "open up" technique or a ball denial, "butt to the ball" method. In the traditional method, when your man throws the ball, you drop step and open your hips so you can see both your man and the ball (see figure 8.4). When your man throws the ball, you don't stand there, turn without moving your feet, and stare at the ball. He could cut in front of you or get underneath of you with a backdoor move. The solution is to always assume the give-and-go and open up to see both the ball and your man.

Another approach to defending the give-and-go is similar to ball-denial, pressure defense. Ball-denial defense is based on the defender not letting his man receive any kind of pass. In this approach, when your man throws the ball, you drop step two to three steps to the ball side with your "butt to the ball." Some teams feel the "butt to the ball" method better anticipates picks and backdoor cuts. We recommend the traditional "open up" as the best method for defending the give-and-go. Once your opponent gives up the ball and you have neutralized any give-and-go maneuver, now you have to focus on off-ball defense. Off-ball defense includes a variety of stick and athletic skills which we will explore in the next chapter.

FIGURE 8.4 Player using "open up" defense.

Dodge Containment: Defending the Dodging Ball Carrier

If your opponent is threatening the goal, your approach will be different. When your opponent makes a move, you should open your hips and take a deep drop step, which adjusts your body so you can get downfield and challenge the dodger at the point of release (or "cut him off at the pass"). If he dodges in a north-south direction toward the goal, you need to adjust your body position (drop-step) and stick position in order to counter the dodge. Your first priority is to get your body weight and momentum going in the right direction and to get up to speed versus your opponent. The drop step gets you going in the right direction, and opening the hips gets you up to speed. To perform a drop step, you drive back or push off with your opposite foot or toe, as shown in figure 8.5. When you drive with your opposite foot, this keeps your body low. You take a step downfield with your ball-side foot. You drive from your opposite hip rather than swing your ball-side hip. When you drive your hips to an open position, you stay low and athletic. Your drop step should get you to a hip-to-hip position on the opponent. Hip-to-hip position allows you to run alongside your man. You want to sprint and stay up with him, matching his speed stride for stride. You must get to a spot downfield where you can challenge the ball carrier when he wants to shoot or feed—and you must get there quickly. You want to give up ground and meet your opponent downfield so you can better defend him when he is threatening the goal. As the dodger gets closer to the goal, you should close down the distance between you and him (reduce the cushion). You need to be in contact with the dodger when he is in a shooting or feeding position, or at the point of release.

As mentioned earlier, you should adjust your body position, and your stick will naturally follow. As you open up your hips and perform a drop step, your hands and stick naturally come across your body so that you lead with your stick. You need to

FIGURE 8.5   Drop step.

get your body's momentum going downfield, since you play defense with your feet. Once you're matching the speed of your opponent, you can adjust your stick to a comfortable position. You want to have your stick head on your opponent's stick side (this is called stick on stick). Your stick should be in between your man and his path to the goal. Do not drag your stick behind your man. If you do, the stick is working against you, and it's not in a position to check. The target for your stick is your opponent's bottom hand, not the head of his stick. You want to be in a position to see the front of the opponent's jersey.

Again, your objective is to pressure the ball carrier but not so aggressively that he turns into a counterpuncher. Don't overcommit and wait for him to make the next move. Depending on your skills, you can apply various stick checks to force the opponent to protect his stick and to try to take the ball away.

At this point, the ball carrier has two options—either pass the ball to a teammate or drive closer to the goal (this second option is discussed in the next section). If the ball carrier passes the ball, you should use the "poke and recover" technique. To execute this technique, you throw a poke check at your opponent's bottom hand. You open your hips and drop-step in the direction of the ball carrier in order to minimize "stepping in" and overcommitting your feet and body (see figure 8.6). You can poke and recover in either direction. Your body weight shifts to the inside of your lead (or front) foot. Having your body weight recover back inside will help you maintain balance.

FIGURE 8.6 Player using a poke check and then drop-stepping in the direction of the ball carrier.

Checks in Lacrosse

A check is the act of impeding or blocking an opponent in possession of the ball with either your body or stick. If you use the stick head or handle to apply pressure against your opponent, then it's a stick check. Stick checks can be used anywhere on the field. If the ball carrier is dodging toward the goal, you should maintain body positioning and execute either a lift check or poke check. The purpose of a stick check is (a) to force your opponent to protect his stick; (b) to apply pressure to the opponent's bottom hand to disrupt a pass, feed, or shot; or (c) to take the ball away from him. Here are some popular types of checks used by lacrosse players:

- *Poke check*—To execute the poke check, you use your bottom hand (which is on the butt end of your stick) to direct your stick forward in order to poke your opponent's bottom hand when he places that hand on the stick. This in turn affects his stick head. If your timing is right, you can control what the offensive player is able to do without overextending or sacrificing your body position. Note that you don't want to step in with your lead foot or reach in with your top hand. This is the most effective check in lacrosse.

- *Inside check*—The inside check is used when you are covering an opponent who is cutting inside to the crease or is stationed on the crease, anticipating a feed and a shot.

- *Lift check*—To execute the lift check, you place the head of your stick under your opponent's glove or forearm. When the opponent is attempting to shoot, you lift up on his glove or forearm. You shouldn't sacrifice body position with this checking motion.

- *Slap check*—The slap check is commonly used in a cross-stick situation such as when a right-handed defender is playing against a left-handed opponent. The defender throws a "slap" across the front of the opponent's body. A slap check is not recommended because you will tend to stop moving your feet when executing this check.

Shot Prevention: Defending Near the Goal

When your man is bearing into the goal and is ready to release the ball (i.e., he is at the point of release), you want to meet him, control him, and be ready to drive him out away from the goal. You need to meet force with force. You don't want the opponent to overpower you, and you can't expect to overpower him. Because the ball handler uses the "big" muscles to do the majority of the work, you've got to match "big" muscles to "big" muscles. Nobody's arms can match the power and strength of another person's legs, so when the opponent is using his legs, you can't expect to stop him with your arms. Driving your man away is similar to cycling.

Your legs provide the power, and your hands guide or steer the bicycle. If the ball carrier is just exchanging the ball with another teammate, you can use your arms to counter his arm movement with a poke check (as described previously). However, if the ball carrier is dodging to the goal and you're driving him out, you must use your legs to counter the leg movement. If the ball carrier is dodging to the goal, you need to match legs to legs.

Reacting to Your Opponent

When the ball carrier is bearing into the goal cage, the pressure is on you to neutralize his body first and then his stick. Specifically, you will use various hold techniques to control your opponent's body, direct him away from the goal, and make him less of a threat.

To drive an opponent away from the goal, you need to stay low with your stance. Your head is up but low so that your helmet is lower than your opponent's. You should use your arms and hands to guide and steer your opponent to where you want him to go. Your arms are more of a steering and guiding mechanism. You can't depend solely on the power in your arms to hold your opponent. You need to drive your opponent with your hips and legs, as shown in figure 8.7. Your hips and legs give you the power to get up and hold your opponent. Your feet have to move, but it's mostly about the hips.

When driving your opponent away from the goal, you must keep your hands apart on the stick in order to control it. Don't bring your hands together to hold your opponent. You can't use any part of the exposed handle between your gloves because you would be guilty of a one-minute penalty for cross-checking.

FIGURE 8.7 Defender driving his opponent with his hips and legs.

Using Holds

You should use holds when the ball carrier is bearing into the goal cage. You need to both control and drive your opponent's hip. Because your hands and stick control your opponent, you should place your bottom hand on your opponent's hips. Your opponent is trying to get his power from his hips and legs, so you want to use your legs to drive through your opponent's hips. You control him with your hands and stick and drive him out with your legs. You can use either a stick-on-stick hold or a cross-stick hold.

An example of a stick-on-stick hold would be a right-handed attacker versus a right-handed defender. In a traditional technique, your arm position is based on a "V" forearm hold and stick-on-stick position, as shown in figure 8.8. You want to control the attacker's bottom hand with either a poke or lift check. The main disadvantages of this are that the "V" forearm hold is difficult to execute, your arms can't adequately match your opponent's legs, and your opponent can always roll back. In the modern technique, you either drive your bottom hand into your opponent's hip and trail with your stick OR have your stick in front of your opponent and trail with your body. Either way, your body and stick are working together to create a balanced "V" position to contain and control your man. Your approach depends on which technique feels more natural and comfortable. Many defenders prefer a body-stick "V" position (e.g., you use your hands to "jam" the attacker); this position is balanced, your stick is not the priority, and you match the opponent's legs with your body. An example of a cross-stick hold would be a right-handed attacker versus a left-handed defender. With this hold, you jab your bottom hand into your opponent's inside near hip, as shown in figure 8.9. This automatically cocks your stick into a position where, if your man shows you some stick, you can come in and throw a check.

FIGURE 8.8 Stick-on-stick hold.

FIGURE 8.9   Cross-stick hold.

Whatever technique you use, you want it to be natural and comfortable to you. At the same time, it needs to be balanced and athletic. If you focus too much on your upper body, you will forget about the most important element of defense: legs and footwork. Your on-ball technique will also depend on where the ball carrier is located on the field. Where he attacks both you and the goal makes a difference in your strategies.

Using Field Position

Playing defense is like buying real estate. It's all about location, location, location. Playing on-ball defense varies based on where the ball carrier is located on the field and where he is going. As mentioned earlier, the defensive half of the field is defined by four lines that bisect the field: the midline, the restraining line, the crease line, and the end line. The goal or crease line runs inside the crease of the goal. If you extend an imaginary line on both sides of the goal line to the sidelines, that's called the goal line extended (GLE). The GLE splits the defensive half of the field into the midfield zone and the attack zone. The area from the midline to the GLE is the midfield zone, and the area from the GLE to the end line is the attack zone. Your defensive strategy will depend on whether your man is located in the midfield zone (above the GLE) or in the attack zone (below the GLE). In the attack zone your man can't score, but, you need to understand the concepts of "closing the gate," the "island," and the inside roll. (These concepts are discussed later in this chapter.) If the ball carrier is located in the midfield zone, he is more danger-ous because he is a triple threat to dodge, feed, or shoot. He is more difficult to cover because you have to give him less cushion and more defensive attention and effort. Especially if you are a short-stick defender in the midfield zone, you are more likely to be a "target of opportunity" for a ball carrier.

In the midfield zone, you should err on the side of defending a dodge first; always assume that your man is going to dodge whenever he has the ball. For example, if the ball carrier has the ball at the center front position (field position #4) and he wants to dodge to the goal, he can take various dodging angles (or paths) to the goal depending on his skills and your ability to apply pressure (figure 8.10).

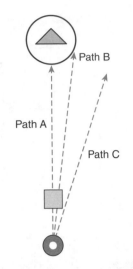

- *Path A*—Center front to center crease. When possible, your opponent wants to go in a straight line from the center front position to the goal for a high-percentage shot.

- *Path B*—Center front to tangent of crease. If you don't use effective driving technique, your opponent will at least get down path B. You allow your opponent's dodge to stay close to the tangent of the crease.

FIGURE 8.10 Dodging angles, or paths.

- *Path C*—Center front to corners of field. Ideally, you want to drive your man away from the goal and toward the corners of the field. You need to drive your man up and out. Once you drive him, you want to keep going in that direction or continue at the same angle.

When the ball carrier is located in the attack zone, he is a double threat to dodge or feed. He is less dangerous because he is not a threat to shoot and score a goal. He is a bit easier to cover because you will give him more of a cushion behind the goal. In comparison to playing a man above the GLE, you can drop back a little more, be more patient, and be less aggressive. Defending a ball carrier behind the goal is a balancing act between defending a feed and defending a dodge. You can afford to play off your opponent behind the goal and give him more cushion because he is not a scoring threat. However, when he runs through the prime feeding area, you need to be within striking distance (poke checking distance) so that you can disrupt any easy feeds to cutters. If you're too concerned about your opponent as a feeder and you overplay him, you may give him the opportunity to become a dodger. If you're too concerned about your opponent as a dodger and you give him too much cushion in the prime feeding area (you "cheat" back toward the GLE), you will weaken your ability to defend him as a feeder.

In the attack zone, you should again err on the side of defending a dodge because the ball carrier is a bigger threat to score when dodging. For example, if the ball carrier has the ball at X-behind and he wants to dodge to the goal, he has various dodging angles or paths to the goal. However, he is facing the back of the goal, so he must first get to the GLE and then drive farther up the field to increase his shooting angle. Because he has no angle through the crease, the ball carrier's best option is to first take a straight line from behind the goal to a tangent of the crease. Ideally, you want to confront him and force him off his straight line, making his path to the goal more of an arc. As soon as you get him off that straight line, the crease becomes more of an advantage to you—as a defender, you can run through the crease (shorter distance), and you're already closer to the goal than the ball carrier is. The following drill can be used to practice playing on-ball defense behind the goal, cutting through the crease, and getting to the GLE.

ONE-ON-ONE DRILL

PURPOSE

To learn proper body position when defending against a dodger.

SETUP

A coach or teammate is positioned on the end line, facing the back of the goal, with a stick and a ball; the player is five yards from the coach or teammate, facing them without a stick.

EXECUTION

The coach or teammate with the ball dodges from the end line to the front of the goal. The player backpedals, drop-steps, and opens his hips once he knows the direction of the ball. The player runs through the crease and meets the coach or teammate at the GLE. He assumes a proper "close the gate" stance and drives the ball carrier away from the goal.

COACHING POINTS

Because the player does not have a stick in this drill, he will learn the importance of body positioning. The player must backpedal, drop-step, and open his hips to counter the dodger. Once he meets the dodger at the GLE, the player practices concentrating on the dodger's body and not his stick. The player can't chase the dodger's stick because he doesn't have one of his own.

A dodging ball carrier in the attack zone has two missions. First, he wants to beat you to the GLE so that you can't muscle him away from the goal cage. If successful, the ball carrier then wants to post you on the "island" (described later in the chapter), where he can go in either direction and where you will need defensive support to counter his moves. You, on the other hand, want to beat the ball carrier to the GLE and take away any close-in shots. If you don't beat the ball carrier to the GLE and he posts you on the island, you should then force him to perform an inside roll.

The GLE on the wings of the goal line, as shown in figure 8.11, can be thought of as a "swinging gate." When you are playing the

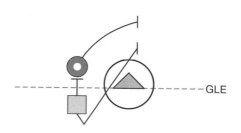

FIGURE 8.11 Closing the gate at the GLE.

ball carrier in the attack zone and he is attacking the goal, your objective is to first beat the ball carrier to the GLE and then meet the ball carrier with body contact. Your job is to get to this imaginary gate first and then shut or close the gate. You want to beat him to this spot (GLE), meet him at this spot, and make physical contact. To properly close the gate, you must have your hips facing the end line or the corner of the field, and you must play the ball carrier's body, not his stick. Don't chase the head of the stick. You need to get up on the ball carrier, turn him, and drive him toward the end line or the corner of the field (meeting force with force).

If the ball carrier runs through the GLE and continues upfield, he may then post you at the island. The island is a spot 5 yards above the GLE and 5 yards wide of the tangent of the crease line (see figure 8.12). It is a defender's no-man's-land. Getting posted on the island is similar to being posted up in basketball by a center playing with his back to the basket. The defender is very vulnerable unless he gets help or forces the ball carrier into the direction he wants the ball carrier to go. In this situation, you want to overplay or shadow the ball carrier's topside, turn him back, and force him to use an inside roll dodge. When you force the ball carrier to use an inside roll, as shown in figure 8.13, you force him into a blind spot because he loses sight of the players and the field. He turns his back to the rest of the action, and he can no longer see the movement of the offensive or defensive players. By forcing the ball carrier to perform an inside roll, you are taking away his opportunity to go to either hand; he may be facing your teammate sliding to him, and your goalie will be taking away the near pipe, thereby cutting down his shooting angle. When forcing the ball carrier to use the inside roll dodge, you must continue to overplay or shadow his topside, play his body and not his stick, and not allow him to roll back.

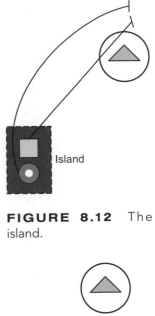

FIGURE 8.12 The island.

Sometimes a ball carrier will use a "rocker step" dodge in which he fakes an inside roll and comes back for his strong-side shot. If he is going to beat you, you should make sure that he beats you with an inside roll dodge and not a topside move.

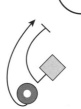

FIGURE 8.13 Forcing the inside roll.

If you are a step behind your attacker at the GLE and you can't get in better position to take away his topside shot, you should drive him up to the midfield corner (see figure 8.14). When you're behind the attacker, the best strategy is to stay there and use proper driving technique to keep pushing him out. Use the proper hold technique, keep your feet moving, and drive the attacker up and out toward the midfield line. If you're trailing the attacker at the GLE, you must avoid trying to suddenly get into the ideal topside position by overcompensating and overcommitting your body positioning. If you overcompensate, the attacker will roll dodge you for a high-quality shot. Whether you're a step behind the attacker at the GLE or you're in good solid position (and you close the gate), you need to keep the ball carrier going away from the goal. In both instances, you're driving your man away from the goal, just in different directions.

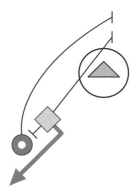

FIGURE 8.14 After losing his position, the defender drives the attacker out.

On-ball defenders need to understand the concepts of cushion, the "snap count," breakdown position at stick's length, and the shadow technique. On-ball defense involves three general strategies. The first approach is to pick up, defend, and release. This is the path of least resistance. The ball carrier is not challenging the goal, and the defender is applying some but not too much pressure on the ball. The second approach is used when the ball carrier dodges to the goal. In this situation, the defender needs to get his body downfield (using a drop step) and get his stick in the proper position. The third approach is used when the ball carrier is near the goal and is challenging the goal. In this situation, the defender must use various types of holds to control the ball carrier's body and drive him away from the goal. The strategies and techniques used for on-ball defense will depend on where the ball carrier is located on the field. If the ball carrier is in the midfield zone, he is a triple threat. If he is in the attack zone, he is a double threat.

CHAPTER NINE

OFF-BALL DEFENSE

Off-ball defense is designed to counter the offensive moves of ball exchange, cutting, and picks. It is geared toward putting defenders in the best possible position to minimize, neutralize, or prevent these potential offensive threats. When you are playing off-ball defense, your man doesn't have the ball, but you must be ever vigilant to all off-ball activity. You will use your body, stick, and vision to anticipate cuts, picks, and ball exchange; and you will use your athletic skills to react to these moves when they are executed. Specifically, off-ball defense is concerned with properly handling a ball exchange and V-cut, defending a cutter for a feed, defending an opponent on the crease, and sliding to an open opponent. Moreover, off-ball defenders try to anticipate and negate two types of picks: inside picks off perimeter cuts and two-man picks inside. This chapter covers some general off-ball concepts and then explores specific fundamentals such as defending the ball exchange, defending a cutter, defending inside, and defending picks.

General Off-Ball Defensive Concepts

When playing off-ball defense, you must remember several key concepts. Most defenders play more off-ball defense (compared to on-ball defense) during a game, so they must be able to successfully execute these general off-ball techniques. The most important concept is using proper body and stick positioning. Also, knowing general rules based on where your man is located on the field is useful. (See figure 9.2 for the three defensive zones to learn various degrees of defensive pressure.) Lastly, defenders need to know the differences between playing on the perimeter and playing inside on the crease.

Stick and Body Position

When you are playing off-ball defense, your stick should always be at a 45-degree angle (in a port position) to knock down passes, take away passing lanes, and check opponents' sticks. The only time that your stick is down is when you're playing the ball and your stick is in the man's gloves. Second, you need to be in an "open" body position between your man and the ball so that you can confidently see your man and see the ball. If you're stationed in a straight line between your man and the ball, and you play squared up directly at the ball carrier, you will become a "ball watcher." Conceptually, you should create a ball-you-man triangle (also called a V-up position) where you can comfortably scan the field for both your man and the ball (see figure 9.1). Your head is constantly moving back and forth so you can see your man and glance or peek at the ball. You can use the "big eye, little eye" concept: Your "big eye" is

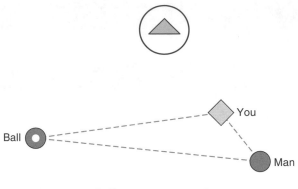

FIGURE 9.1   Ball-you-man triangle.

on your man, and your "little eye" is on the ball. The farther your man is from the goal and the ball, the more your big eye can concentrate on the inside and the ball. The closer your man gets to the goal and to the inside, the more your big eye concentrates on your man. Be sure to listen and talk constantly to your teammates (regarding picks, slides, and so on). On defense, you must be constantly aware of your surroundings and must not lose focus. You can't relax on defense. When the ball is in the air and not in the stick of one of your opponents, the other team can't really hurt you. You can use this time to adjust your position, play ball side, and be one step ahead of the flow of the ball (adjust on the flight of the ball).

Location on the Field

When playing off-ball defense, a general rule is that the closer your man is to the goal, the more of a threat he is to receive a pass—and the more you have to focus on him (compared to focusing on the ball). You adjust to where your man is located on the field in relation to the goal. The fundamentals include vision or focus (man versus ball), body position (square versus opened up), and cushion (tight or loose). Your mental and physical focus changes depending on where your man is located in relation to the goal and to the ball. Your vision, body position, and cushion will change based on where your opponent is on the field.

The area of the field in front of the goal is a place of keen defensive interest. Off-ball defenders have to balance watching their man and watching the ball based on their man's distance from the goal. This area can be broken up into three zones (see figure 9.2), and each zone has specific rules for off-ball defenders to apply.

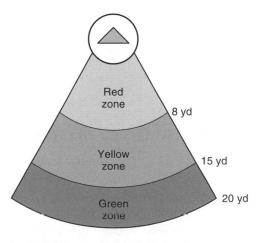

FIGURE 9.2   Off-ball defensive zones.

- *Red zone (GLE to 8 yards out)*—If your man is in the red zone, you should have 90 percent of your attention on him and 10 percent on the ball. Even inside, you still have 10 percent of your attention on the ball. You can never solely focus only on the ball or on your man. Your body position is square to the opponent. In the red zone, you get really tight, provide no cushion, and automatically switch.

- *Yellow zone (8 to 15 yards out)*—If your man is in the yellow zone, your focus is now 50-50 (50 percent on your man and 50 percent on the ball). You start to open up your hips into a "half" body position. You tighten it up but provide more cushion than in the red zone. A pick may be a bit more urgent than in the green zone because an attacker can pop for the ball and then catch and shoot. The rule on switching is that it's up to the discretion of the defenders.

- *Green zone (15 to 20 yards out)*—If your man is in the green zone, your attention is 70 percent on the ball and 30 percent on your man. You use an opened-up body position. In the green zone, you provide lots of cushion. Defenders have no need to automatically switch on picks because there is a lot of cushion and defenders can get through the picks.

In addition, off-ball defense is about adjusting to the movement of your man and the movement of the ball. Your man will move along the perimeter, from the perimeter to the inside, and from the inside back to the perimeter. Here are some rules to follow based on whether your man is on the perimeter or on the inside:

- If your man is on the perimeter, you should play between your man and the goal, shading to the ball side. You can afford to allow some cushion.

- If your man is on the crease inside and the ball is out front, you should play between your man and the ball (topside) and allow very little cushion. If your man is inside and someone throws the ball to him, you want to be in the passing lane and minimize the direct path of the ball to him. If you play behind him, he can cut directly to the ball, meet the ball, and then turn and shoot. If you play behind him and you need to slide upfield to help a teammate, your slide will be longer, and you may be sealed off more easily by opponents on the crease.

Let's look at a few scenarios to illustrate these concepts. The first scenario explains how an off-ball defender will adjust his approach based on the movement of his man from the perimeter to the inside. The second scenario explains adjustments on movement from the perimeter to the inside with a give-and-go. The third scenario explains adjustments on movement from the perimeter to the inside and then back to the perimeter.

Scenario 1

Midfielder 1 has the ball out top; midfielder 2 is on the perimeter with his defender. If midfielder 2 takes his defender to the crease (cuts inside), the defender must turn and adjust his position so that when he is inside and the ball is out front, he is now playing top-side with no cushion. If the defender doesn't adjust his position and continues to play between midfielder 2 and the goal, midfielder 2 can cut back for the ball and shoot (see figure 9.3).

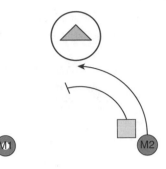

FIGURE 9.3 Perimeter cut inside.

Scenario 2

Midfielder 1 is out top; midfielder 2 has the ball out top with his defender. Midfielder 2 throws the ball to midfielder 1 on the perimeter and cuts down for the ball (give-and-go). The defender uses proper give-and-go defense by opening up to the ball and his man. As midfielder 2 starts to cut, the defender plays between his man and the goal, shading to the ball side. As midfielder 2 gets closer inside, the defender needs to adjust to a topside position with no cushion because midfielder 2 can pop out from the crease to get the ball (see figure 9.4).

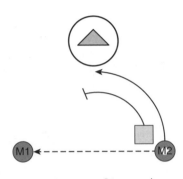

FIGURE 9.4 Give-and-go.

Scenario 3

The attackman has the ball behind the goal at position 2 (see chapter 10 for more information about field positions). The midfielder is at position 3 on the perimeter with his defender. The defender drops his midfielder and gives him cushion. The defender is playing between his man and the goal (man-goal position), giving the midfielder a lot of cushion. The midfielder cuts directly toward the attackman. If the defender plays man-goal, the midfielder has a clearer path to the feed. If the defender plays man-goal, but "shades" more to the ball side, then the midfielder has to arc away from the feed. If the midfielder is not open for a feed, he will go back out top to the perimeter. The defender recovers out top, giving the midfielder more cushion, and changes from playing ball side to playing the man-goal perimeter position. The following drill will help players learn the proper technique for making adjustments on defense (see figure 9.5).

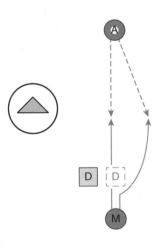

FIGURE 9.5 Perimeter and inside adjustments.

ADJUSTMENT DRILL

PURPOSE

To learn to adjust your body position based on where your opponent is located.

SETUP

The player is defending a teammate out top; the coach has a ball in his stick.

EXECUTION

The player assumes a proper position between his man and the goal. The coach has the ball out top in an adjacent position. The teammate cuts to the inside crease area. The player changes his defensive position from playing between the man and goal to playing between the ball and his man (topside) and giving less cushion (see figure 9.6). The coach tries to feed the teammate. The player tries to prevent an open passing lane and deflects or intercepts the pass inside.

COACHING POINTS

- The player must adjust his position as he reacts to the opponent's movement.
- The player uses a V-up body position so he can see both the ball and his man. He keeps his head on a swivel.
- The player keeps his stick up in the passing lane to prevent a dangerous feed inside.
- A defender must be constantly aware of his surroundings.

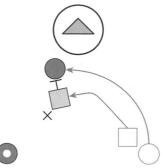

FIGURE 9.6 The player adjusts in order to see the ball and his man.

Defending the Ball Exchange

Most opponents will be stationed along the perimeter around the goal. These players will move the ball around the perimeter in order to get the off-ball defenders to move and adjust their position. For the offense, the objective of this is to eventually create a favorable matchup. As an off-ball defender, you can apply various degrees of defensive pressure based on how much cushion you give your opponent. If your man is not a scoring threat on the perimeter and is not making any aggressive moves to the goal, you can give him a comfortable cushion. You will pick up your man when he gets the ball, maintain some pressure on him, and release him when he passes to another teammate. If your man is more of an offensive threat, you will give him less cushion and apply more defensive pressure. Your man will probably execute a V-cut to get open for an exchange pass. He will accelerate toward the inside crease and then cut back to the perimeter in a 45-degree cutting pattern. You have to respect his forward motion inside and give ground because you don't know his intentions (you must assume the worst). Applying pressure is a balancing act. You want to apply enough pressure to make the opponent work for the exchange pass, but you don't want to apply too much pressure because you will be vulnerable to a backdoor cut. The following drill will help players learn the technique for defending V-cuts.

DEFENDING THE V-CUT DRILL

PURPOSE

To learn the proper technique for handling a V-cut maneuver by the opponent.

SETUP

A teammate or coach has the ball at field location 5. The player and another teammate (the opponent) are stationed at field location 3.

EXECUTION

The opponent uses a V-cut, cutting hard to the inside and then reversing back to the perimeter and toward the coach. The player must defend the V-cut and make proper adjustments. The coach throws the ball to the opponent if he is open.

COACHING POINTS

- The defender has to be careful not to apply too much pressure.
- The defender's objective is to make the opponent work for the pass, not to deny the pass.
- To be successful, the defender must use proper off-ball techniques for body position, stick position, and vision.

Defending a Cutter

A cutter is an off-ball opponent who uses change of direction and change of speed to create space, to break open for a pass, or to get open for a feed. Sometimes an opponent will cut merely to create space for a teammate or to balance up the field. As mentioned earlier, an opponent may cut (using a V-cut) in order to get open for an exchange pass from a teammate. The biggest threat to an off-ball defender is an opponent who can cut to set himself up for a feed—with the intention of catching and shooting. The focus here is on this type of cutter running toward the crease in anticipation of a feed for a possible shot (cut to the goal).

As soon as you recognize the cut, you must change your vision, body position, and stick position. If your man is cutting, you have to focus on your man, and you have to be able to look ahead and see if there is a pick. Your attention needs to be on the cutter and potential picks. Your head needs to be moving back and forth on a swivel so you can see both your man and the ball. The more you can see, the more you can anticipate. You yell "Cutter" to alert your goalie and your teammates.

You listen for a "Check" call from your goalie or a "Pick" call from your teammates. If your man makes a move, the first thing you need to do is drop-step and open up your body position. You want to see if there is a pick coming and then see if you are told to switch. You try to get hip to hip with the cutter so you can run stride for stride with him. Ideally, you will play ball side on the cutter and will be able to see the front of his jersey.

In a traditional inside checking position, your stick is straight up and down with your shoulders squared up toward your opponent (see figure 9.7a). In a modern checking position, your stick is in a port position (if you're left-handed, your stick is off your left shoulder) with your opposite shoulder pointing toward your opponent (see figure 9.7b). By turning your shoulders, you automatically load up your stick.

FIGURE 9.7 Player in the (a) traditional and (b) modern checking position.

You want to be able to throw checks with your big shoulder muscles rather than just your arms. If you're a right-handed defender playing a right-handed cutter, when you run hip to hip, your stick automatically comes over toward your lead shoulder (so you lead with your stick); you are also able to see the cutter's numbers, and you're ready to check down on his arms. If you're a right-handed defender playing a left-handed cutter, when you run hip to hip, your stick is in a port position; you listen for a check call, and you're ready to check down on his arms.

Whether it's a settled or unsettled situation, you are responsible for covering the cutter because he is cutting toward the most dangerous area of the field. You can't let him go unless a switch call is made. If you're playing a man-to-man defense and your man cuts to the goal, you have to cover him unless there is a switch call. In an unsettled situation, you should always go with your cutter, and you should be ready to be bumped off the crease and play someone else. You can't just let your man cut by you because you assume that somebody is there to help out inside or you assume that it's a "dummy cut." Defensively, you must always expect or anticipate the worst-case scenario. That way, you'll be ready for it.

Defending Inside

Defending a single opponent inside on the crease is an off-ball task that requires intensity, attention, and vigilance. For an off-ball defender, the inside crease is the most dangerous area of the field because a completed feed means a very high-percentage shot. Defenders need to be always vigilant to players inside because they can become a potential scorer very quickly. If you let your guard down for even a second, it can cost you a goal.

Defending inside can also be a physically demanding task. Defenders have to be willing to throw checks and make body contact in the most dangerous area of the field. It's a given that there will be a lot of moving, pushing, and shoving inside. If there is a loose ball or rebound shot on the crease, you must body-check your opponent, drive him off the crease (i.e., clear the crease), and let the goalie pick up the ball. The offense has a distinct officiating advantage inside. Officials don't call moving picks inside as they do on the perimeter. Officials let more go on the inside, and they encourage defenders to let the attackers move inside. You won't hear the officials saying, "Watch the moving picks" to the offense.

When defending a single opponent inside, you need to maximize your ability to quickly maneuver inside and deliver decisive checks. You want to be able to knife through the crease area and change positions quickly with either a shuffle or hip-to-hip movement. You must be able to maneuver inside, adjusting and getting through the tight spaces. You can use any of three stick positions inside on the crease: traditional, box, or opposite shoulder. In a traditional stick position, you hold your stick in an upright, vertical position, and your bottom hand is a little farther out and away from the body than your top hand (see figure 9.8a). Most of your checking power comes from your arms. In a "box" position, similar to the "box" position described earlier in the book, you hold your stick in a port position at 45 degrees (see figure 9.8b).

FIGURE 9.8 Player's stick position inside on the crease: *(a)* traditional, *(b)* box, and *(c)* opposite shoulder.

You always have your elbows down and out and your stick in a ready position to get through tight spaces inside and to throw checks. In an opposite-shoulder stick position, you rotate your shoulders toward your opponent and place your stick in a loaded position (see figure 9.8c). You turn your shoulders, which cocks your stick and allows you to use your shoulder muscles to check. This method is very effective. You should never have your stick at your waist or side because the stick will not be in a ready position to check. Having your stick in these positions will also make you wider, make it difficult to get through traffic, and therefore decrease your ability to effectively change positions inside.

When checking, you should always check inside with the handle or shaft and not the plastic head of your stick. If you focus on checking with your shaft, you will be closer to your man and in a better field position to check. If you rely on the handle and you're a little out of position, you can still use the plastic head of your stick to get a piece of your opponent. This gives you a margin of error because you still make contact. Players who use the plastic head of their stick for checking inside will miss their opponent's stick altogether if they are late. You should aim for the opponent's arms between the elbows and the cuff of the glove. On defense, you focus on the opponent's bottom hand (not the head of his stick). Inside checking should be a driving force with your shoulders where you lead with your shoulders and follow through with your arms (see figure 9.9). The closer your check is to your top hand, the more leveraged force will be applied. Your follow-through motion is toward the ground. It's like driving a spike into the ground with a sledgehammer (not a roundhouse motion). Once you make contact, you should continue to drive that check toward the ground. Don't tap and release. You want to drive your opponent's arms toward the ground ("bury the check").

FIGURE 9.9 Player driving toward the ground with his shoulders when checking.

When your man is inside, your "big eye" should be focused on your man. The closer your man gets to the goal, the more attention you must pay to him (instead of the ball). If you want to take a quick glance or peek at the ball, you can temporarily place your stick on your man, turn, and look for the ball. That way, if your man tries to move, you will feel it, and you can refocus on your man. This technique is especially useful when you have sliding responsibilities from the crease and you need to constantly locate both the ball and your man. However, you don't want to overuse this technique. If the goalie makes a "check" call when you're using this technique, you will have to lift up your stick to check your opponent, and you might not have enough time to prevent the shot. There's no penalty call for making contact as long as you don't hold your opponent and prohibit him from moving.

If your man is standing directly in front of the goal, your back is to the ball, and you're almost forced to listen rather than look. When defending inside, you don't really get a chance to look for the ball, so you have to depend on your listening skills. You listen to improve your "sightability." You need to listen to your goalie for directions (e.g., ball locations and check calls) and listen to your teammates for help on defense (e.g., picks, cuts, switches). If you hear a "check" call, you must be able to deliver a decisive check and come down with your stick in a driving motion.

Defending Picks

As mentioned earlier, picks and posts are screens used by offensive players to block a defender. One offensive player positions his body near a teammate's defender in order to obstruct that defender. The other offensive player uses the pick to get free for a dodge, feed, or shot. Off-ball defenders must identify a pick, communicate a pick, and negate its impact.

Picks come in two varieties: on-ball and off-ball picks. In the case of an on-ball pick, the play involves the additional component of a defender playing a ball carrier and using on-ball techniques. Both on-ball and off-ball picks are discussed here because what makes the pick play unique is the off-ball pick setter. Sometimes the pick user has the ball, and sometimes he doesn't. In an on-ball pick situation, a ball carrier is using the pick. In an off-ball situation, a cutter is using a pick for a feed. In either case, the defense typically wants to open a lane and let the defender get through the pick and not switch. However, as a defender, you may have to switch, especially when you are closer to the goal. Both the defender playing the ball and the defender playing the pick setter will shadow their men and play sides as the pick develops. The former is ready to switch, and the latter is preventing the pull-back move.

Defenders' Roles on Picks

The defender roles discussed in this section apply to picks in both the attack zone and the midfield zone. You can afford to have a cushion on a pick behind the goal or out top. If your man sets a pick in the attack zone, you can afford to be 1 1/2 yards below the pick because your man can't score. When you go underneath a pick, you can give the attacker a wider cushion because he can't score but he has his hands free in the most dangerous feeding area of the field. If your man sets a pick in the midfield zone (10 to 12 yards above the crease), you can afford to be 1 1/2 yards below the pick because your man is not dangerous as a shooter.

If you're the defender playing the pick user, you should run with your man and give him a cushion, especially on a sweep. You shouldn't try to be all over your man, because if he shoots the ball and you're within a stick's length, you can get a piece of his gloves and cause a turnover (bad shot). You can afford to give your man a cushion and get through a lane on a pick because he is not dangerous as a shooter. If you're the defender playing the pick setter, be aware that your opponent is not in a real dangerous area, so you can afford to give him a 1 1/2-yard cushion. You can drop back and create an open pick lane for your teammate. You give your man that much cushion because you can switch if necessary and you can close down on your man if he receives the ball. If you are the defender playing the pick setter, your first task is recognizing and communicating a pick. If your man sets a pick, you should shadow or trail him to minimize a front swing or backdoor cut, and you should be ready to switch. You must communicate the pick to your teammate by using concise and descriptive language such as "Pick left" or "Pick right." You should keep repeating the call (instead of just calling out one time). Ideally, you want to create an open lane for your teammate to run through the pick. You create a 1 1/2-yard cushion below the pick and a 1 1/2-yard cushion to the off-ball side of the pick. If you have to switch, then you're already two steps ahead of the man with the ball, and you are stepping up into his path to the goal. If you don't position yourself 1 1/2 yards below the pick, you become a double pick. If you don't position yourself 1 1/2 yards to the off-ball side, you will be trailing the man with the ball if you have to switch.

By rule, your man has to be stationary when setting the pick, but you don't want to be stationary. If you stop and then have to switch, you can't expect to go from a standing still position to effectively covering another man who is sprinting by you. As your man sets the pick, you are already anticipating the switch and moving away from the pick (cheating for the switch). You use your momentum to be leaning and moving in the direction of the oncoming ball carrier. You are ready to explode in that direction. When your man sets the pick, you're ready to recover. You drop-step and open up your hips so you can run hip to hip and match the opponent's speed. This also gives you the angle you need to take in order to get on your attacker.

When your teammate gets near the pick, you have to decide whether you want him to stay or switch. "Get through" tells your teammate to take the open lane through the pick and not switch. You lift your stick vertically to allow your teammate to get through the pick smoothly. "Ready" tells your teammate that you are going to switch (e.g., "Pick left, ready, ready"). The defensive rule is that only the defender whose man is setting the pick can initiate a switch call.

Note that a "help" call is the only time that the defender playing the ball can initiate a switch. The defender whose man is using the pick may make a "help" call if he falls down or loses the ball carrier and can't recover. This defender will call "Help," which means SWITCH. You should always expect the worst on defense (e.g., open lane closes down on the pick, teammate gets picked off). If your man sets a pick, you should always anticipate the switch and anticipate changing direction but keep your feet moving. You need to be in the proper field position to effectively play the ball once you do switch, and you want to use your momentum to your advantage.

If you are the defender playing the pick user, your first task is recognizing the pick. You hear your teammate yell, "Pick left" or "Pick right." Once you recognize a pick, you drop-step and open up your hips so you can see the pick coming and can run hip to hip. If your man sprints, you can run hip to hip (not a shuffle) and match your man stride for stride. You shadow or trail your opponent toward the pick to minimize a pull-back or cut-back move. If your opponent slows down, then you slow down (you should mirror your man). You lift your stick vertically so it doesn't get caught up with the pick. Your job is to choose the optimum path through the pick (see figure 9.10):

- *Path A (over the pick)*—This path is the worst-case scenario. You never want to go over or above the pick because you will always be trailing your man.
- *Path B (through the gap)*—This path is the best-case scenario. In this case, you run through the open lane or gap. If you can, you want to get through an open lane on a pick, but the switch is always a safe play (safety valve). The defender playing the pick setter is a yard over and a yard back so that he can anticipate and make a switch.
- *Path C (under the pick)*—This path is your second best option. In this case, if you go low or under the pick, your man will have his hands free with the ball.

If you go underneath the pick in the attack zone, your opponent can step back and pop out to be a feeder. You have to close that gap or cushion. You close down the distance, move your stick from a port to a poke position, and get into the opponent's gloves. However, by closing down the distance, you are stepping away from the goal. Whenever you step away from the goal or GLE, you leave yourself vulnerable to a dodge. You don't want to turn a feeder into a dodger. If you go underneath the pick in the midfield zone and your opponent pops out, he will be 15 yards out and not in a position where he can shoot the ball right away. You can close down that distance before he becomes dangerous as a shooter.

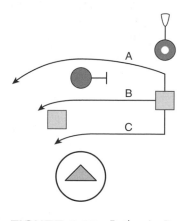

FIGURE 9.10 Paths A, B, and C through the pick.

Pick Maneuvers

Off-ball defenders will have to deal with two main types of offensive pick maneuvers: perimeter cuts to inside picks and two-man inside picks. Perimeter cuts to the inside include a classic cut and pick, a wing or topside mumbo, a pop, and a fishhook. These types of picks revolve around one opponent cutting from the outside toward his teammate on the inside. Either player can set a pick and the other player uses the pick to get open for a feed and shot. Off-ball defenders usually negate the effects of this pick by taking sides. The other major type of pick maneuver happens when two offensive players are stationed on the crease. The two offensive players set picks for one another and try to get open for a feed and shot. Off-ball defenders use squared-up, bookend, or ball-side positioning to counter these moves.

Perimeter Cuts to Inside Picks

As an off-ball defender, if your man cuts from the perimeter to set an inside pick, you should expect something coming back out top or on the wings. Your man may cut you inside, but you're not necessarily going to follow him inside. You shadow your man and play sides. You need to adjust or recover to your area of responsibility. The offense is trying to seal the inside defender with a pick. The offense will use a mumbo, classic, pop, or fishhook.

Mumbo A "mumbo" maneuver is when two players cut toward one another from opposite directions and the perimeter player sets a pick for the inside player. The offensive objective is to get the inside player open for a feed and shot. Off-ball defenders must be alert and prepared to take sides on the pick. Let's take a look at a couple scenarios where this type of pick might be used.

Let's assume that attackman 2 has the ball behind the goal. Defender 1 is covering attackman 1 on the wing. Defender 3 is on the crease and is covering midfielder 3. Defender 1 is playing between his man and the goal. Attackman 1 cuts inside and picks for midfielder 3, who cuts to the perimeter and looks for a feed from attackman 2. Defender 1 shadows attackman 1 because defender 1 needs to be ready to switch with defender 3. Defender 1 switches with defender 3 and has to fight to get topside versus midfielder 3 cutting out to the wing (see figure 9.11).

For the next example, let's assume that midfielder 2 has the ball out top. Defender 1 is covering attackman 1 on the wing. Defender 3 is covering midfielder 3 on the crease. Defender 3 is playing topside on midfielder 3, and defender 1 is playing between his man (attackman 1) and the goal. Attackman 1 starts to cut inside, and defender 1 has to get to a topside position (playing between the man and the ball). Attackman 1 continues to cut inside and picks for midfielder 3, who cuts to

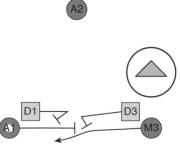

FIGURE 9.11 Wing mumbo defense: ball behind.

the perimeter and looks for a feed from midfielder 2 out top. Defender 1 shadows attackman 1 because defender 1 needs to be ready to switch with defender 3. Because defender 1 and defender 3 are both topside, they can play sides (two-man zone) and switch on the mumbo pick (see figure 9.12).

A third scenario for a mumbo is a topside maneuver. For example, let's assume that midfielder 2 has the ball out top. Defender 1 is covering midfielder 1 out top. Defender 3 is playing topside on midfielder 3, who is on the crease. Midfielder 1 cuts down to the crease and picks on top for midfielder 3, sealing off defender 3. Defender 1 follows midfielder 1 inside and expects something coming back at him. Midfielder 3 cuts up top for a feed from midfielder 2, and defender 1 and defender 3 switch (see figure 9.13).

Classic Pick and Cut A classic "pick and cut" is used when an inside player moves up to set a pick for his teammate who is cutting from the perimeter. The perimeter player's intention is to catch a feed from another teammate and shoot if possible. If the pick is successfully executed, then the off-ball defenders must be ready to switch.

For example, let's assume that attackman 2 has the ball behind the goal. Midfielder 1 is out top and is being played by defender 1. Midfielder 3 is on the crease and is being played by defender 3. Midfielder 3 sets a high-crease pick for midfielder 1, and defender 3 plays ball side of midfielder 3. Midfielder 1 makes a classic cut to the crease pick set by midfielder 3, looking for a feed from attackman 2. Defender 1 follows midfielder 1 and has to drop down to the crease to play sides. Defender 3 switches with defender 1 and covers midfielder 1 on the cut. Defender 1 switches off to cover midfielder 3, who is "cutting off the tail" of midfielder 1's cut (see figure 9.14).

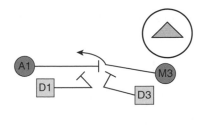

FIGURE 9.12 Wing mumbo defense: ball out top.

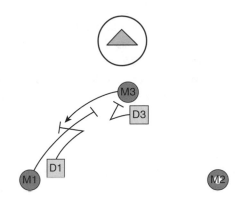

FIGURE 9.13 Topside mumbo defense.

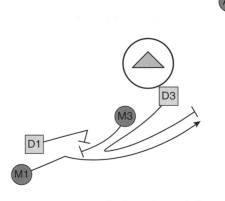

FIGURE 9.14 Pick and cut defense.

Pop A pop move is a variation of the classic pick and cut. If the off-ball defender playing the cutter goes below the pick, the cutter reverses and pops back out to the perimeter for a feed and shot.

For example, let's assume that attackman 2 has the ball behind the goal. Midfielder 1 is out top and is being played by defender 1. Defender 3 is defending midfielder 3 on the crease. Midfielder 3 sets a high-crease pick for midfielder 1, and defender 3 plays ball side of midfielder 3. Midfielder 1 makes a classic cut to the crease pick set by midfielder 3, looking for a feed from attackman 2. If defender 1 goes underneath the crease pick, then midfielder 1 can pop out for a spot feed and shot. Defender 3 switches and covers midfielder 1 on the pop move (midfielder 1 is dangerous as a shooter). Defender 1 switches and covers midfielder 3 on the crease (see figure 9.15).

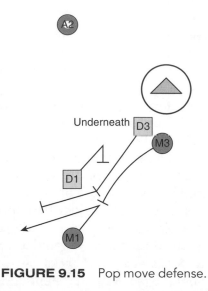

FIGURE 9.15 Pop move defense.

Fishhook If a fishhook cut takes place in the red zone, it's an automatic switch for the defenders. When you have two men inside, you've got to be ready to switch because it's too difficult to stay tight to your man when he is in the most dangerous part of the field. If a fishhook takes place in the yellow zone, the defender should mirror his opponent. If a fishhook takes place in the green zone, the defender should again mirror his opponent. However, you won't see many fishhooks in the

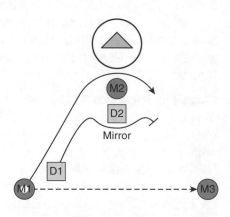

FIGURE 9.16 Traditional fishhook defense.

green zone. The general rule is that you never follow an opponent's fishhook move underneath the pick because you will lose that topside advantage. Two methods are used for defending a fishhook: traditional and modern approach.

In the traditional approach, the defender "mirrors" the fishhook move of his opponent, as shown in figure 9.16. For example, assume that midfielder 1 has the ball out top and is being covered by defender 1. Midfielder 2 is on the crease. Midfielder 3 is out top and adjacent to midfielder 1. Midfielder 1 throws to midfielder 3 and cuts inside and underneath the pick set by midfielder 2 on the crease. Defender 1 takes away midfielder 1's give-and-go move with proper body positioning, follows midfielder 1 on the cut inside, and yells, "Fishhook." He adjusts his position from playing between his man and the goal to playing between his man and the ball (topside) and then mirrors midfielder 1 across the top of the pick. Ideally, defender 1 wants no cushion inside, but a defender has to give some cushion on a fishhook.

Midfielder 1 executes a fishhook move and is momentarily open for a feed when coming out at the pick. Defender 1 must close down the gap or cushion immediately because midfielder 1 is in a dangerous position. Defender 1's stick is in a ready position prepared to check; defender 1 is listening to the goalie for a "check" call.

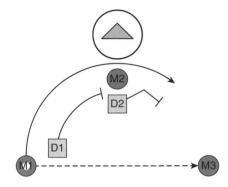

FIGURE 9.17 Modern fishhook defense.

In the modern approach, whenever two attackers go inside, defenders play sides and are ready to switch because they can't give any cushion. For example, let's assume that midfielder 1 has the ball out top and is being covered by defender 1. Midfielder 2 is on the crease and is being covered by defender 2. Midfielder 3 is out top and adjacent to midfielder 1. Midfielder 1 throws to midfielder 3 and cuts inside and underneath a pick set by midfielder 2. Defender 1 follows midfielder 1 on the cut inside, and defender 1 and defender 2 play sides on the inside pick. When midfielder 1 executes the fishhook move and comes out of the pick, defender 2 switches and plays midfielder 1 (see figure 9.17).

Two-Man Picks Inside

The general rule inside is that you should defend your opponent topside. Also, when defending inside (from the crease to 10 yards out), you can't afford to have a cushion. The inside crease area is the most dangerous area of the field because attackers are so close to the goal. If the offense gets the ball in their stick inside, they are dangerous immediately. If you give your opponents a cushion through a pick, they could pop out for a spot feed and quick shot. Defenders have to automatically switch inside because it's just too difficult for a defender to stay with his man and play man-to-man inside. If your man separates from you or you give him a cushion to maneuver inside, you have to close that distance immediately. You must close the gap, anticipating the check call from the goalie, and must have your stick ready to check down. The defensive strategies against two-man picks inside include playing squared up, bookend, or ball side.

Squared Up In this strategy, defenders play squared up on their men on the crease (see figure 9.18). Both defenders are vulnerable to being sealed off by a pick on their outside shoulder, and the attackers can pop out for a quick shot. For example, let's assume that attacker 3 has the ball behind the goal. Attacker 2 is on the crease and is being played by defender 2. Attacker 1 is on the crease and is being played by defender 1. Attacker 1 sets

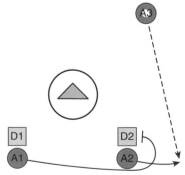

FIGURE 9.18 Squared-up defense.

a pick on the outside shoulder of defender 2, and attacker 2 cuts off the pick toward the wing area. It's difficult for defender 2 to fight through the pick and cover attacker 2 on the cut, and both defenders get "backed up" on the crease.

Bookend In the bookend strategy, both defenders position themselves on the outside shoulders of their opponent. Each defender positions himself so that the opponent can't get to his outside shoulder to set a pick. Both defenders play sides (two-man zone) on the crease and are ready to switch on picks. For example, let's assume that midfielder 3 has the ball out top, as shown in figure 9.19. Attacker 1 and attacker 2 are both on the crease; defender 1 and defender 2 play bookends or sides. Attacker 1 sets a pick on defender 2, and attacker 2 cuts behind the pick and curls out, looking for a feed from midfielder 3 out top. Defender 1 switches and covers attacker 2 on the cut. Defender 1 and defender 2 are expecting something coming back the other way, so they are playing sides and are ready to switch.

In another example, as shown in figure 9.20, attacker 1 has the ball behind the goal. Attacker 2 and attacker 3 are both on the crease; defender 2 and defender 3 play bookends or sides. Attacker 2 sets a pick on defender 3, and attacker 3 cuts behind the pick and curls out, looking for a feed from attacker 1 behind the goal. Defender 2 switches and covers attacker 3 on the cut. The main weakness is that the two defenders can't satisfactorily cover a middle cut.

In a third example, attacker 1 again has the ball behind the goal. Defender 2 and defender 3 bookend attacker 2 and attacker 3 on the crease. Attacker 2 drives toward attacker 1, and defender 2 covers attacker 2. Because defender 2 is bookending attacker 2, attacker 2 can cut through the middle and has an unobstructed path to the ball (see figure 9.21).

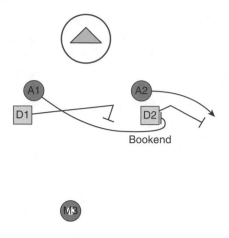

FIGURE 9.19 Bookend defense: playing sides when the ball is out top.

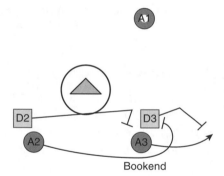

FIGURE 9.20 Bookend defense: playing sides when the ball is behind.

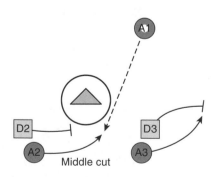

FIGURE 9.21 Bookend defense: open middle cut.

Ball Side In this strategy, the ball-side defender plays on the outside shoulder of his man, and the off-ball defender plays topside on his man. For example, let's assume that attacker 3 has the ball behind the goal. Defender 1 and defender 2 play ball side versus attacker 1 and attacker 2 on the crease. Attacker 1 carries the ball toward defender 2 and defender 2 gets to the outside shoulder on the ball side of attacker 2. Defender 1 splits attacker 1 and attacker

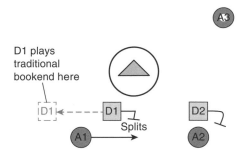

D1 plays traditional bookend here

FIGURE 9.22 Ball-side defense.

2, and he plays more ball side (topside) on attacker 1 (not bookend). Defender 1 and defender 2 stay relative to one another. Defender 1 and defender 2 overplay ball side (not bookend), and they don't allow a gap to occur between them where attacker 1 could cut to the ball in the gap (see figure 9.22).

2V2 INSIDE PICK DRILL

PURPOSE

To learn how to defend a pick on the crease.

SETUP

Four players are on the crease, and a coach has the ball out top.

EXECUTION

Two players are on offense, and the other two players are on defense. The two offensive players set picks for each other and try to get open for a feed from the coach. The two defensive players must communicate with each other to locate the pick ("Pick right" or "Pick left") and to indicate whether their teammate should "switch" or "stay" with his man.

COACHING POINTS

During the first part of the drill, the defensive players are learning how to communicate, how to get through a pick, and how to switch on a pick. For the second part of the drill, the coach tells the defensive players that they can't switch. The two defenders are forced to fight through every pick, which makes the drill more difficult.

Off-ball defense is based on many fundamental concepts, including vision, body positioning, stick positioning, awareness of field location, and perimeter-inside adjustments. Specific off-ball defensive techniques include playing the ball exchange, playing the cutter, and playing an opponent on the inside crease area. One of the most important off-ball skills is defending the pick. Off-ball defenders must understand the various types of picks and how to defend them. The defender playing the pick user and the defender playing the pick setter have to be in sync—physically and mentally—in order to handle these moves.

TEAM PLAY

Part II reviews the aspects of team offensive and defensive play. Chapter 10 focuses on team offense: two-man offensive plays, three-man plays, and 6v6 offensive formations. The 6v6 formations are based on your personnel, balancing the field, and reacting to what the defense imposes on them: slides or no slides. Regardless of the formation, the objective of team offense is to score a goal. Chapter 11 concentrates on team defense: two-man plays, three-man plays, and 6v6 team defense. The 6v6 defense is based on forcing the ball carrier to his weak side or control the middle of the field, extend to the perimeter or slough inside, or slide to the ball carrier. Some teams want to create mistakes and force turnovers, while other defenses wait for their opponent to make a mistake and repossess the ball. The goal of team defense is to prevent goals. Chapter 12 covers transition offense, the movement of the ball from your defensive half of the field to your offensive half of the field. Transition offense has to balance ball possession with quick ball movement to take advantage of any break situation. Chapter 13 concludes with transition defense: the movement of players from your offensive half of the field to your defensive half of the field. If it's a break situation, then the defense wants to get back into the hole, identify the situation, and adjust manpower to the opponent's player and ball movements.

CHAPTER TEN

TEAM OFFENSE

The purpose of team offense is to score goals. Team offense starts with individual skills such as dodging, feeding, and shooting. Next, players must execute off-ball skills involving two or more players, such as using and setting picks, cutting to a feed, ball exchange, and proper off-ball movement. Team offense is based on several general concepts such as the advantage of the "snap count," ball possession, ball movement, the straight-line principle, high-quality shots, tempo of play, and the use of field position. Organized team offense starts with two-man plays, three-man plays, and then full 6v6 team offense. For the 6v6 offense, strategies are designed to balance the field, and teams use various offensive sets to take advantage of their personnel strengths. In team offense, players often have to react to whatever the opponent's defense imposes on them. The two biggest reactions are based on whether the opponents are sliding or not and whether they are playing a zone.

General Offensive Concepts

Team offense is based on various underlying principles. "Snap count" is a football analogy that means the ball carrier always has an advantage over his defender. Ball possession and ball movement are trademark virtues of team offense. If you are the ball carrier, you want to use a straight line to drive directly to the goal. If you don't have the ball, you want to keep your defender in a straight line between you and the ball. This forces the defender to make a choice—watch you or watch the ball. The objective of a team offense is to take a high-quality shot at the right time. Offense may have either a fast-paced or slowed-down tempo of play. Finally, offensive players need to understand field position so that player and ball movement are planned and coordinated.

Snap Count

The biggest advantage that the offense has is the "snap count." In football, the advantage for the offense is based on them knowing where the set play is going and when the play will be initiated with the center snap to the quarterback. In lacrosse, the player with the ball knows where he is going and when he will be attacking. Ideally, he can threaten the goal in either direction with his right hand or left hand. This gives the man with the ball an extreme edge over his defender.

Ball Possession

Offense is determined by who has the ball. Sometimes the ball is loose on the ground—but it won't be for long because both teams will vigorously compete for possession. Once your team has the ball, you are on offense. Gaining possession of the ball and maintaining possession are the essence of offense. The question of who handles the ball is an important issue. This role is analogous to a quarterback in football or a point guard in basketball. A team must have leaders who can decide when to push the transition and when to control the ball.

Ball Movement

Lacrosse is a game of running and ball movement. You want to share the ball. The ball moves faster in the air than any defender can move or slide. Ball movement and player movement can minimize the obvious defensive slide, create mismatches, and disrupt the defense. If you throw the ball to a teammate, you should then move without the ball and keep your feet moving. Many offenses (e.g., motion offense) are based on everyone moving on every pass (e.g., "Pass and cut" or "You throw, you go"). When catching the ball from a teammate, you need to keep your head up, watch the ball, and never lose sight of the ball. Everybody on offense should think ahead and look ahead: You should always think about the next step and open up your body to see the next play.

Straight-Line Principle

On-ball offensive principles are based on the straight-line principle. You want to use "north-south" dodges (e.g., bull, face, roll, split) to attack the goal. Off-ball offensive principles are also based on the straight line. You want to keep your defender in a straight line between you and the ball so that he can't V-up and see both you and the ball. If your defender focuses on you, you should pull the defender away from the action. If your defender focuses on the ball, you want to be close enough to your defender so that if he turns, you can cut and be dangerous and open in three steps.

High-Quality Shots

The primary objective of a team offense is to get a high-percentage, high-quality shot in the area from the crease to 12 yards out. Offensive players need to be very selective. The best shot may not be the first shot or the shot that the defense wants you to take (low-angle or high-perimeter shot). Sometimes you must be willing to take that extra step and take a physical hit from a defender in order to get a better shot. For example, you may have to fight for the middle of the field.

The best shots tend to be in the middle, but that is where most of the defenders are located. Shooting involves accuracy, velocity, deception, and changing the plane of your shot (e.g., shooting the ball high to low). You want to shoot to the goalkeeper's weaknesses. Some goalies are weaker high, and some are weaker low, but all goalies are weaker to the off-stick side. A shot that is located between the off-stick shoulder and off-stick hip is the most difficult shot to save.

Tempo of Play

The major distinction between various offensive philosophies is the desired tempo of play. Slow-tempo offenses are designed to control the ball. In the game of soccer, turnovers happen all the time. In lacrosse, fewer turnovers occur (compared to soccer), and when they do, they are very costly. This places a premium on ball possession. Ball control offense is the best way to prevent turnovers. This type of offense can be thought of as your best defense because it keeps the ball away from the opponent. It also allows your defense to regroup. Ball control lets you settle the flow of the game. Ball control offense creates an environment that enables you to recognize a mismatch or create a mismatch by forcing a switch on a pick. This offense makes it easier to set up a desired matchup or to isolate the defender on the perimeter. Fast-tempo offenses are designed to push the transition game. Run-and-gun offenses will maximize any numerical advantages on the field and place lots of pressure on the defense in order to create a high-percentage shot. Offenses will rely more on either set plays or freelance movement depending on personnel and game experience.

Field Position

For 6v6 offense around an opponent's goal, it is useful to designate specific field locations around the goal to describe player and ball movements. The 6v6 system described in this section is used by most college programs. This system uses a clock analogy in which the opposing goal is the center of the clock; lacrosse field positions are assigned based on the various clock positions (see figure 10.1).

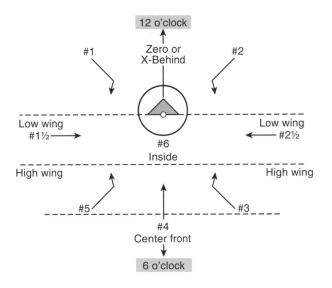

FIGURE 10.1 Field positions around the goal: using clock hands to understand them.

Behind

The location directly behind the goal corresponds to the 12 o'clock location. In lacrosse, this position is called zero or X-behind. Two other important field positions are also located behind the goal. The location corresponding to the 10:00 clock position is referred to as the 1 position in lacrosse, which is primarily used by a right-handed feeder. The location corresponding to the 2:00 clock position is referred to as the 2 position, which is primarily used by a left-handed feeder.

Low Wing

The low wing is located from the GLE to 10 yards above the GLE. When an offensive player is in this area, he wants to be a couple of yards above the GLE. He can either dodge or swing behind the goal to exchange the ball from one side of the field to the other. The location corresponding to the 9 o'clock position is referred to as the 1 1/2 position, which is primarily used by a right-handed dodger. The location corresponding to the 3 o'clock position is referred to as the 2 1/2 position, which is primarily used by a left-handed dodger.

High Wing

The high wing area stretches from 10 yards above the GLE to the restraining line. In this area, an offensive player has the opportunity to redirect the ball out top (his primary look is out top). The location corresponding to the 7:30 clock position is referred to as the 5 position, which is primarily used by a right-handed dodger. The location corresponding to the 4:30 clock position is referred to as the 3 position, which is primarily used by a left-handed dodger.

Center Front

The most difficult position for a team to defend is the area out top at the center of the field. When a ball carrier is in this area, the defense has to anticipate defending the ball carrier going in either direction. The location corresponding to the 6 o'clock position is referred to as the 4 position. Whether the ball carrier is right- or left-handed, this is usually a prime offensive location.

Inside

The most dangerous offensive position on the field is inside. Lacrosse position 6 is on the crease directly in front of the goal.

Lacrosse offenses are always trying to stay a step ahead of their adversary. Traditional offenses were based on topside midfielders sweeping across the middle of the field for a strong-hand shot. For example, if an attacker at the 5 position is right-handed, he would sweep across the middle of the field, as shown in figure 10.2; a left-handed attacker at the 3 position would also sweep across the middle of the field.

Some defenses took away the sweep across the middle of the field and forced the dodger down the alleys. When the defense forces the ball carrier down the side alley, the ball carrier is forced to his weak hand and has a lower-angle shot. For example, if a ball carrier at the 5 position is right-handed, the defender would force him down the side to his weak hand and a lower-angle shot (see figure 10.3).

When defenses started taking away the middle of the field, offenses reacted by switching their strengths (i.e., switching the side of the field that a right-hander or left-hander would line up on). For example, if a ball carrier at the 5 position is a left-hander, then forcing him down the alley allows him to use his strong hand; the tradeoff for the defense is that forcing him down the alley still causes him to have a lower shooting angle (see figure 10.4).

In response, some defenses began forcing players to their weak hand and to the middle of the field. For example, if the ball carrier at the 5 position is left-handed, the defender will force the ball carrier to his weak hand and the middle of the field. The defender can't overplay him so much that the ball carrier gets back underneath the defender for his left-handed shot. The tradeoff for the defense is that they are forcing the ball carrier to his weak hand but they are also giving him the center of the field where he has all kinds of options.

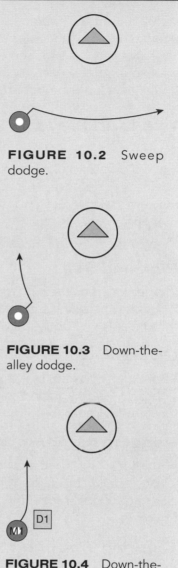

FIGURE 10.2 Sweep dodge.

FIGURE 10.3 Down-the-alley dodge.

FIGURE 10.4 Down-the-alley dodge using the strong hand.

Team Offensive Plays

Individual offense begins with a single ball carrier and a single defender. Team offense begins with two-man plays, and it progresses to three-man plays and 6v6 offensive sets. This section covers basic two-man plays, which are the core of team offense, and proceeds to three-man plays on the perimeter and inside (near the goal). Next, information is provided on 6v6 team offense.

Two-Man Plays

Basic team offense starts with two-man plays. The purpose of two-man plays is for two offensive players to act in a synchronized manner to create an advantage against the defense. This advantage can be created by the confusion of a pick or the surprise of a give-and-go. Also, this advantage can be maximized if the offensive player reads his teammate's movements and clears through for the ball carrier, thereby minimizing the opportunity for one defender to play two offensive players.

Pick-and-Roll

Midfielder 1 has the ball at position 5, and midfielder 2 is at position 3. Midfielder 2 cuts left and sets a pick; midfielder 1 dodges over this pick. Midfielder 2 then rolls back for an outlet pass (see figure 10.5).

Give-and-Go

Midfielder 1 has the ball at position 5, and midfielder 2 is at position 3. Midfielder 1 throws the ball to midfielder 2 and quickly cuts right, looking for a return pass from midfielder 2 (see figure 10.6).

Reading the Teammate's Movements

Midfielder 1 has the ball at position 5, and midfielder 2 is at position 3. Midfielder 1 uses a split dodge from left to right. Midfielder 2 moves left and then right to clear space for midfielder 1. Midfielder 2 mirrors midfielder 1's movement (see figure 10.7).

Clearing Through

Midfielder 1 has the ball at position 5, and midfielder 2 is at position 3. Midfielder 1 uses a right-handed sweep dodge across the front of the goal, while midfielder 2 cuts underneath midfielder 1 (see figure 10.8). Midfielder 2 wants to cut hard and occupy his defender instead of "drifting" underneath his teammate, midfielder 1. Midfielder 2 wants to open up the dodging area.

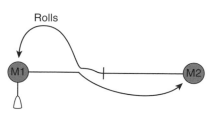

FIGURE 10.5 Two-man play: pick-and-roll.

FIGURE 10.6 Two-man play: give-and-go.

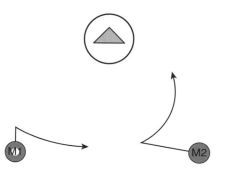

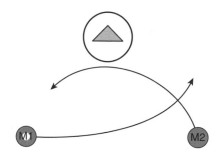

FIGURE 10.7 Two-man play: reading the teammate's movements.

FIGURE 10.8 Two-man play: clearing through.

Three-Man Plays

The basics of three-man plays are similar to the two-man plays: picking, faking a pick, clearing out, and so on. However, adding a third player to the tactical mix increases both the reward and the risks of the maneuver. The plays provide more offensive opportunities, but there are also more defenders involved who want to break up the play. Some three-man plays are designed for the inside, and some are geared for the perimeter.

Three-Man Plays on the Inside

A three-man play on the inside is a set play designed to feed the ball from the perimeter to the inside crease area. The two off-ball offensive players are setting various picks (pick, overload, and pop) to get each other open, and the ball carrier behind the goal wants to feed the ball to the crease. The purpose of this progression is to get a high-quality shot from the crease.

Pick-and-Roll   Attackman 1 is on left crease, attackman 2 is on right crease, and attackman 3 has the ball at position 2. Attackman 2 cuts left and sets a pick for attackman 1. Attackman 1 cuts over the pick, looking for a feed from attackman 3 behind the goal. Attackman 2 rolls to the crease as a secondary target (see figure 10.9).

Overload   Attackman 1 is stationed low (nearer the crease), and attackman 2 is stationed higher (farther from the crease). They are in an I formation on the crease. Attackman 1 cuts low to the right, and attackman 2 cuts sideways to the right. Attackman 1 and attackman 2 overload one side of the crease (right side), and attackman 3 tries to feed the open cutter (see figure 10.10).

Pop   Attackman 1 and attackman 2 use the same I formation on the crease as in the previous overload play. Attackman 2 makes a high cut off of attackman 1 and pops off the crease (see figure 10.11).

Three-Man Plays on the Perimeter

Three-man plays on the perimeter are an offensive progression in which the unit tries to get an off-ball teammate open for an offensive opportunity—catch and shoot, catch and feed, and so on. If unsuccessful, the off-ball players then create space and clear out for the ball carrier. The three-man plays on the perimeter are either traditional or modern in style.

Traditional Three-Man Plays

The traditional three-man plays were prevalent from the 1960s through the 1990s. This offensive progression is based on five maneuvers: pick, pop, repick, fake pick, and clear-through. This progression is described here with a midfield unit in the midfield area. The five-play sequence can also be used with the attack unit and the ball starting out behind the goal.

Pass, Pickaway, and Cut   Midfielder 1 is at position 5, midfielder 2 has the ball at position 4, and midfielder 3 is at position 3. Midfielder 2 passes the ball to midfielder 3. Midfielder 2 then cuts to midfielder 1 and sets a pickaway for midfielder 1. Midfielder 1 cuts over the pick for a pass from midfielder 3 (see figure 10.12).

Pop   The players use the same setup as for the "pass, pick away, and cut." Midfielder 2 passes the ball to midfielder 3. Midfielder 2 then cuts to midfielder 1 and sets a pick for midfielder 1. Midfielder 1 cuts to the pick and then pops out for a feed from midfielder 3 (see figure 10.13).

Repick   The players use the same setup and sequence as for the "pass, pick away, and cut." When midfielder 1 cuts over the pick (for a pass from midfielder 3) but is not open, he then sets a repick for midfielder 2. Midfielder 2 cuts over the repick for a pass from midfielder 3 (see figure 10.14).

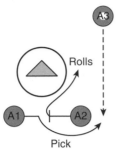

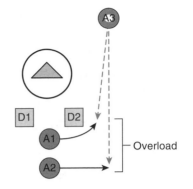

FIGURE 10.9 Three-man play on the inside: pick-and-roll.

FIGURE 10.10 Three-man play on the inside: overload.

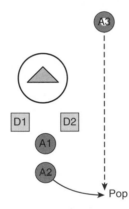

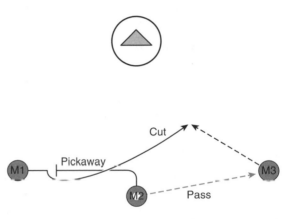

FIGURE 10.11 Three-man play on the inside: pop.

FIGURE 10.12 Traditional three-man play: pass, pickaway, and cut.

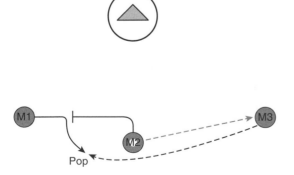

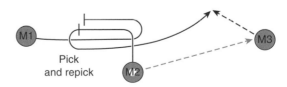

FIGURE 10.13 Traditional three-man play: pop.

FIGURE 10.14 Traditional three-man play: repick.

187

Fake Pick   The players use the same setup as for the "pass, pick away, and cut." Midfielder 2 passes the ball to midfielder 3. Midfielder 2 cuts toward midfielder 1 but fakes a pick and cuts back for a feed from midfielder 3 (see figure 10.15).

Clear-Through   The players use the same setup and sequence as for the "pass, pick away, and cut." Midfielder 2 passes the ball to midfielder 3, and they run the off-ball sequence; however, no one is open. Midfielder 1 and midfielder 2 then cut underneath midfielder 3, and midfielder 3 dodges to the left and sweeps across the front of the goal (see figure 10.16).

Modern Three-Man Plays

Modern three-man plays are a reaction to opposing defenses executing two strategies. First, defenses began to slide from the crease to the midfield ball carrier before he had a premium shot. Second, defenses began to take away the midfield ball carrier's outlet pass to X-behind. As a result, the ball carrier redirected the ball out front, looking for an opening.

Midfield Roll-Back Pass   The offense uses a 1-4-1 offensive set. Midfielder 2 and midfielder 3 are on the crease, and midfielder 1 is out top with the ball. Midfielder 1 executes a right-handed dodge to the goal, midfielder 3 cuts to position 4, and midfielder 2 cuts to position 5. If the defense slides from the crease to the dodging midfielder (1), then the offense has an advantage out top. Midfielder 1 throws a roll-back pass to midfielder 3 out top, and midfielder 3 feeds midfielder 2 for a shot (see figure 10.17).

Fargo   Fargo is used to take away the second defensive slide (midfielder 3 cuts through underneath). Midfielder 1 is at position 5. Midfielder 2 has the ball at position 4 and is covered by defender 2. Midfielder 3 is at position 3 and is covered by defender 3. Midfielder 3 cuts underneath to the crease, and defender 3 follows him inside. Midfielder 2 passes the ball to midfielder 1 and cuts toward position 3. Midfielder 1 catches the ball and makes a right-handed move toward the middle of the field, attacking defender 2. When defender 2 slides, midfielder 1 makes an outlet pass (a pop pass) to midfielder 2. There is no second slide to midfielder 2 (see figure 10.18).

Early   Early is used when the defense forces a ball carrier to the middle of the field and to his weak hand. Midfielder 1 is at position 5 and is covered by defender 1. Midfielder 2 is at position 4. Midfielder 3 is at position 3 and is covered by defender 3. Midfielder 3 has the ball and makes a left-handed move because defender 3 is forcing him into the middle of the field. Midfielder 2 clears through "early" and curls underneath to open up the middle of the field. When midfielder 2 curls underneath midfielder 3 and midfielder 3 is forced into the middle, the defense may want to switch. If the defense tries to switch, midfielder 3 throws the ball back to midfielder 2. If defender 1 slides, midfielder 3 passes to midfielder 1. If the defense slides from the crease, then midfielder 3 dumps the ball inside (see figure 10.19).

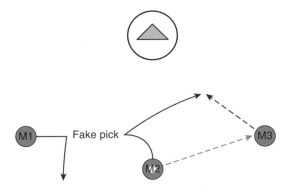

FIGURE 10.15 Traditional three-man play: fake pick.

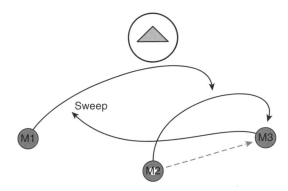

FIGURE 10.16 Traditional three-man play: clear-through.

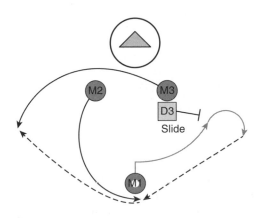

FIGURE 10.17 Modern three-man play: midfield roll-back pass.

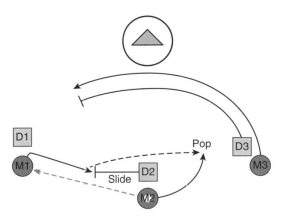

FIGURE 10.18 Modern three-man play: fargo.

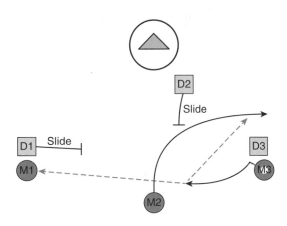

FIGURE 10.19 Modern three-man play: early.

6v6 Offense

Now let's move on to 6v6 offensive lacrosse. The full 6v6 offense is based on certain principles. One principle is the need to maintain a balanced playing field, which requires offensive players to understand three primary "boxes" on the field. Another important principle is using effective offensive sets based on the strengths of the team.

Balance on the Field

Offensive players need to occupy three primary "boxes" on the field: behind, inside, and out top (see figure 10.20). Players should stay in their boxes to help the offense maintain field balance. Offenses need to be evenly spaced and not congested in a particular area of the field. Offensive players must have space in order to execute critical functions such as maintaining ball possession, getting high-quality shots, and minimizing fast break opportunities for the opponent.

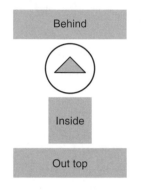

FIGURE 10.20 Primary boxes for offensive players to occupy.

Behind This box is primarily occupied by feeders and dodgers. Their primary field responsibility is backing up shots and maintaining ball possession for the offense. Remember that lacrosse is a unique game because it has a large area behind the goal. When positioned in the area from behind the goal to the GLE, players are a double threat to dodge or feed. The advantage of the ball being behind is that the defensive players have to turn their back on players in front of the goal. This makes it difficult for the defense to watch both the ball and their man, and it opens up off-ball effectiveness and the feeding and cutting game. This area is an advantage for feeding and cutting, but it's a disadvantage for dodging because the defender can run through the crease and make up ground (the attacker can't run through the crease). Behind the goal, the prime feeding area is on each side of the goal.

Zero or X-behind is the position directly behind the goal. Directly behind the goal is not the best place for offensive players to be because the goalkeeper is in their feeding path. Transferring the ball from one side of the field to another behind the goal is an important offensive maneuver. If the offense is playing a 1-4-1 and has only one player behind the goal, that player will have to adjust his position frequently. Any time a team uses an offense with just one player behind the goal, the player has to know how to play that position and use that position to his advantage.

Inside This box is primarily occupied by shooters. Their primary field responsibility is to occupy the most dangerous offensive position on the field. In this box, players are a single threat to shoot. Typically, the position is occupied by off-ball players and finishers. A shot from the inside is the highest-percentage shot, so the goalkeeper must make a great save in order to prevent a goal. To get these high-percentage shots, the offense often sets picks to get a teammate open.

Inside players are always away relative to the ball. They are opposite the ball and far away from the ball. If the ball is behind the goal, inside players are positioned high in order to open up dodging lanes and to have room for cutting. If the ball is out top, inside players are positioned low in order to open up dodging lanes.

Also, the offense never wants to have too many players inside, causing a congested crease area. If someone cuts to the crease, then somebody else needs to bounce off the crease and get on the perimeter. When a player cuts to the inside, he must create an offensive opportunity or get out ("cut and get out"). When in doubt, the player should get off the crease and balance up the offense: If in doubt, then get out. The rule for playing inside is like the three-second rule in basketball—players don't want to loiter in front of the basket.

Traditionally, the inside position was used for screening outside shots. A player would intentionally try to line up with the head of the shooter's stick and the goalie's position. The player would provide a stationary screen for the shooter, and the shooter would bounce the shot low at the screener's feet. In the contemporary game, the screening role is minimal because of the artificial turf and safety concerns. Most games are played on artificial surfaces. If a shooter bounces the ball on turf, the turf provides a predictable "true bounce" for the goalkeeper (unless the turf is wet), and the ball slows down once it makes contact with the ground. Therefore, most players tend to shoot high. It's tough to screen a goalkeeper when everybody shoots high. More important, the threat of a shot to the chest is extremely dangerous to the screener. In the past, players bounced outside shots, and the shots were slower. But today's shots are faster because of stick design. Sometimes offenses create unintentional screens. For example, attackers may be cutting through the inside, and this distracts the goalkeeper. Also, when a cutter clears through the inside, he brings his defender to the inside, so it becomes a two-man screen for the goalkeeper.

Out Top   This box is primarily occupied by triple-threat players. Their primary field responsibility is to minimize the counterattack. When an offensive player shoots the ball, the offensive players out top have to be ready to run back into the hole and play defense. These players are the first line of defense. When positioned in the area from the top to the wings above the GLE, players are a triple threat to dodge, feed, or shoot. As long as the ball is in front of the GLE, the offensive player becomes a triple threat.

Offensive Sets

The offensive sets used by a team should be chosen based on the team's personnel. Each team has certain strengths. The team should use these strengths by placing them in certain positions on the field. Also, teams should position players on the field based on how well they work together and complement each other's abilities. When determining which offensive sets your team will use, you should consider how many players you want to have in each of these areas of the field: behind the goal, on the crease, at the wings, and out top.

Behind the Goal

Do you want one or two players behind the goal? (Offenses normally don't have three attackmen behind the goal.) Do you have an attackman who can work effectively by himself behind the goal? A team's primary ball handler can operate anywhere around the goal, but this player is often an attackman working behind the goal. If you have an ace attacker behind the goal and he controls the offense, you might not want to put a teammate back there with him to get in his way. If you have two attackmen behind the goal, you must ensure that they work well together. When you bring another attackman behind the goal, he will bring another defender behind the goal with him. Now a total of four players are behind the goal instead of two. The same rule applies out top.

Crease

How many players do you want on the crease? You could have three players in this area, but you don't want to get too much congestion on the crease. Do you have more perimeter players or inside players? For example, if you have one strong attackman and one strong midfielder, you could use a 1-4-1 set. If you have two strong midfielders, you can use a 2-2-2 or 1-4-1. If you have two strong attackmen, you can use a 2-2-2.

Wings and Out Top

How many triple-threat players do you have? Do you want to put all of them on one midfield unit, or do you want to spread out the talent to two or more midfield units?

Based on all of these factors, teams will decide which offensive set or sets will work best for them. Offenses used by contemporary teams include the following sets:

- 1-4-1 (as shown in figure 10.21)
- 2-3-1 (as shown in figure 10.22)
- 3-1-2 (as shown in figure 10.23)
- 1-3-2 (as shown in figure 10.24)
- 2-2-2 (as shown in figure 10.25)
- 4-2 (as shown in figure 10.26)

The number designations begin with the players out top, then the wings and crease, and lastly, the players behind the goal. Team offense depends on the abilities of your personnel, so your offensive sets should be selected based on your personnel. You accomplish your offensive objectives (high-percentage shots) by putting your personnel in positions where they feel comfortable and confident and where they will be the most effective. You want to play toward your players' strengths and get the ball into the hands of your most effective dodgers, feeders, and shooters in preferable field positions. One useful tool is to ask the players, "Where do you want the ball when you need to initiate a dodge or finish a play (shoot) to win the game at the end of the fourth quarter?" The coach has a sheet of paper with a diagram of a goal on it.

Each player puts his number on the paper where he wants to be and what he wants to do: dodge or shoot. If dodging, he would include his preferred dodging maneuver, where it would begin and where it would end. If shooting, he would indicate where on the field he would like to receive a feed to shoot. The coach then tries to "connect the dots" in the most efficient manner.

1-4-1 The advantage of a 1-4-1 is that the offense has wide dodging lanes above the GLE.

The center midfielder has the whole "out top" box to operate. If you have a strong midfielder, this player can dodge in either direction from out top. Players on the wings have excellent locations to initiate a dodge. The player behind the goal has the whole "behind" box to operate which allows for greater individual dodging freedom. In the 1-4-1, the two players on the crease can work together to get open for an offensive opportunity. The disadvantages include longer outlet passes and less defensive capability. See figure 10.21 for an example of a 1-4-1 offensive set.

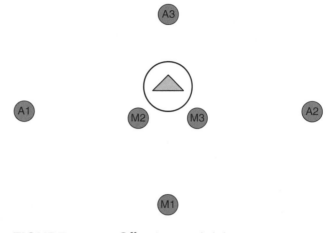

FIGURE 10.21 Offensive set: 1-4-1.

2-3-1 The advantage of a 2-3-1 is that it has five potential dodger/shooters above the GLE.

The two players out top can work together to create some offense. Like the 1-4-1, a lone player is positioned behind the goal for dodging and feeding from behind and the wings have lots of room for the players to maneuver for a scoring opportunity. The 2-3-1 set is a very popular formation in today's game because it lends itself to a "motion- style" offensive pattern. The advantage of a motion offense is that it gets the players moving. The motion offense is better suited for less experienced players because it provides more structure. The disadvantage is that players are moving for the sake of moving. Players may be moving in one direction when they would be better off moving in another direction. See figure 10.22 for an example of a 2-3-1 offensive set.

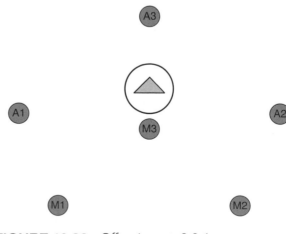

FIGURE 10.22 Offensive set: 2-3-1.

3-1-2 The advantage of the 3-1-2 is the three midfielders can work together in the "out top" box. This is a prime alignment to run three-man midfield plays. Also, the two attackmen can work together behind the goal. This alignment provides the most defensive capability. The disadvantage of the 3-1-2 is the "top" box can become congested, there isn't much opportunity for wing play, and there are longer outlet passes to and from the midfield and close attack. See figure 10.23 for an example of a 3-1-2 offensive set.

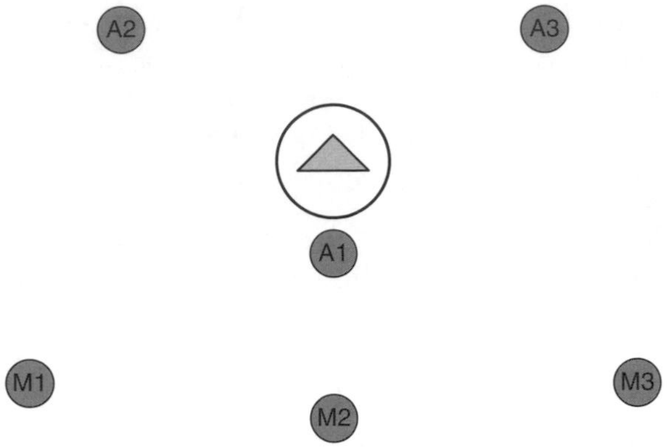

FIGURE 10.23 Offensive set: 3-1-2.

1-3-2 The advantage of the 1-3-2 is it has wide, uncongested dodging lanes above the GLE. Like the 1-4-1, the center midfielder has the whole "out top" box to operate and the other two midfielders are positioned in the wing areas. Like the 3-1-2, it has two attackmen who can work together behind the goal. Like the 1-4-1, its disadvantage is long outlet passes and less defensive capability. See figure 10.24 for an example of a 1-3-2 offensive set.

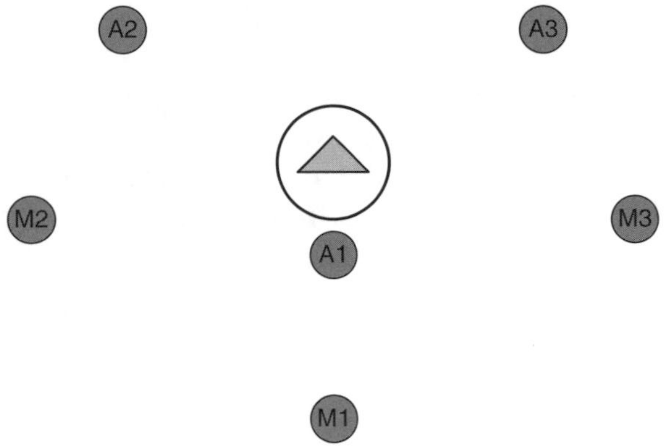

FIGURE 10.24 Offensive set: 1-3-2.

2-2-2 Players out top, inside, and behind work in pairs to create offensive opportunities for each other. Players set and use picks to free each other's hands to feed, shoot, or dodge. See figure 10.25 for an example of a 2-2-2 offensive set.

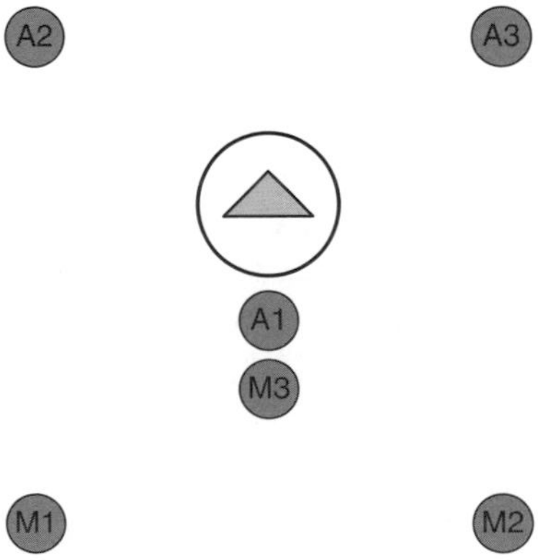

FIGURE 10.25 Offensive set: 2-2-2.

4-2 This formation uses a pick alignment on both sides of the crease with two feeders behind the goal. The two feeders work the ball back and forth, quickly changing sides of the field and looking for any defensive lapses on a pick above the goal. The objective is to feed a player cutting off a pick near the crease for a close-range shot. See figure 10.26 for an example of a 4-2 offensive set.

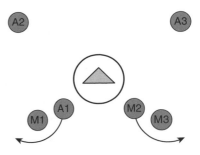

FIGURE 10.26 Offensive set: 4-2.

Offensive Reaction to Defenses

Offenses tend to take what the defenses give them. Typically, team defenses take away the middle of the field (forcing attackers down the alleys) OR take away strengths or strong hands. For example, when the offensive team's players predominantly play one-handed, the defense would focus on taking away strengths. Team offenses have to react to two important defensive strategies. The first question is whether the opponent will slide or not. The other question is whether the opponent is playing man-to-man or zone defense.

A lot of team defenses try NOT to slide. This is called island defense: The defender is all alone on an island with his man. If the defensive team thinks that they are athletically superior to an opponent, they are not going to slide. Coaches will tell their defenders that they are responsible for their man and should expect no help. However, the majority of teams do slide, especially to the ball carrier. Sliding teams assume that all on-ball defenders will get beat because the attacker has a distinct advantage. Therefore, the defense double-teams or slides to the ball before the attacker is a threat to shoot or feed; the defense forces the attacker to pass the ball. Slides typically come from the crease, from an adjacent defender, or from across the crease (coma slide). Most defenses will slide a crease defender to the ball carrier, and the defender covering the ball carrier will recover back to the crease and help out on the crease (slide and recover).

Offenses always want to make the defense slide and rotate. If the ball carrier is double-teamed, he should pass the ball and not risk the turnover. Offenses want to attack the expected slide. They want slides from the obvious defender or the only defender possible. For example, if it's an adjacent slide, this creates space for a dodger. If it's a crease slide, the offensive players don't want to jam the ball inside. They want to work the ball to the backside and take advantage of any defensive lapses. Offenses will attack a defense differently depending on whether the defense slides to the ball OR only "shows" (the defender fakes a slide and recovers back to his man or area of responsibility).

Offenses must react to various defensive sliding schemes. The two primary defensive techniques are (1) slide and recover and (2) show or fake a slide. If a defense slides, they will usually plan to slide more than one player. The offense wants to take away the second slide. Defenses are always going to be in position to get the first slide, but the offense should minimize the opportunities for a second slide. In the example shown in figure 10.27, the ball carrier (midfielder 1) is at field position 3 and is covered by defender 1. Midfielder 2 is at field position 5 and is covered by defender 2. Attackman 3 is behind the goal at field position 1 and is covered by defender 3. The ball carrier dodges to his left and across the middle of the field. Ideally, the defense wants defender 2 to slide to the ball carrier and wants defender 3 to slide to midfielder 2. However, when the ball carrier makes his move, attackman 3 front swings to the front of the crease and takes defender 3 with him on the cut. When defender 2 slides to the ball carrier, there is no second slide.

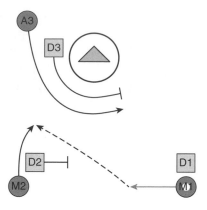

FIGURE 10.27 Front swing negates second slide.

Offensive Strategy: Offense Reacts to Slide and Recover

If a defense uses a slide and recover defense, the offense wants the defense to continue to slide and rotate while the offense moves the ball forward, looking to create a 2v1 opportunity.

In the example shown in figure 10.28, the ball carrier has the ball at position 3 and is covered by defender 4. Attackman 3 is on the crease and is covered by defender 3. Attackman 2 is behind the goal at field position 2 and is covered by defender 2. Attackman 1 is at field position 1 and is covered by defender 1. Defensively, the opposing team will have defender 4 force the ball carrier down the alley. Defender 3 on the crease will slide to the ball carrier, and defender 4 will recover to the crease and cover attackman 3 (see figure 10.28).

Offensively, the ball carrier wants the defense to slide and continue to rotate. In this example, the ball carrier will try to get defender 2 to adjacent slide to him so that defender 1 is forced to coma slide across the goal and pick up attackman 2. The offensive objective is to get the entire defense rotating and then take advantage of any lapses in coverage by moving the ball. In this case, the offense would move the ball to attackman 2 and then attackman 1 (see figure 10.29).

Offensive Strategy: Offense Reacts to "Show" Defense

If a defense uses a show (fake slide) defense, the offense wants to force the entire defense to rotate or wants to take away the expected second slide. The defense wants to fake a slide, recover to their man, and NOT have the defense rotate. For example, the ball carrier has the ball at field position 3 and is covered by defender 1. Attackman 2 is behind the goal at field position 2 and is covered by defender 2. Attackman 3 is behind the goal at field position 1 and is covered by defender 3. The ball carrier dodges down the alley. Defender 2 shows (fakes a slide to the ball carrier and recovers to attackman 2). In essence, defender 2 is playing two attackers: the ball

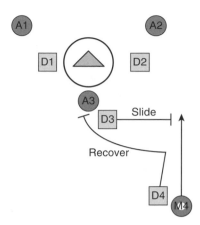

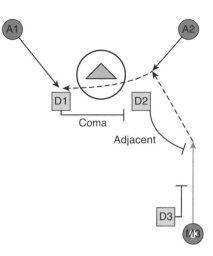

FIGURE 10.28 Slide and recover.

FIGURE 10.29 Offense wants defense to slide and rotate.

carrier dodging down the alley AND attackman 2 receiving a pass behind the goal. If attackman 2 is way out in no-man's-land, then it's easy for defender 2 to "show" to the ball carrier and still recover to attackman 2 (see figure 10.30).

Offensively, the ball carrier wants to force defender 2 to slide to him or get the next defensive slider to commit to another offensive cut to the goal. The key for the offense is to keep moving the ball forward, to get defenders to adjust their positions, and to then take advantage of any defensive lapses in coverage. In this example, the offense wants attackman 2 close to the goal so that when defender 2 shows, attackman 2 can take off toward the front of the crease and draw defender 3. Then, the ball carrier skips the ball to attackman 3. Attackman 3 catches the ball and attacks the backside, and the defense has to rotate (see figure 10.31).

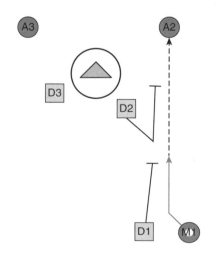

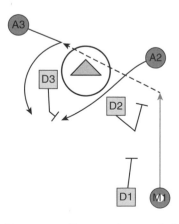

FIGURE 10.30 Defensive strategy: Defense shows or fakes the slide.

FIGURE 10.31 Front swing and skip ball to backside.

Zone Defense

The offense needs to attack a zone defense from all 360 degrees around the cage. Each attacker must be dangerous and force his opponent to defend him. Attackers must occupy their defender; otherwise, the defender will slough inside and be able to help out teammates. Offenses want to change formations by moving the ball on the perimeter and cutting to various positions. The formation change is a recognition problem for the defense, especially if it ends up in an unusual set such as an overload. Offenses want to be dangerous inside on the crease. Specifically, they want to attack the inside crease defender who is trying to play the ball-side cutter. Zone defenses try to play one defender inside, and this crease defender's main responsibility is to cover the ball-side cutter or inside shooter. Also, they want to force an adjacent or coma slide.

For example, assume that attackman 1 is at X behind; attackman 2 is at position 2 1/2; attackman 3 is at position 3; attackman 4 is at position 4; attackman 5 is at position 5; and attackman 6 is at position 1 1/2. Offenses may run a circle play and move the ball around the perimeter. Attacker 6 has the ball and draws defender 1. Attacker 6 passes to attacker 1 cutting to the front of the goal. Attacker 1 draws coma slide from defender 2. Attacker 3 cuts to the crease looking for a feed from attacker 1 and draws crease defender 6. If cutter is not open, attacker 1 passes to attacker 2 cutting behind the goal. Attacker 5 cuts to crease, looking for a feed from attacker 2. If cutter is not open, attacker 2 can pass to attacker 4 drifting to position 3 (see figure 10.32).

Zone defenses tend to follow the ball, not men. Sometimes defenders will be aggressive to the ball carrier and adjacent outlets to the side. Player movement and ball movement are important against a zone defense. For example, one successful tactic is to change the plane of the field by passing the ball quickly from the ball side to the help side.

However, some teams think that if they just move the ball against a zone, they will be effective. If the offense is just banging the ball around the perimeter, most defenses are pretty good at adjusting to the ball movement. The offense needs to attack the seams in the zone to force the defense to rotate. Seams are the field positions between each defender's position. In the example shown in figure 10.33, midfielder 2 has the ball at position 3;

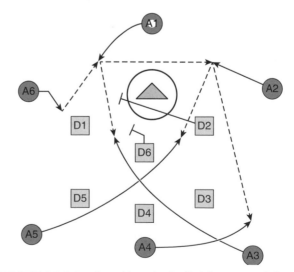

FIGURE 10.32 Attacking the ball-side crease defender.

midfielder 1 is at position 4 and is covered by defender 1. Midfielder 2 drives to the left and attacks a seam between positions 3 and 4. If defender 1 steps up to play midfielder 2, the offense has the defense rotating.

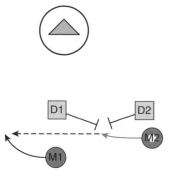

FIGURE 10.33 Attacking the seams of the zone.

Against a zone, the most important thing is that the offense must attack the zone. Specifically, the offense can dodge one of the two short-stick defenders. Offensive players should dodge a zone and force a defender to slide to them. When an attacker dodges and draws another defender, this forces the zone to rotate. When defenders rotate, they are in unfamiliar positions. The offense wants to get a couple of high-quality shots from the rotation of the defense. They shouldn't settle for outside shots. If an offense is having difficulty with the zone defense, one remedy is to force the transition and beat the defense downfield before they can set up the zone.

The objective of team offense is to score goals. Players need to understand the various offensive principles that underlie the Xs and Os of team offense. This chapter started with two-man offensive plays and progressed up to 6v6 offense around the goal. In lacrosse, 6v6 team offense is based on balancing the field and using various sets to take advantage of the team's personnel. To be successful, team offenses must be able to react to certain defensive strategies. Specifically, they need to react to island defenses, sliding defenses, and zone defenses. Successful team offenses are able to adapt to any situation.

CHAPTER ELEVEN

TEAM DEFENSE

The purpose of team defense is to prevent goals. Team defense, like team offense, starts with individual skills and builds up from 1v1 to 6v6 defense. Individual defenders need to focus on their on-ball defensive skills versus dodgers, feeders, and shooters. Once players develop their individual skills, they can move on to team defense. Off-ball skills such as defending a cutter, pick, or ball exchange usually involve working with a teammate. Team defense starts with two-man plays and progresses to three-man plays and then 6v6 defense. However, all defense begins with the individual defender matching up against an individual dodger in a 1v1 struggle.

General Defensive Concepts

Team defense is founded on many underlying fundamentals. Defending the snap count means forcing the ball carrier in the direction you want him to go. Team defense is about adjusting to ball movement and eventually gaining possession of the ball. The defense needs to prevent high-percentage shots. Because of the playing area behind the goal, defenders have to adjust to defending the goal from 360 degrees. Defense requires constant communication, and defenders must always be vigilant to the opponent, especially when there is a break in the action.

Snap Count

Just like in football, the player with the ball has a distinct advantage over his defender because he knows his "snap count." He knows where he is going and can attack when he is ready to do so. Much of team defense is based on the assumption that the man with the ball will eventually beat his defender because he has such an advantage. Defenses respond by sending a teammate to help out the on-ball defender. The defense strives to take away the dodger's strong hand or take away the middle of the field (in order to create a poorer angle for the shot). In either case, the defense is taking away the 50-50 chance that the dodge could go in either direction and is forcing the dodger in the direction they want him to go.

Ball Possession

If your team doesn't have the ball, you should follow this general rule: "When in doubt, play defense first." You can look for an opportunity to regain possession, but you must always use proper body and stick positioning. You don't want to step away from the goal (i.e., take a "fatal step"). Anytime you take a step away from the goal, you leave yourself vulnerable to being dodged. If you're stepping away from the goal line and your attacker is stepping toward the goal line, that immediately puts you two steps behind the attacker—it's like two trains passing each other, going in opposite directions. As a defender, you want to be going in the same direction as the attacker. Playing defense means playing the percentages, even on turnovers. A turnover doesn't always have to involve a defender taking the ball away from an attacker. For example, if you force a low-percentage shot with pressure (e.g., a shot from 12 yards out with your stick in the shooter's gloves) and it's an easy save for the goalie, the result is the same as a turnover. When a defender poke-checks the ball carrier and the ball goes out of bounds, that's a turnover.

Defending Ball Movement

Lacrosse is a game of running and ball movement. The defense relies on athletic running skills to neutralize the effect of ball movement. In football, the offense's advantage is the snap count, and the defense's advantage is that they can move around before the snap count. In lacrosse, team defense is all about how fast the defenders can cover the offensive players compared to how fast the offense can move the ball.

Defending Shooting

The defense should not try to prevent every shot. If a defense tried to do this, they would spread themselves so thin that it would open up more dodging opportunities for the offense. Playing defense is more about preventing high-percentage shots (such as layups) and giving up more lower-percentage outside shots. Good offenses will be able to shoot the ball, and the goalie will need to come up with some saves. Defenders must avoid turning a nonthreat into a threat. As a defender, you shouldn't take chances at the restraining line in an effort to prevent the shot or take away the ball. If you get too aggressive at 20 yards, you may turn a low-percentage 20-yard shot into a high-percentage 15-yard shot. And if the defense must slide, your overaggressive play can result in a higher-percentage layup.

Ball Behind

Lacrosse is a unique game because of the large playing area behind the goal. When the offense has the ball in this area, defenders in front of the goal or above the GLE will have difficulty seeing both the ball and their man. In this situation, defenders should use V-up body positions with their sticks up in the passing lane. They must constantly adjust their position as the ball is moved around the perimeter. When the ball is behind the goal, defenders are at a disadvantage in the feeding and cutting game because they will lose sight of the ball or their man. However, defenders have an advantage in the dodging game because they can run through the crease (and the offensive players cannot).

Communication

Defenders need to be animated and constantly talking and moving. As a unit, the defense should communicate what the offense is doing and should adjust accordingly. Talking can be one of the most effective weapons in a team's defensive arsenal. Defenders can sometimes intimidate an offense into not employing a move or set play because the defenders are telling the on-ball defender that he will be adequately backed up on either side.

Tempo

Team defenses have two distinct paces. Some teams like to create mistakes, while others like to wait for the offense to make mistakes. Defenses that try to create mistakes are focused on taking away the ball and creating transition offense. More and more teams are attempting to create transition goals because of the success of 6v6 settled defenses. Other teams focus more on containment and wait for the offense to make a mistake. Teams measure the risk and reward of taking chances on defense, and most teams lean toward playing the percentages. Playing defense is not about taking the ball away. Just as a team doesn't want selfish players on offense, the team also doesn't want selfish players on defense. A team doesn't want one defender trying to be the hero by taking the ball away if he also risks giving up a layup by missing the check. Dislodging the ball from an opponent's stick is very difficult for defenders to do.

Vigilance

Defenders must always be aware of the opponents' positions and must be alert to sudden movements with or without the ball. Vigilance is most important when play has been temporarily suspended. For example, if you're playing defense and the ball is shot out of bounds, the referee will blow the whistle. Players tend to relax on the whistle. Then, the referee suddenly restarts play, and the players aren't ready. You can't relax on the whistle, especially with current rules where there's an immediate restart of play. You need to be ready before the whistle blows to restart play. Defenders should use the time between whistles to communicate with their teammates by "checking up" to get into the proper field position and to get their sticks up. Checking up refers to calling out the jersey number of your opponent so that everybody knows whom you are covering on defense.

Reaction

Everything in lacrosse is a reaction to something else. In the past, defenders played squared up on their man and allowed ball carriers to sweep dodge into the middle of the field for a premium shooting opportunity. In the 1990s, team defenses started to overplay the ball carrier to take away the middle of the field. The defense would force the ball carrier down the side of the field for a lower-angle shot opportunity. Offenses then began to put their strong-hand players in the 3 and 5 alley positions, and team defenses reacted by forcing these players to their weak hand and into the middle of the field.

Team Defensive Plays

Individual defense begins with a single defender playing a single ball carrier. Team defense begins with two-man plays and progresses to three-man plays and eventually 6v6 team defense around the goal cage.

Two-Man Plays

Two-man plays are the building blocks of team defense. The most important ingredients are communication, anticipation, and the mind-set of assuming that the worst can happen. Two-man defensive plays revolve around how to handle an offensive pick. Picks are a major instrument in the offensive toolbox. Team defenses use many mechanisms for minimizing the impact of picks. The following are some of the tactics employed by a team defense to counter various offensive picks.

No Switch and Open a Lane

In a classic offensive pick scenario behind the goal, the defense creates a lane for the defender playing the pick user, and the defenders do not switch. In the example shown in figure 11.1, attackman 1 has the ball behind the goal and is being played by defender 1. Attackman 2 is off ball and is being played by defender 2. Attackman 2 sets a pick at X-behind. Defender 2 sets up 1 yard from attackman 2 and 1 yard to the

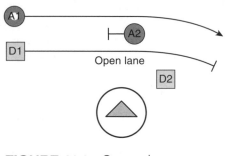

FIGURE 11.1   Open a lane.

help side of the field. Defender 2 opens up a lane between himself and attackman 2 so that defender 1 can run through the lane and continue to play attackman 1. If defender 1 gets picked off, then defender 2 has time and room to switch and play attackman 1.

No Switch and Compress

Another "no switch" technique is when the defense compresses the pick and the defenders don't switch men. For example, let's assume that attackman 1 has the ball and is defended by defender 1, who is a long-stick defender. Attackman 2 is off ball and is defended by defender 2, who is a short-stick defender. The offense wants the defenders to switch so they get a desired matchup. If the defenders switch, attackman 1 has the advantage of dodging a short-stick defender instead of a long-stick defender. Attackman 2 sets a pick for attackman 1, but defender 2 (short stick) compresses the pick by positioning himself right on the backside of attackman 2. Attackman 2's pick becomes one large pick (see figure 11.2). Attackman 1 uses the pick and goes over the pick. Defender 1 (long stick) takes a deeper drop step to stay in good position, gets underneath the pick, and has the advantage of defending the ball with a long stick.

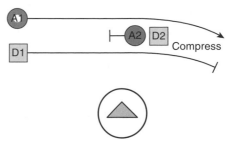

FIGURE 11.2 Compress the pick.

Switch

A switch can be either reactive or proactive. Sometimes a switch is reactive because the defender playing the pick user is successfully picked off by the opponent (see figure 11.3). Sometimes a switch is proactive because the defense's strategy is to switch on all picks in an effort to minimize any breakdown of coverage.

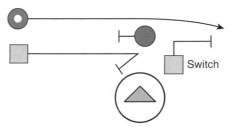

FIGURE 11.3 Switch.

Jump Versus Double

Some defenses double some or all picks, especially behind the goal, with the intent of taking away the ball. Defenders can double from the front (jump) or the back (blindside) of a pick. Typically, the off-ball defender lets the ball carrier run through the pick and then tries to blindside the ball carrier from behind (see figure 11.4).

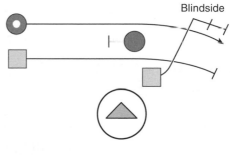

FIGURE 11.4 Jump.

Three-Man Plays

Opponents will typically use either their close-attack unit or a midfield unit in a three-man offense to run picks, pops, repicks, fake picks, and clear-outs. In a three-man play, one defender is watching the ball, and the other two defenders are anticipating something happening in their direction. The on-ball defender will force the man with the ball away from the center front of the field and toward X-behind. The off-ball defenders will be alert to off-ball activity (e.g., picks, pops, fakes) and will use their vision, body, and stick to help out their on-ball teammate.

For example, the offense may run a "pick away" offensive play, as shown in figure 11.5. Midfielder 1 is at field position 5 and is being defended by defender 1. Midfielder 2 is at field location 4 and is defended by defender 2. Midfielder 3 is at field position 3 and is defended by defender 3. Midfielder 2 has the ball; he passes it to midfielder 1 and then picks for midfielder 3. Once midfielder 2 passes the ball, defender 2 drops back to respect any give-and-go maneuver. Defender 2 recognizes the pick and communicates the oncoming pick to defender 3. Defender 2 and defender 3 neutralize the pick by using effective communication and proper body and stick positioning.

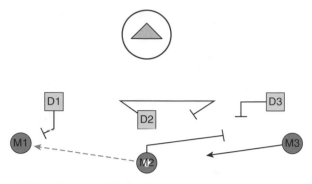

FIGURE 11.5   Defending a pick away.

6v6 Team Defense

Many of the decisions regarding team defensive strategy will be made based on the team's personnel. Usually, the decisions are based on the players' athletic skills and the team's willingness to take risks: Some defenses want to create mistakes or turnovers, while others wait for the offense to make a mistake. A team's defensive approach can be either proactive or reactive, and this is determined by three key decisions: Does the defensive unit want to extend and pressure the offense on the perimeter or slough inside and protect the most dangerous area of the field? Does the defense want to take away the offensive players' strength (strong hand) or take away the middle of the field? Will the team use an island type defense or the more traditional slide and recover style?

Extension and Sloughing

Team defense is always putting some type of pressure on the ball carrier and any adjacent teammates. The question is how much pressure. It's a balancing act. If you extend and put a lot of pressure on the ball carrier, you can create more turnovers, but you may also open up the inside for easier goals. If you slough back and defend more of the crease area, you are defending the most dangerous area of the field, but you are also giving the opposing team more time and space to execute any offensive maneuvers.

Defensive extension is designed to pressure the ball and pressure the adjacent outlet. The purpose of extending is to disrupt the flow of the offense and especially their timing. For example, the defense may deny any passes to X-behind. Offenses that rely on set plays and cutting and feeding are most affected by extending. Extending gives the defense opportunities for big poke checks and turnovers. If the defense extends but creates a break situation for the offense, the defenders will be farther out on the perimeter and will have a longer distance to travel to get back into the hole (see figure 11.6). Teams that extend are usually not in a position to slide and recover.

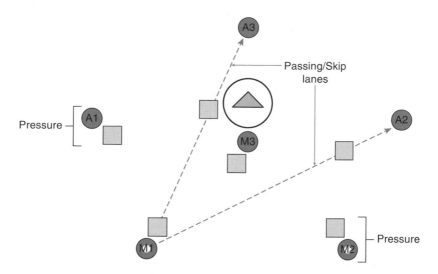

FIGURE 11.6 Extending on the perimeter.

Sloughing defense is more hole conscious and relies on slide and recover. For example, if the ball is above the GLE, the wing defensemen want to be positioned above the GLE so they are available to help out inside (see figure 11.7). If the ball is above the GLE, the defensive midfielders want to get "underneath" the ball. That way, if the on-ball defender is beat, the midfielders are able to help out inside instead of worrying about their own man. With a sloughing strategy, the defense tries to put as many defenders in front of the goal as possible, taking away the most dangerous area of the field. Sloughing allows the offense to throw the ball around the perimeter, but this strategy takes away dodging lanes and forces an outside shot.

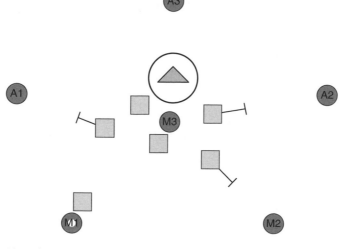

FIGURE 11.7 Sloughing inside.

Strength Versus Field Position

Team defenses are primarily designed to either take away strength (player's strong hand) or take away field position (middle of field). At times, a defender can do both. The shadow technique is used to take away strength or field position. The defender overplays the man with the ball and forces him into a desired direction. The shadow technique keeps the attacker going in the same direction whether it be away from his strength OR away from a preferred position on the field. Typically, a shadow technique is a way to funnel an attacker into an area so that he can't turn back. The defender is playing the attacker's hip and not allowing him to roll back. If the defender gets up on the man, sees the front of his jersey, and chases the head of his stick, this will enable the attacker to roll back and have a good shooting angle.

Strength

In this case, the defender forces the opponent to his weaker hand. The team defense is taking away the ball carrier's strength no matter where he is on the field. To force the opponent to his weak hand, the defender must overplay his strong hand. Once the defender forces him toward the desired direction, the defender continues to shadow the opponent so that he can't roll back to his strength. Again, the defender shadows the attacker by staying on his hip. The defender is not playing stick on stick and cannot see the front of the attacker's jersey. The defender is slightly trailing the attacker to funnel him toward a teammate who is sliding (sometimes called funneling into a squeeze).

Field Position

In this case, the defender forces the opponent away from the middle of the field in order to decrease his shooting angle. The team defense is forcing the man down the side no matter what. To force the attacker down the side, the defender must overplay his topside position. Once the defender forces him down toward the desired direction, the defender continues to shadow the attacker so that he can't roll back to the middle of the field. The defender uses the same shadow techniques described in the previous section. The defender is slightly trailing the attacker to funnel him toward a teammate who is sliding toward him.

Shadowing Dodges Behind the Goal   Let's look at three scenarios that illustrate how to properly shadow a ball carrier behind the goal. In the first example, the ball carrier has the ball at position 1 and is covered by his defender. The ball carrier dodges to the GLE. The defender beats the ball carrier to the GLE and positions himself with his feet pointing toward the corner of the field or the end line. The defender wants to "close the gate" and take away the ball carrier's topside shot. The defender shadows or overplays the ball carrier's top hand and forces him to perform an inside roll. The inside roll causes the ball carrier to turn his back to both the offensive and defensive players. The defender forces the ball carrier into playing blindly because he loses sight of the field and can no longer see the movement of the offense or defense (see figure 11.8).

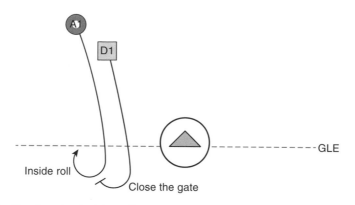

FIGURE 11.8 Forcing the inside roll.

In the next example, the ball carrier has the ball at the 1 1/2 wing position and is covered by his defender. The defender wants to force the ball carrier to X-behind (see figure 11.9). The defender shades to the ball carrier's backside hip. The defender shadows the ball carrier's movement behind the goal. With every step, the ball carrier is losing his dodging angle. The defender doesn't want the ball carrier to get topside on him.

Note that the defender doesn't want to "chase" the ball carrier to X-behind because this may put the defender in a bad position if the ball carrier plants at X-behind and rolls back. With the shadow technique, the defender is in proper position if this occurs. Also, if the ball carrier runs through X-behind and drives to the cage through the 1 position, the ball carrier has to arc out, but his defender can cut through the crease and beat the ball carrier to the GLE (see figure 11.10).

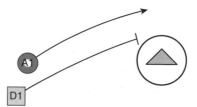

FIGURE 11.9 Forcing a ball carrier to X-behind.

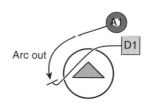

FIGURE 11.10 Shadowing (not chasing) to X-behind.

Shadowing Dodges Above the Goal When a defender is shadowing a dodge above the goal, the main difference from shadowing behind the goal is that the ball carrier has the potential to shoot on cage. The defender wants to force the ball carrier either to his weak hand or away from the middle of the field. Let's look at two scenarios: One illustrates how to properly shadow a dodge above the goal, and the other illustrates how not to do so. In the first example, the ball carrier is a right-hander at position 3 and is covered by his defender. The defender wants to take away the ball carrier's strength (right hand). The defender shades or shadows toward the outside of the ball carrier. The defender forces the ball carrier to his weak hand and into the middle of the field (see figure 11.11).

In the second example, the ball carrier is a right-hander at position 3 and is covered by defender 1. Defender 2 is on the crease. Defender 1 forces the ball

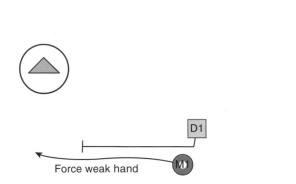

FIGURE 11.11 Taking away the ball carrier's strong hand.

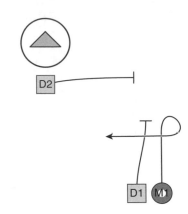

FIGURE 11.12 Ineffective slide.

carrier down the side (see figure 11.12). However, defender 1 gets up too high on the ball carrier and loses his shadow position. Defender 2 (crease defender) slides to the ball carrier. The ball carrier rolls back to the middle of the field. Even though the ball carrier goes to his weak hand (left hand), the defense has committed two defenders to the ball carrier, and they did not funnel him properly.

Island Versus Sliding

Some teams don't slide, especially if they think they are superior athletically to the other team. Everybody is responsible for stopping their own man. Defenders are solely responsible for their men, and they will get no help. If everybody does their job, the defense will be effective. However, the majority of teams slide to the ball and either recover or stay. Defenses try to force the ball into an area where they plan to slide a teammate. The on-ball defender will shadow the ball carrier and force him in a specific direction. Shadowing takes away the 50-50 element of a dodger being able to go in either direction. The defender who slides is forcing the attacker to shoot the ball from the outside or move the ball to a teammate. Either way, the attacker is giving up the ball. The slide takes away the opportunity for a high-percentage shot, and the defense has some control over the movement of the ball and can anticipate the next pass. Some teams will slide whenever the man with the ball turns his back to the defense.

Types of Slides

Defenses use three types of slides depending on field position: near man, adjacent, and crease. Near man means that whoever is closest to the ball carrier is sliding to the ball first. An adjacent slide is usually executed from the perimeter and the side of the ball carrier. A crease slide commences from the crease area and is currently the most prevalent style in lacrosse.

Near Man   Whoever is the closest defender to the ball will slide, either from an adjacent or crease position. For example, if an offense is using a circle set with no one on the crease, the defense may use a near-man slide (see figure 11.13).

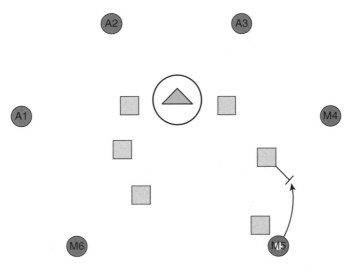

FIGURE 11.13   Near-man slide.

Adjacent   Traditional defenses primarily used adjacent slides because the crease area was the most dangerous area of the field and the defense could not afford to leave anyone on the crease undefended. The traditional perspective on crease slides was based on the thinking that the help-side defender behind the crease defender was "pulled" to the crease by the sliding movement of the crease defender to the ball (the first slide pulled the second slide to the crease). Adjacent sliding is perimeter sliding (see figure 11.14). Another example of an adjacent slide is a cross-crease slide (see figure 11.15), which is called a coma slide—the defender is COMing Across the crease.

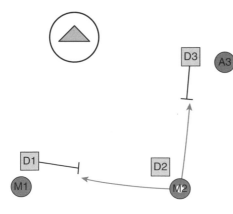

FIGURE 11.14   Adjacent slide.

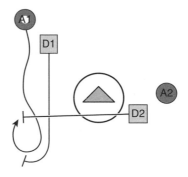

FIGURE 11.15   Coma slide.

Crease Current defenses primarily use crease slides, which involve a more complicated process than adjacent slides. The current perspective on crease slides is based on the thinking that the help-side defender behind the crease defender "pushes" (frozen rope) the crease defender to slide upfield (the second slide pushes the first slide upfield) (see figure 11.16). Because the crease defender is leaving the most dangerous area of the field, the other off-ball defenders pinch inside to help out.

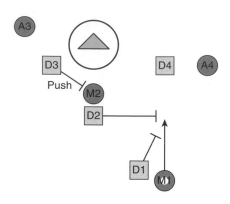

FIGURE 11.16 Crease slide.

Slide and Recover or Slide and Stay

A coach, goalkeeper, or on-field defender will be responsible for making slide calls. This person will see a matchup and yell "Early," "Slow," or "Stay." If any on-field defender hears the bench call, that player will repeat the call so that everybody is on the same page. An "early" call indicates that the ball carrier is an imminent threat to score so the defense wants him to give the ball up quickly. In this case, the defense will use the slide and recover, which is the most prevalent defensive strategy used by defensive units. A "slow" or "stay" call indicates that the defense perceives the ball carrier as less of an offensive threat.

Slide and Recover This strategy is basically a zone because the defense is forcing the ball into an area. The on-ball defender forces the ball carrier to the side or to his weak hand. The crease defender slides to the ball, and the on-ball defender recovers back to the crease. The defense can triple-team the most dangerous player on the field using second-slide, pop, and adjacent defenders. If the defense doesn't like their matchup, they should slide early. The functions of individual defenders include the following:

- *First slide:* Usually the crease defender ("Hot")
- *Second slide:* Pushes the first slide. The second slide is the most important slide on defense.
- *Pop:* Defends any pop-out move off the crease
- *Adjacent:* Protects skip lanes
- *Backside:* Defends the attacker farthest from the ball

In the example shown in figure 11.17, the ball carrier has the ball at position 3 and is

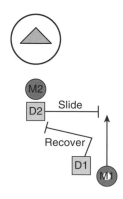

FIGURE 11.17 Slide and recover.

covered by defender 1. The ball carrier's teammate, midfielder 2, is on the crease and is covered by defender 2. Defender 1 forces the ball carrier down the side (the alley). Defender 2 slides from the crease to the ball carrier. Defender 1 recovers to the crease and does not double the ball carrier.

Slide and Stay If the defense likes their matchup (e.g., long-pole defender versus midfielder), they will be slow to go OR will fake a slide from the crease. In the example shown in figure 11.18, the ball carrier is at position 3 and is covered by defender 1. Midfielder 2 is on the crease and is covered by defender 2. Defender 1 forces the ball carrier down the side (the alley). The crease defender (2) starts to slide to the ball carrier, and the ball carrier gives the ball up early. Defender 2 yells "Stay," and defender 1 recovers back to the ball carrier.

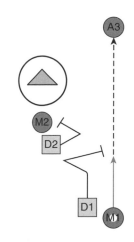

FIGURE 11.18 Slide and stay.

Slide Package Versus Offensive Sets

Slide packages are based on whether the defense is taking away strength or field position and on who is making the first, second, and third slide. A slide package is a predetermined set of reactions by a defense to an offense. A defense may select the sequence of slides based on the opponent's strengths, and the sequence can be anything that the defense wants to implement. For example, the first slide can come from the crease, and the second slide can come from an adjacent defender. The following are examples of slide sequences versus specific offensive sets.

2-2-2 Midfielder 1 is at position 5; midfielder 2 is at position 3; midfielder 3 is at the right-hand crease; attackman 4 is at the left-hand crease; attackman 5 is at position 1; and attackman 6 is at position 2. Midfielder 2 has the ball. Defender 2 forces midfielder 2 down the side. Defender 5 slides to midfielder 3 and supports defender 3. Defender 3 slides to attackman 4 and supports defender 4. Defender 4 slides to midfielder 2, and defender 1 recovers to the crease. Defender 1 drops down and looks for a pop pass inside. Defender 5, defender 3, and defender 2 are collapsing to the crease (see figure 11.19).

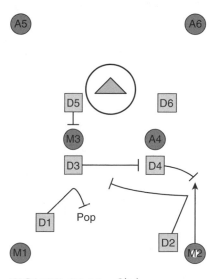

FIGURE 11.19 Slides versus a 2-2-2 set.

1-4-1 Midfielder 1 is at position 4; midfielder 2 is at the left crease; midfielder 3 is at the right crease; attackman 4 is at the 1 1/2 position on the wing; attackman 5 is at the 2 1/2 position on the wing; and attackman 6 is at the X-behind position. Midfielder 1 has the ball. Defender 1 forces midfielder 1 to his weak (left) hand. Defender 5 slides to midfielder 3 and supports defender 3. Defender 3 slides to midfielder 2 and supports defender 2. Defender 2 slides to midfielder 1, and defender 1 recovers to midfielder 3. Off-ball defenders collapse on the crease and take away midfielder 2 and midfielder 3 (see figure 11.20).

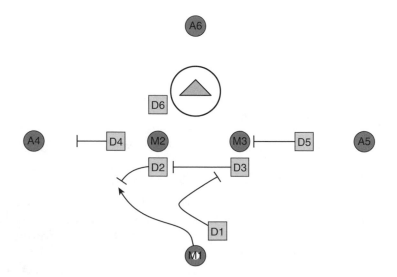

FIGURE 11.20 Slides versus a 1-4-1 set.

2-3-1 Midfielder 1 is at position 5; midfielder 2 is at position 3; attackman 4 is at the 1 1/2 position on the wing; midfielder 3 is on the crease; attackman 5 is at the 2 1/2 position on the wing; and attackman 6 is at the X-behind position. Midfielder 2 has the ball. Defender 2 forces midfielder 2 down the side. Defender 5 stays on attackman 5. Defender 4 and defender 6 support defender 3 on the crease. Defender 3 slides to midfielder 2, and defender 2 recovers to the crease. Defender 1 drops in and looks for a pop pass inside. Off-ball defenders collapse on the crease and take away midfielder 3 (see figure 11.21).

Zone Defenses

Zone defenses are primarily designed to contain strong dodging teams. Zone defenses will jam the inside with bodies, minimize feeds into the crease, and force outside shots. In a zone defense, defenders follow the ball, not the man, and they tend to be aggressive on the ball and adjacent outlets. Zone defenses have various styles. In some zones, defenders don't go behind the GLE and address the ball carrier. These defenses want to put more bodies above the GLE to protect the crease. In other zones, defenders do go behind the GLE because they want to put

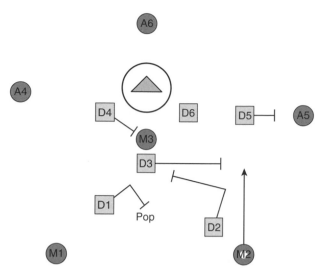

FIGURE 11.21 Slides versus a 2-3-1 set.

some pressure on the ball carrier. If the behind-the-goal ball carrier dodges above the GLE, the defense has to decide who will slide to him: an adjacent defender or a backside "coma" defender. If a ball carrier carries the ball from one zone to another, defenses have to decide whether the defender stays with the ball carrier or releases him to his neighboring teammate in another zone. All zones try to hide their short-stick defenders because they are a prime target for dodgers. If the short-stick defender gets dodged, the defense can slide from either the adjacent or crease area. If defenders in the zone are forced to rotate, they will follow basic man-down defensive principles: Stay tight in your formation, keep your sticks up in the passing lanes, keep your head on a swivel so you can see the ball and the man, and keep rotating into the ball.

The objective of team defense is to prevent goals. Players need to understand fundamental defensive concepts such as defending the snap count, ball movement and ball possession, defending shooting, ball behind, communication, vigilance, tempo of play, and whether to extend or slough. Team defense begins with two-man defensive plays such as defending picks with or without switching. Defense progresses to three-man plays and 6v6 team defense. Team defense is based on either taking away the ball carrier's strong hand or taking away the middle of the field. The strengths and weaknesses of the team's personnel will dictate whether the team employs an island defense, sliding defense, or zone defense.

CHAPTER TWELVE

TRANSITION OFFENSE

Lacrosse has been called the "fastest game on two feet." The transition game is one of the most exciting parts of lacrosse. Because settled 6v6 team defenses have become so effective at limiting scoring opportunities, teams are relying more and more on the transition game to provide a lot of their goals. Transition is defined as the movement of players and the ball from the defensive end of the field to the offensive end, and vice versa. The transition game includes—but is not limited to—break situations in which the offensive team has a numerical edge and seeks to take advantage of this edge by getting a high-quality shot.

Transition Principles

The offensive transition game is based on three principles: turnovers, ball possession, and ball movement. The transition game starts when a turnover occurs. Turnovers can be either unforced errors by the opposing team or forced errors caused by your team. Once your team has ball possession, you are on offense. Ball possession defines offense, and the job of the offense is to move the ball downfield toward the opponent's goal to create a scoring opportunity.

Turnovers

Turnovers are the "light switch" of offensive transition. Once your team has the ball, the transition light is on. Turnovers can be unforced errors committed by the other team. The offensive player may drop the ball, throw an errant pass, or fail to catch a pass from a teammate. The bottom line is that the offense loses possession. At that point, desire and scooping skills become very important. A forced turnover can be caused by a stick check, a body check, or a goalkeeper's save. Turnovers will be covered in more detail later in this chapter.

Ball Possession

Transition is a balancing act. You want to push transition, but at the same time, possession is the key; therefore, you don't want to make foolish decisions and throw the ball away. The chances of scoring on a 4v3 break are good, but if you do something too daring, you will risk blowing a good opportunity. Different teams have different philosophies. Some are very aggressive, and others are more con-servative. Between the restraining lines, some teams want their defensive "rope" midfield unit (two defensive short sticks and one long pole) to stay on the field and push the transition into the attack area (see figure 12.1). Other teams want their defensive midfield to substitute out so they can get their offensive midfield on the field (see figure 12.2). No matter what the approach, you should focus on possession first and then take advantage of any breaks second. Scoring goals in a settled 6v6 situation is very difficult, so it's great to have the opportunity to score in the unsettled situation. However, you shouldn't sacrifice your ability to maintain possession in order to go for the transition.

Ball Movement

As soon as your team gets possession, the first thing you need to do is bust upfield quickly. Whoever has the ball looks upfield to see if he has any teammates he can throw the ball to. The goal is to push the ball forward. For example, if a close defenseman has the ball, he should look for a teammate who is in front of him and make a pass to a teammate who is ahead of the ball.

When running with the ball in the open field, you want to be as efficient, com-fortable, and athletic as possible. But you must always be ready to adjust your body and stick in order to make the next play, which might be a pass to an open

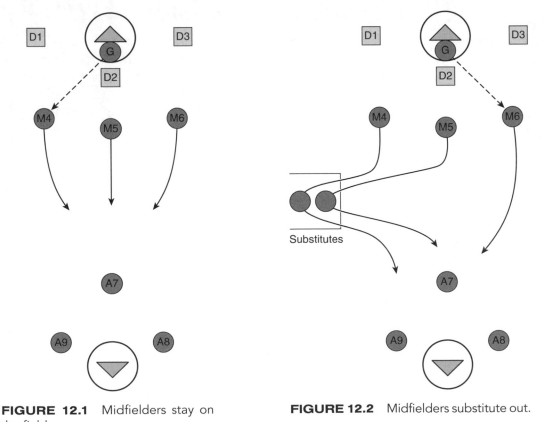

FIGURE 12.1 Midfielders stay on the field.

FIGURE 12.2 Midfielders substitute out.

teammate or a shot on goal. In a transition situation, there is a good chance that somebody will be open; thus, if and when a defender slides to you, you should always look toward where the slide came from and move the ball to the teammate who was previously defended by the slider.

If you don't have the ball, you should look to get into an open area. You don't want to be in a position where a pass to you would be a high risk of a turnover. You want to help your teammate make a good decision, a good play, and a high-percentage pass.

Remember that the ball travels faster than the man. When offensive players carry the ball, the defenders can match them step for step, so the offense may not be gaining any advantage. If the offense moves the ball by passing it, the ball is moving faster than the defense, and the offense has a better opportunity to get underneath the defense for a good scoring attempt. If the opposing team has dropped back to take away any breaks, the offense should move the ball into the attack area without any high-risk passes. If the opposing team has not dropped back on defense, the offense might have a break opportunity, so they should move the ball upfield quickly and try to get underneath the other team's defense. In any case, ball movement up the field is a valuable asset.

Types of Turnovers

Offensive transition starts with a turnover by the opposing team. The turnover can be a missed pass that rolls toward the midline (and becomes a loose-ball fight), a save by the goalie, or a turnover that occurs in the open field.

An open-field turnover can be an unforced error such as an errant pass, or it can be a forced turnover such as an intercepted pass or a loose ball caused by a checked stick. This section examines three prominent scenarios involving turnovers: a loose ball at the midline, a save by a goalie, and a loose-ball pickup in the open field.

Midline Play

If the opposing team has possession of the ball in a 6v6 situation in your defensive half of the field, your close defense and defensive midfield will be playing active defense, and your close attack will be positioned behind its own midline. The close attack is set up in a triangle; two attackmen are at the midline, and one attackman drops back so that the centerline isn't congested (see figure 12.3). The two upfield attackmen don't want to go all the way to the edge of the centerline. They should stop at 1 to 1 1/2 yards from the centerline and break down. That way, if they get nudged by their opponent, they will not go over the centerline and create a penalty. The two

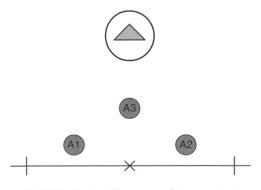

FIGURE 12.3 Close attack's positioning at the midline.

upfield attackmen follow the ball and adjust their positions so that if the opposing team's pass or feed goes through, they can back up the rolling ground ball at the midline. The close attack needs to know what their responsibilities are before the break. When the ball is at the other end, they have to communicate and make sure they are on the same page regarding who is going where on a break. The close attack will communicate who has point, right, and left (see figure 12.4). If the ball is down on the defensive end of the field and the coach decides to substitute someone into the game, the substitute needs to check in with his other two attackmen so they are all on the same page. Lack of communication or miscommunication can prevent a team from taking advantage of a fast break.

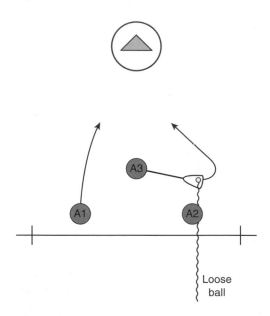

FIGURE 12.4 Close attack's reaction to a ball at the midline. A2 lifts his opponent's stick, A3 goes for the loose ball, and A1 goes to the goal.

If the opposing team loses possession and the ball rolls to the midline, one attackman will check up on his defender's stick and let the ball run through the midline. Another attackman goes for the ball (if he gets the ball, he may have a 2v1 opportunity), and the third attackman goes to the goal.

Goalie Save

When the opposing team takes a shot on goal, the goalkeeper's job is to prevent the goal. If the goalie makes a save and yells, "Break," the entire defense will execute a breakout pattern, spreading out and away from the goal (this is called inbounds clearing). The defensive midfielders need to "bust up and bust out," cutting upfield and spreading the field to provide an upfield outlet pass. They need to bust upfield to separate themselves from their defender. By executing a quick burst, the midfielder gets a head start on his defender. This gives the midfielder a cushion and makes it easier for the goalie to see him. Having a cushion also allows the midfielder to slow down and gather himself to handle the pass if necessary. The midfielders want to be in a position where they feel comfortable catching the ball. Some teams will have the close defense crash the crease to minimize any rebound opportunities for the opposing team (see figure 12.5). On goalie possession, the two wing defenders will cut behind the GLE and provide a safety valve for an outlet pass. Other teams will have one defender protect the crease, and the other two defenders will "banana" out along the GLE for an outlet pass (see figure 12.6).

The goalkeeper has three primary looks once he gains possession of the ball after the shot. The goalie's first look is upfield where the shot came from. When the other team takes a shot, the midfielder covering the ball tries to get a piece of the shooter and then starts to release and get up the field, looking back for the ball. However, this player shouldn't be running upfield with his back to the ball; if there is a rebound, he will have created a 6v5 for the opposing team. The goalie's second look is to any upfield teammate for an outlet pass. If the goalie has a choice, he should stay away from the box side of the field (this minimizes the opposing team's opportunities to substitute their rope unit out). The goalie's third look is an outlet pass to the close defense as a safety valve. If there are no available outlets, the goalie can circle around the crease area and set up a settled clear. Some adventurous goalies may even carry the ball upfield and create their own transition offense. See figure 12.7 for a goalie's first and second look; see figure 12.8 for a goalie's third look.

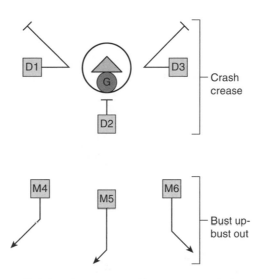

FIGURE 12.5 Defensive midfielders bust up and bust out, and close defense crashes the crease.

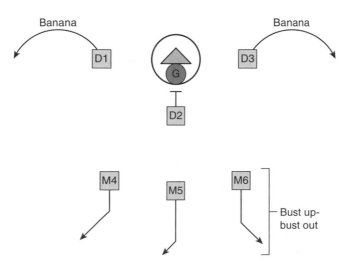

FIGURE 12.6 Close defense "bananas out" on the wings.

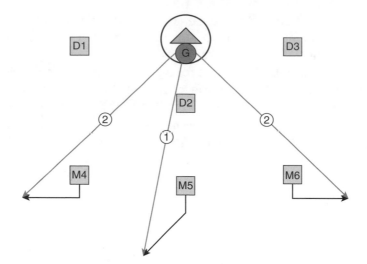

FIGURE 12.7   Goalie's first and second look.

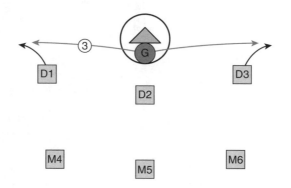

FIGURE 12.8   Goalie's third look.

Open Field

On any kind of turnover in the open field, players will use many of the same principles that they use during inbounds clearing after a goalie save. An open-field turnover can happen in your offensive half of the field or in your defensive half of the field. Sometimes the opposing team has gained possession of the ball because their goalie saved a shot. However, because of the hard "riding" of your attack or midfield unit, your team causes a turnover. In this case, the opposing team is especially vulnerable, and once you gain possession, your first look is inside to the crease for a quick shot opportunity.

Most often, your team will cause an open-field turnover in your defensive half of the field. Typically, a close defenseman or midfielder will gain possession of the ball by scooping up a loose ball or intercepting a pass and then carrying or passing the ball from the defensive half of the field into the offensive half of the field.

Two-on-One Strategies

Once your team gains possession of the ball, you will often encounter a 2v1 situation. Whenever you have a man-advantage situation, you want to take advantage of it. A man-advantage scenario can present itself anywhere on the field, but they are especially critical near the opponent's goal. In essence, all man-advantage situations stem from a simple two-on-one numbers advantage over your opponent. The two offensive players have to coordinate their actions: One has the ball, and the other may provide an outlet or a better offensive opportunity. The two players can coordinate their action by using nonverbal or verbal communication to maximize the connection, or they can do it instinctually because of a field sense gained from game experience. The off-ball offensive player can maximize the advantage by using one of the following offensive calls: "early," "draw," "one more," or "right away." These offensive calls typically apply to a 4v3 fast break near your opponent's goal ("early" or "draw") or even closer to the goal in either a 3v3 or 2v1 fast break situation ("one more" or "right away"). The main thing is for the off-ball teammate to communicate with the ball carrier to execute the right play.

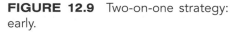

Early

This is an effective strategy when the offense has a 2v1 situation and the ball carrier is a stronger offensive threat. The off-ball teammate yells, "Early." The ball carrier passes the ball early to his teammate so that the defender must turn his attention and energy to the teammate; the original ball carrier then looks for a return pass (see figure 12.9).

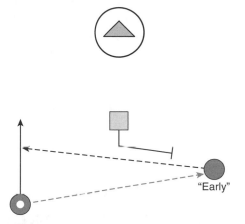

FIGURE 12.9 Two-on-one strategy: early.

Draw

This strategy is used when the offense has a 2v1 situation and the defender is playing "cat and mouse" (i.e., the defender is not committing to either offensive player). The off-ball teammate yells, "Draw." The ball handler then forces the defender to commit to him (draws the defender to the ball) so that the off-ball teammate is open for a pass and a scoring opportunity (see figure 12.10).

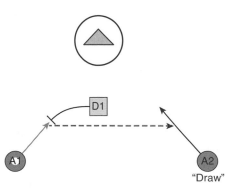

FIGURE 12.10 Two-on-one strategy: draw.

One More

In this play, the ball carrier has a pretty good scoring opportunity and is ready to take the shot. However, the off-ball teammate is open and yells, "One more." This indicates that the teammate thinks he has a better opportunity if the ball carrier will make one more pass. In this situation, the ball carrier has the freedom to choose which option to execute—take the shot or make the pass (see figure 12.11).

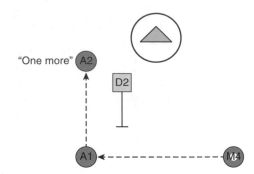

FIGURE 12.11 Two-on-one strategy: one more.

Right Away

This play is used when the defender is sliding and charging hard at the ball carrier. The off-ball teammate yells, "Right away." This indicates that the ball carrier should get rid of the ball right away because he does not have the best opportunity to move the ball or shoot. The "right away" call is the most urgent call on offense (see figure 12.12).

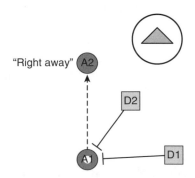

FIGURE 12.12 Two-on-one strategy: right away.

Reaction of the Close Attack

Once the team gains ball possession, the team's close-attack players have to anticipate some type of break. These players should sprint from the centerline to their positions or spots near the goal and set up as soon as possible in case a fast break develops.

An attackman who has an outside position at the centerline (e.g., attackman 2, attackman 3) should sprint to his lower position near the goal line extended (see figure 12.13). He should turn to the inside, open up so he can see the ball, and then "feel" for his spot. He must always have his head on a swivel—seeing the ball and

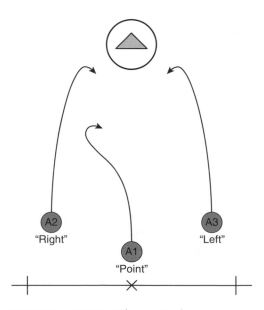

FIGURE 12.13 Close attack's reaction to a break.

feeling for where his spot is on the field. The attackman should never take his eyes off the ball to find his spot on the field. If he does, he is no longer an outlet for a pass, and this may encourage the opponent to jump the ball carrier. The close attack wants to get in near the goal and then come back for the ball. Sometimes a close-attack player is already near the goal when the team gains possession of the ball. Close-attack players should not run up to the midline and act as an outlet for their teammates. If they do, they may allow their opponent to play two (defend two players at the same time).

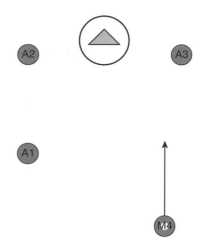

FIGURE 12.14 Close attack in a triangle formation.

The close attack as a unit needs to set up in a triangle-shaped formation near the goal, anticipating a teammate bringing the ball toward them (see figure 12.14). The following sections provide details on the proper field positioning for the three at-tackmen who make up the close-attack unit. In these descriptions, attackman 1 is covered by defender 1, attackman 2 is covered by defender 2, and attackman 3 is covered by defender 3.

Point Attack

The starting position for attackman 1 (called the point attackman) should be at or near the restraining line and 10 yards from the center of the field, as shown in figure 12.15. Attack-man 1 wants to open up and V-up where he can see the ball, think a pass ahead, and feel the defensive pressure around him. Attackman 1 has his "big eye" on defender 2, reading his movements, and his "little eye" on the ball. He should tuck his inside shoulder; the inside shoulder should always be low so that the attackman can look inside and be ready to make the next play. The attackman's arms are extended and loose to maneuver his stick,

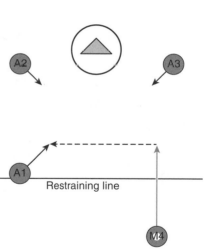

FIGURE 12.15 Upper position: point attack.

his hands are back, and his stick is loaded and protected from the defender. The attackman should not be square to the ball and should not stare at the ball. Being square to the ball or having tunnel vision will cause the attacker to lose the advan-tage of using his peripheral vision to see and anticipate the next play. Attackman 1 must maintain his spacing and not go toward the goal; otherwise, he may end up shortening the slide for defender 2 if defender 1 slides to the midfielder car-rying the ball.

Lower Attack Positions

Attackman 2 is positioned in the low right-hander's position near and above the GLE. The point attackman (attackman 1) and attackman 2 should be on the same imaginary line. The point attackman mirrors attackman 2's position. Attackman 3 is positioned in the low left-hander's position near and above the GLE. Because attackman 2 and attackman 3 are above the GLE, they both have to anticipate a missed shot and chase the ball out to the end line. Attackman 2 and attackman 3 should not make it easy for their defenders to know where they are located. The attackmen should keep the defenders guessing. Remember, defenders are taught to V-up so they can see both the ball and their man. If the attackman is positioned in a straight line between the ball and his defender, the defender will not be able to V-up (see figure 12.16).

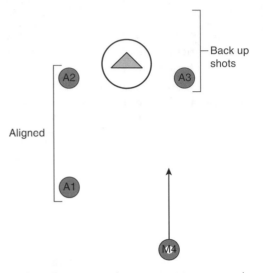

FIGURE 12.16 Lower positions: attackman 2 and attackman 3.

Transition Between the Restraining Lines

The restraining lines are 20 yards out from the goal line extended, running parallel to the GLE on both ends of the field. These lines define the perimeter of a team's attack area as well as the team's defensive area. Much of the transition action in lacrosse happens between the restraining lines: A loose ball is picked up, a pass is intercepted, a shot is saved by your goalie and he makes an outlet pass to a teammate running upfield. As previously mentioned, transition offense is the movement of the ball from your defensive end of the field to your offensive end of the field. This can be an even-up (no break) situation where your opponent has matched up with your offensive players and there is no apparent numbers advantage. On the other hand, your team may have a numbers advantage. The numbers advantage can take many forms, such as a 6v5, 5v4, or 4v3 situation.

4v3 Fast Break

The classic break in lacrosse is the 4v3 fast break because normally there are three close attackmen near the goal when the ball carrier is bringing the ball into the offensive area on a break. The starting point for the classic 4v3 fast break is the ball carrier. Typically, this is a close defenseman or midfielder who has possession of the ball and is carrying it in the defensive half of the field. For this discussion of the 4v3 break, we will assume that the ball carrier is a midfielder, but it could be anyone, including a close defenseman or even a goalkeeper. The midfielder wants to get the ball downfield securely and set up his waiting point attackman on the close attack.

Ball Carrier Sets Up Point Attackman

The ball carrier running in the open field should always try to set up the point attacker's strength, which in most cases is the right hand. For example, the goalkeeper saves the ball and throws the ball to a breaking midfielder. The midfielder catching the ball needs to choose a side, preferably the side opposite his point attackman's strength. If the midfielder catches the goalie's outlet pass and runs down the middle of the field, his point attackman (attackman 1) can't read him and go opposite (see figure 12.17). The midfielder needs to establish a side of the field as early as possible so his point attackman can read his intentions and know which way to go to set up for the ball (see figure 12.18). If the point attackman's strength is the right hand, but the goalie throws the midfielder an outlet pass on the SAME side of the field as his point attackman, the midfielder then has to make a decision: The midfielder must decide whether he has enough of a lead on the opposing chaser that he can diagonally cut across the field, keeping the chaser on his back. If not, the midfielder needs to go down the sideline, which will force his point attackman to his weak hand (left hand). If the midfielder has enough time and room, he should angle up the field, beat the chaser to the offensive area, and set up the point attacker's strength (see figure 12.19). If the midfielder is forced to come down the left side and does not set up his point attackman's strong hand, the point attackman needs to adjust and move to the left-hander's point attack position (see figure 12.20).

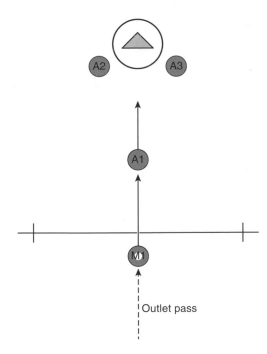

FIGURE 12.17 Ball carrier should avoid the middle of the field.

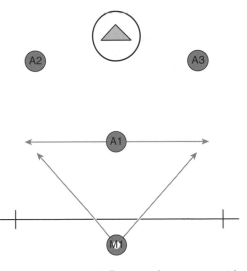

FIGURE 12.18 Ball carrier chooses one side of the field so the point attackman can react.

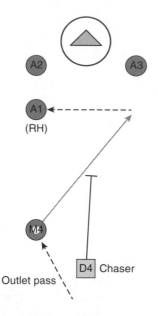

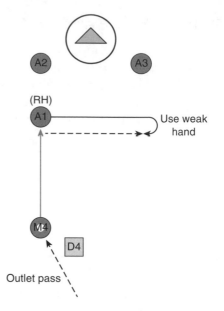

FIGURE 12.19 Ball carrier crosses the field to set up the point attackman's right hand.

FIGURE 12.20 Ball carrier sets up the point attackman's left hand.

Ball Carrier Enters the Attack Area

Once the midfielder crosses into the offensive half of the field, the close attack should be getting into their triangle-shaped formation near the goal. The midfielder doesn't come straight down the middle of the field. He chooses a side in the offensive area because he is an option for a return pass, especially if the defense holds (does not slide). The midfielder must be able to think while on a dead sprint. Some midfielders will slow down and look for open teammates, which allows their defender to catch them. When the moment arrives for him to throw the ball, the midfielder must be able to gather himself and make an accurate pass. John Wooden always said, "Be quick but don't hurry." If defender 1 does not commit and slide to the midfielder, the midfielder should keep on coming to the cage and be prepared to shoot (see figure 12.21). Otherwise, the midfielder has two options: pass to attackman 1 (point) or pass to attackman 2 (see figure 12.22).

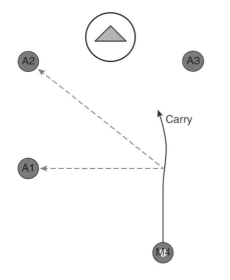

FIGURE 12.21 Midfielder drives to the cage.

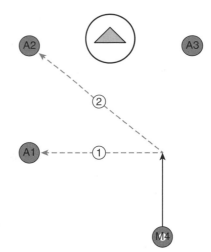

FIGURE 12.22 Midfielder's pass options.

Midfielder's First Option: Pass to Point Attackman

The point attackman (attackman 1) can make two calls to help the midfielder choose the best play. To make the proper call, the point attackman must know the team's personnel. In this situation, the point attackman can call "early" or "draw." If the point attackman does not communicate, the "draw" call is the default call.

Early Situation As discussed earlier, the "early" call means that the ball carrier should give up the ball early to a teammate and then look for a quick return pass. The "early" call is made to set up the midfielder for a shot. If the offense has a talented midfielder carrying the ball into the offensive area, then this player is a valuable shooter and feeder. In this case, attackman 1 may make an "early" call (see figure 12.23). Attackman 1 will shake or pump his stick, which means "Give me the ball now." The midfielder gives up the ball to attackman 1, and defender 1 holds and does not slide to the midfielder. Attackman 1 and the midfielder reverse their roles: The midfielder becomes the point attacker.

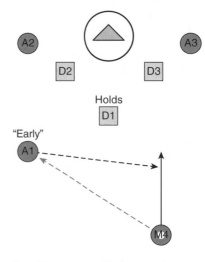

FIGURE 12.23 Early situation.

However, in some situations, an "early" call is not a good option. For example, if the midfielder (with a long pole) is carrying the ball and his defender (defender 4) is right on his back, then attackman 1 should not call "early." If the midfielder throws to attackman 1 and then attackman 1 throws back to the midfielder, defender 4 will be there to execute a lift check on the shot. Therefore, in this situation, the midfielder should keep coming even though his defender is on his back. Defender 1 may "show and hold," as shown in figure 12.24, thinking that defender 4 is going to get the midfielder or baiting the midfielder to throw to attackman 1; this helps open a lane for the midfielder to keep coming.

Note that in an "early" situation, the attackman must be sure to communicate his intentions and make the call. He must communicate what he

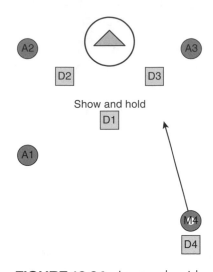

FIGURE 12.24 Long-pole midfielder wants to draw D1 but will keep the ball if D1 holds.

wants to do on the field and should never assume that his teammate will be able to guess his intentions. Also, timing is very important. The attackman must not make the call too late—that is, when it's too late for the midfielder to execute the move. The play doesn't have to be executed exactly when the "early" call is made. For example, let's assume that the midfielder is carrying the ball in a break situation. Attackman 1 yells "Early" when the midfielder crosses the centerline. At that moment, the midfielder is 25 to 30 yards from attackman 1. The "early" call doesn't mean that the midfielder has to throw the ball to attackman 1 immediately. It just means that the offense is in an "early" set: The midfielder can run downfield and throw to attackman 1 when he's ready to give up the ball. It's up to the man with the ball (in this case, the midfielder) to make the right decision. Remember that the man who has the ball is ultimately responsible for the ball. All offensive players are encouraged to call for the ball, but it's up to the man with the ball to make the right decision on whether a teammate is open. Some players often call for the ball when they are not open.

Draw Situation As mentioned earlier, the "draw" call is used when a defender is splitting coverage between two offensive players; the play is designed to force the defender to commit to one of the offensive players—usually the ball carrier. If the midfielder has a defender close on his back (defender 4), attackman 1 will make the "draw" call (see figure 12.25). All the decision making is in the hands of attackman 1, and he will use hand signals for "draw." If

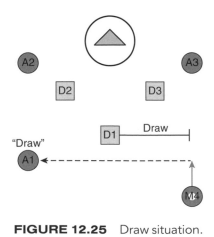

FIGURE 12.25 Draw situation.

the offensive midfielder bringing the ball down the field is handling a long-pole stick, the draw play is usually called no matter what. The offense doesn't want to use an "early" call and have the ball going back to the long-pole offensive midfielder. If the long-pole midfielder gives the ball up early, defender 1 will hold, and this puts a long-pole midfielder into a position where he is a point attackman, which is not a long-pole midfielder's strength.

There are exceptions to this rule. If a team has a very talented long-pole offensive midfielder, he might be effective on the "early" call. The midfielder would throw the ball to the point attackman and then get a return pass for a shot at the goal.

If the midfielder chooses to pass to attackman 1 on the draw play, as shown in figure 12.26, the midfielder must first get the point defender (defender 1) to commit to him, but he should not let defender 1 get into his gloves. The midfielder has to make defender 1 take one or two steps toward him and turn his hips to the ball. He can't allow defender 1 to play two defenders: attackman 1 and the midfielder. Once defender 1 commits, the midfielder turns and looks at attackman 1's stick target. Attackman 1 needs to give a good target just like a catcher in baseball. When it's time to give the ball up to attackman 1, the midfielder turns his body, looks at the target, and delivers the ball on target with a 10-yard pass. This is not the time for a deceptive look-away pass. He delivers the ball, slows down, and is ready for a return pass. He keeps his stick in his right hand.

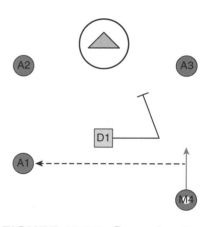

FIGURE 12.26 Draw situation: pass to the point attackman.

Midfielder's Second Option: Pass to Attackman 2

If the midfielder chooses to pass to attackman 2, as shown in figure 12.27, he first wants to get a feel for how aggressively defender 2 is going to slide to attackman 1. He wants to keep defender 2 honest on his slides. The midfielder should look at defender 2 and attackman 2 and see if defender 2 is cheating on his slide to attackman 1. If defender 2 sees the midfielder looking at him, defender 2 may decide to hold. Defender 2 may worry about getting beat by attackman 2's underneath move. If so, this would buy more time for the point attack (attackman 1). If defender 2 is cheating a lot, then the midfielder can pump fake to attackman 1 and feed underneath to attackman 2. Unfortunately, the skip pass from the midfielder

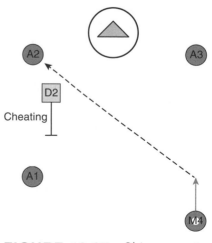

FIGURE 12.27 Skip pass to attackman 2.

to attackman 2 is an "all or nothing" pass. It's either a home run play or a strikeout.

Remember, the offense can use deception in the transition game. For example, when the midfielder is coming down the field, he may look at attackman 1. He makes it appear to defender 2 that he is going to make a lazy pass to attackman 1. Defender 2 takes off prematurely on his slide to attackman 1. The midfielder then skip passes to attackman 2. He sets up defender 2 by getting his attention. He makes it look as if he is going to make a lazy pass that defender 2 can intercept, but then he zips it behind him to attackman 2 (see figure 12.28).

Point Attackman Catches the Ball

Attackman 1 should go at a 45-degree angle, meet the ball parallel to the restraining line, and catch the ball on the tangent of the crease (see figure 12.29). If defender 2 is coming at attackman 1 out of control, this creates a great opportunity for a split dodge and a 3v2 break. A dodge in this situation keeps defender 2 honest. Attackman 1 needs to see space, see openings, and feel for the passing lanes. Finding an open lane is mostly the responsibility of the off-ball offensive players, but it's also the responsibility of the man with the ball. Attackman 1 never wants to catch the ball while standing still; he needs to be a moving target for defender 2.

Point Attackman's First Option: Diagonal Pass to Attackman 3

Attackman 1's first look is a diagonal pass to attackman 3 (see figure 12.30). To cover the passing lane from attackman 1 to attackman 3, defender 1 must stop on his slide to the midfielder, perform a drop step, and then go opposite. This is the toughest job for the close defense to manage. Some defenses

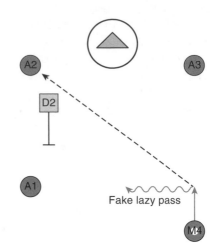

FIGURE 12.28 Deceptive pass to attackman 2.

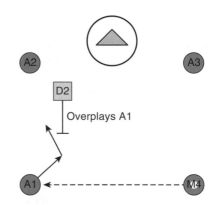

FIGURE 12.29 Point attackman catches the pass.

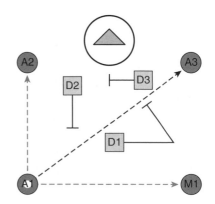

FIGURE 12.30 Point attackman's diagonal pass to attackman 3.

drag defender 3 across the crease until defender 1 gets back into the passing lane, but most teams can't afford to drag defender 3. Attackman 1 needs to read defender 3. Defender 3's crease positioning will determine whether attackman 1 will attempt to pass to attackman 2 OR attackman 3: If defender 3 is on the right side of the crease, attackman 1 will pass to attackman 3. If defender 3 is on the left side, the pass will go to attackman 2. Attackman 1 is keying in on defender 3 and is not really looking at his defender (defender 2).

Point Attackman's Second Option: Return Pass to Midfielder 4

Attackman 1's second look is a return pass to the midfielder. Midfielder 4 should keep his stick in his right hand. If he receives a cross-chest pass, having the stick in his right hand sets up his strength and allows his body to protect his stick from any defenders behind him. If he switches hands to his left hand, he will lose his strength and stick protection. After receiving the ball, midfielder 4 can throw a diagonal pass to attackman 2, throw a pass to attackman 3, or pass back to attackman 1.

Attackman 3 Catches the Ball From the Point

Attackman 3 has two options for getting into scoring position based on reading defender 1 (see figure 12.31). Attackman 3's first move is underneath. If defender 1 can't get back into that passing lane, attackman 3 goes underneath, looking for a feed and a shot. However, if defender 1 gets back into the passing lane quickly, then attackman 3 "shows" underneath but goes opposite. Attackman 3 pops out, looking for a feed behind defender 1, and takes a 7-yard shot.

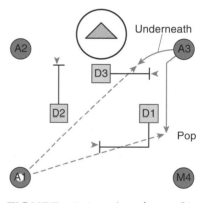

FIGURE 12.31 Attackman 3's two options.

Transition is a key component of lacrosse offense. Transition offense involves many principles, including turnovers, ball possession, and ball movement. Turnovers play a large part in the transition game. This chapter described three common situations that illustrate the impact of turnovers: midline play, goalie saves, and open-field scenarios. The basis of transition is taking advantage of a 2v1 somewhere on the field. When this happens, the close attack must react and get into their triangle positions around the goal so they are ready to take advantage of the play. Most transition opportunities occur between the restraining lines. The classic break in lacrosse is the 4v3 fast break, and this chapter examined how the various principles are put into use.

CHAPTER THIRTEEN

TRANSITION DEFENSE

Transition defense, like transition offense, has two components. Transition defense may involve managing an all-even movement of the opposing team (neither team has a numerical advantage) from your offensive side of the field to your defensive side of the field. Transition defense may also involve defending *the* opposing team when they have a man-advantage or break situation that gives them a great opportunity to score a goal. For the defense, the objective is to limit any breaks and make the offense play 6v6. Transition defense in lacrosse is like transition defense in basketball: You're trying to beat your opponent back up the court so you can set up your defense.

Principles of Transition Defense

Lacrosse players need to understand the core principles of transition defense. These principles include ball possession, defending ball movement, communication, and the value of numbers on the field. Team defenses should try to get the ball back but not at the cost of risking a larger break for the opponent. Defenses want to force the offense to move the ball across the field instead of vertically up the field. Defenses want more bodies or numbers in the defensive area to counter any numerical advantage the opponent may have.

Ball Possession

By definition, your team is playing transition defense when the opposing team has gained possession of the ball through a turnover or save. You should try to get the ball back but not at the risk of creating a man-advantage for your opponent. In transition defense, players need to be smart, aggressive, and athletic. As a defender, you want to turn the ball carrier back whenever possible. You can often use the sidelines as an extra teammate to force the opponent to pass the ball backward.

When defending breaks, you need to play the percentages. You usually can't prevent the offense from shooting, but you can force them to shoot low-percentage shots. You want to force the offense to shoot the ball from as far away as possible. If you get a piece of the shooter's gloves, that's even better. The offensive player may get a shot, but he must make it from the outside and must try to make it under pressure. The defense is trying to prevent high-percentage shots and layups.

Defending Ball Movement

In transition, your opponent will be trying to move the ball upfield quickly to take advantage of any breaks. For your defense, the task is to slow down the opponent and limit any breaks. You want to force your opponent to pass the ball across the field instead of up the field. Again, you should use the sidelines whenever possible as an extra teammate to force the ball backward.

Numbers

Transition lacrosse is all about numbers. Offenses want low numbers, and defenses want high numbers—on the field and near the goal. The greater the numbers on defense and the more defenders the team can get back into the hole, the lower the chances that the offense will score a goal. For example, a 6v5 is better for the defense than a 3v2. On defense, you want to get as many teammates back into the hole as possible. If your team has six players in the hole, then it doesn't matter what numbers your opponent has because you can match up with them. In a worst-case scenario, you want to make sure all six of your defenders have fallen in toward the hole and you're playing 6v6. If the offense gets a shot, it misses the goal, and the ball goes out of bounds, the opposing team will retain possession, but the defense has done its job. By that time, the cavalry has arrived—the defense can now regroup, match up, and play settled 6v6.

Communication

In a game situation, defenders should call out the jersey number of the opponent they are covering before, during, and after play has been suspended (this is called checking up). Because every player has a different number, this helps ensure that two defenders are not playing the same opponent. In a transition situation, a defender may end up playing more than one opponent, so it's even more important for defenders to communicate about whom they are covering. If defenders fail to communicate, this can give the offense a temporary advantage. When defenders are sliding or scrambling, they need to minimize any lapses in defensive coverage.

Functions of Team Defense

Consider this scenario: The opposing team has caused a turnover via a goalie save or has gained possession of the ball from an intercepted pass, a take-away check, or a loose-ball pickup. Each unit of the team defense has a job to do to react to the loss of possession, play smart athletic defense, and attempt to regain possession. Let's look at the role of each defensive unit in this situation.

Close Attack

Most teams depend on their close attack to do their aggressive riding. Because the three close-attack players are matched up against the opposing goalie and three defenders, each attackman plays two opponents (see figure 13.1). If the goalie makes a save, the close attack's first job is to screen the goalie with their body and stick to take away any quick and accurate outlet passes. After the first pass, the close attack's responsibility is to chase down and turn back any ball movement up to the centerline. Riding is about desire and attitude. The riding executed by the close attack is analogous to fore-checking in hockey, which is about tenacity and taking good angles. Riding attackmen are like rushing defensive linemen reacting to a screen pass. Football linemen have to brake, turn, and chase down the play.

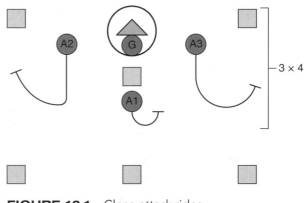

FIGURE 13.1 Close attack rides.

Midfield Unit

Most teams tend to be more conservative because they don't want to take a lot of chances in the open field and risk turnovers. They don't want to make "all or nothing" heroic plays that could result in giving the opponent a man-up advantage (not via penalty). They don't want to create unsettled situations for the opponent by making foolish decisions. Therefore, midfielders rarely slide upfield when they don't have much opportunity to steal the ball. Midfielders must know when to concede the clear, turn and drop back, and play 6v6 defense (figure 13.2). Whether it's an all-even transition or a break situation, defenders need to set up in the hole.

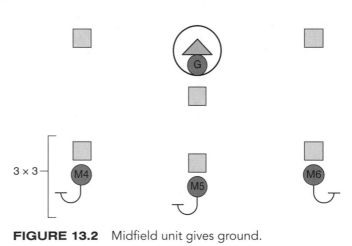

FIGURE 13.2 Midfield unit gives ground.

Close Defense

The close defense unit needs to closely guard the opponent's close-attack players from the midline back to the goal (figure 13.3). If these defenders are looking to challenge for the ball, they need at least a 50-50 chance to secure possession of the ball. When in doubt, they play defense first. The most important task for this group is to get back into the hole and minimize any breaks.

Goalkeeper

The goalkeeper is the quarterback of the defense and the eyes of the defense. The

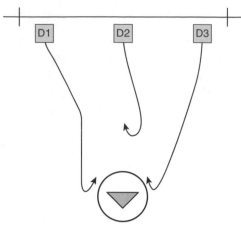

FIGURE 13.3 Close defense unit gets back into the hole.

goalie recognizes the break situation and communicates the proper defensive formation. For example, a defender may slip in the open field; a defender may break his stick and have to get a replacement before he can continue to play defense; or the opposing team may gain possession on an intercepted pass or loose-ball pickup and have a numbers advantage between the restraining lines. In these circumstances, the defense is in a scramble situation. Whenever there is a break situation, the goalkeeper will recognize the situation and yell "Fire" or "Break." If the goalie yells "Break," then there is no debating the issue—the defense immediately reacts and drops back to the hole.

Once the defenders hear the "Fire" call, everybody must turn and sprint (fire), dropping back into the hole. As soon as defenders hear "Break" or "Fire," they are no longer playing one man. They're playing a zone. At this point, it doesn't matter what defensive package they are in; all bets are off, and the Xs and Os go out the window. The defenders need to sprint back into the hole, jam the inside, and take away a dangerous situation. The "Fire" call communicates this message to the defenders: "We are in trouble here, and we're trying to stop the bleeding until we're all-even, playing 6v6 team defense." Depending on the break, the goalkeeper will yell out the following defensive calls:

- 5v4 break: Goalie yells, "Five on box."
- 4v3 break: Goalie yells, "Four on triangle."
- 3v2 break: Goalie yells, "Three on stack."

Open Field

Defenses can encounter a man advantage for the opposing team in either their offensive half of the field or their defensive side of the field. In either case, much of defensive transition is in the open field and a defender in the open field needs to set realistic goals. If the defender gets too aggressive, he will open up the lanes for layups. If the defender is not aggressive enough, then the opponent will have no resistance clearing the ball from one end of the field to the other.

In the open field, the defense is at a distinct disadvantage because the opposing team has a lot of field to work with; therefore, the defender is forced to give ground in order to better defend this situation. Nearer the goal, the defender will eventually be forced to commit to the ball carrier.

Offensive Half of Field

In your offensive half of the field your opponent has both the ball possession due to a turnover and a numerical advantage of 7 versus 6 with the addition of the goalkeeper in the action. However, your opponent will be controlling the ball with three long-stick, close defenseman, who may or may not be agile ball handlers, and a goalkeeper who may or may not want to come away from his goal. In your offensive half of the field, a defender needs to remember that he is playing a zone and essentially playing two opponents at the same time while always rotating into the flight of the ball. The defender needs to anticipate the next pass and get involved with the defensive rotation. In the offensive side of the field, some teams try to take away the ball and create their own break while other teams do not. We recommend you not try to take the ball away and wait for them to make a mistake.

Defensive Half of Field

In your defensive half of the field, your opponent no longer has an inherent numerical advantage because of the offside rule, but they can still pose a threat due to any unsettled situation. If the defender gets disoriented and can't find his man, the first place he should look is on the crease. If the defender is trailing his man, he should not chase his man unless he thinks he can check him. If the defender is trailing the ball, he shouldn't chase the ball because someone will be sliding to the ball. The defender wants to find any open man so any teammate positioned near the crease doesn't have to slide upfield. As a defender is getting near the crease, he should not stare at the ball

First, he should pay close attention to any opponents near the crease. Second, he should look away from the ball and see what can hurt him coming down the backside with any possible backdoor cuts. Third, if he doesn't need to pick up anybody off ball, he can watch the ball and check up on a single opponent (figure 13.4). "Checking up" means clearly identifying an opponent's number and actively defending his movements.

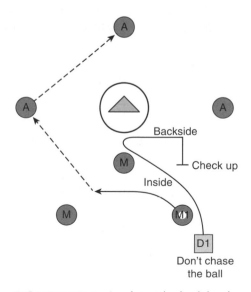

FIGURE 13.4 Look inside, look backside, then check up.

Types of Breaks

The defensive transition game involves defending various types of breaks: 6v5, 5v4, 4v3, 3v2, and 2v1. The defense wants to compress the area that they have to defend by getting back into the hole (see figure 13.5). The hole is an area stretching 12 yards out from the GLE and directly in front of the goal. If defenders beat the ball back to their goal, they should go to the hole and see if they need to pick up anybody inside. Defenders should always be quicker to get into the hole and slower to come out to play the opposing team on the perimeter (quick in, slow out). A defender must get into the hole, make sure this is a secure area, and then check out to his man. The defender shouldn't be looking for his man out at the restraining line even though he might be there. Transition defense is based on "circling the wagons" around the goal. The defensive team wants to pack as many of their players in the hole as they possibly can in transition and unsettled situations; the players then check out. The defense should maintain a tight formation so that there are not a lot of passing lanes. This also maximizes the effects of slides. Defenders should have their sticks up in order to take away passing lanes. Defenders have their head on a swivel, and everybody is looking around. Everybody is talking, listening, and helping each other out. The defense is working together as a unit, and nobody needs to be heroic and try to make a big play.

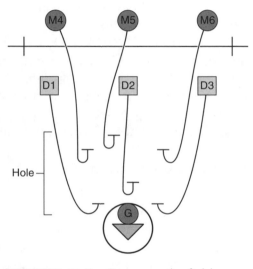

FIGURE 13.5 Compress the field.

6v5 Break

A 6v5 break (figure 13.6) may not be as apparent to the defense as other breaks because of all the player traffic. All defenders need to identify their matchups and communicate regarding which offensive player they are defending. If there is a 6v5 break, the defense has numbers to compensate for being one down on defense. However, if the defense is not aware of the break situation, a 2v1 opportunity can happen very quickly. The trailing defender should not yell "All even" until he is inside and checking out. At that point, the team is playing 6v6 team defense.

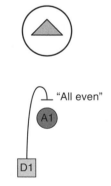

FIGURE 13.6 Defending a 6v5.

5v4 Break

Against this break, the defense uses a box formation (figure 13.7). Typically, the close defense sets up in a triangle, and defender 4 comes down and sets up in the box. Defender 1 or defender 4 must first stop the ball carrier and make him pass. On the first pass, the defense will rotate into the flight of the ball. The defense must make sure they have the crease covered and have the ball carrier covered because he is the most dangerous player. The adjacent defenders should be in skip lanes. The defense is leaving the farthest man from the ball open, but defenders are trying to split two attackers if they can. *On each pass, the defense continues to rotate into the ball.* Low defenders stay in front of the GLE because the defense doesn't go behind the goal. If an opposing attackman drives to the cage from behind the goal, a help-side defender may slide across the crease (coma slide) to play this attackman. If an off-ball player cuts inside, a defender should cover him and release him to a crease defender so that the first defender can get back into the rotation. If a defender is trailing the ball, he will go away from the flow of the ball.

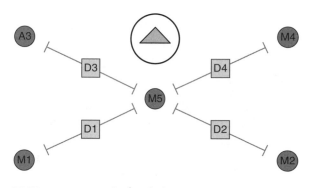

FIGURE 13.7 Defending a 5v4.

4v3 Break

In this situation, the defensive formation is a tight triangle (figure 13.8). Defender 1 is out top covering the point attackman (attackman 1). Defender 2 is down low covering the right-handed shooter (attackman 2). Defender 3 is down low covering the left-handed shooter (attackman 3). Everybody will slide to the inside hub (imaginary hat) first and then out to the opponent. Sliding in this manner keeps the triangle tight and helps with the passing lane angles.

Defender 1 is positioned at 12 yards out. Defender 1 slides across to pick up midfielder 4. His objective is to force midfielder 4 to give up the ball to attackman 1. If midfielder 4 doesn't pass, then defender 1 must eventually stop the ball. If midfielder 4 starts to wind up at 12 yards, the defender would invite the shot and try to get a piece of his gloves. A shot at that distance is not a high-percentage

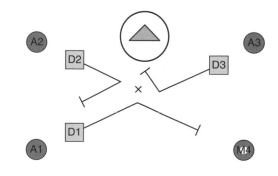

FIGURE 13.8 Defending a 4v3.

shot. If midfielder 4 passes the ball to attackman 1, defender 1 will slide inside to the hub and then down to attackman 3. The slide from midfielder 4 to attackman 3 is the toughest one to execute on the defensive break. Defender 1 has to slide across the field, stop midfielder 4, drop-step, and with two steps get into the passing lane from attackman 1 to attackman 3.

When midfielder 4 passes to attackman 1, defender 2 slides inside to the hub and then out to attackman 1. Defender 2 wants to come out at a good angle and under control with his stick in port position to knock down passes and poke-check when within range. The last thing he wants is to be dodged by attackman 1.

When midfielder 4 throws the ball, defender 3 slides to the inside hub and then out to attackman 2. When defenders slide, they must slide under control so they don't get dodged. Some teams like to drag defender 3 across the crease to help out with the passing lane from attackman 1 to attackman 3, but defender 3 should not screen the goalkeeper.

3v2 Break

The defensive formation is a stack (figure 13.9). Defender 2 is positioned on the crease, and defender 1 is positioned 10 to 12 yards out. Defender 1's job is to hold and stop the ball at 12 yards out. On the first pass, defender 2 takes the ball, and defender 1 turns to the inside, gets down, and looks opposite.

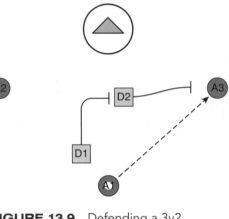

FIGURE 13.9 Defending a 3v2.

2v1 Break

When defending a 2v1 near the goal (figure 13.10), the defender needs to drop down into the crease and compress his area of the defense. He wants to make his two opponents continue to come inside where their area to handle the ball is tight (instead of being out top where they have too much space). The defender is trying to buy some time so that help can arrive. The defender should use a V-up body position: He opens up so he can see both the ball (attackman 1) and the other man (attackman 2). He must not stare at the ball. He's playing "cat and mouse"

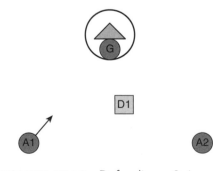

FIGURE 13.10 Defending a 2v1.

between attackman 1 and attackman 2. On a 2v1, the defender is not playing the man with the ball (attackman 1). He is shading toward attackman 2 and is really playing attackman 2. Although the defender is off ball and can't make contact with the ball carrier (attackman 1), his stick is in a port position, ready to knock down a pass. As the defender closes, he is staying in that port position until he can get a piece of the ball carrier's glove. Eventually, the defender has to stop the ball. As attackman 1 gets closer, the defender will have to come in and get a piece of the attacker's gloves, whether attackman 1 throws or shoots the ball. The defender will eventually have to slide to the ball, but he doesn't want to do it too early. He doesn't want to make the decision for the man with the ball. The defender should make the ball carrier decide what his best option will be: pass or shoot.

Transition defense is based on certain fundamentals, including ball possession, defending ball movement, communication, and trying to get more numbers near the goal to counteract the break situation. When your team commits a turnover, each unit has a function in trying to regain possession in a smart, efficient, and non-risky manner. Transition defense boils down to how a team and its individual players handle a 2v1 advantage for the other team. In the open field, defenders are more likely to give ground first before challenging the ball carrier. Near the goal, the defenders might not have that choice. Usually, the best policy is to compress the field so that defenders need to use minimal slides to chase the ball. This chapter examined various break situations and showed the importance of communication, patience, and working as a coordinated unit.

REFERENCES

Chapter 1

U.S. Lacrosse. 2011. Participation survey. www.uslacrosse.org.

Weyand, A., and M. Roberts. 1965. *Lacrosse story*. Baltimore, MD: H&A Herman.

ABOUT THE AUTHORS

Don Zimmerman has over 31 years of experience in coaching lacrosse and has been a Division I college head coach for over 25 years. Coach Zimmerman's career has taken him to Princeton University, the University of North Carolina, Johns Hopkins University, Loyola University Maryland, and the University of Maryland at Baltimore County (UMBC), a position he has held since 1994.

Zimmerman was instrumental in winning NCAA national championships at North Carolina (1981 and 1982) and Johns Hopkins (1984, 1985, and 1987). He led the UMBC Retrievers to four consecutive NCAA Division I tournament appearances from 2006 to 2009, a feat accomplished for the first time in the school's Division I lacrosse history.

Zimmerman is considered one of the preeminent teachers of the game and has taught lacrosse on four continents: North America, South America, Europe, and Asia. In 2002 he was honored with induction into the Greater Baltimore Chapter of the United States Lacrosse Hall of Fame. Zimmerman was named America East Conference Coach of the Year by his colleagues in both 2008 and 2009 and was the 2008 Coach of the Year in *LaxPower* men's lacrosse Fan Awards. He achieved career win 200 in 2010 and is 10th among active coaches with 202 victories in 24 campaigns.

Zimmerman lives in Baltimore, Maryland.

Peter England was a member of Coach Zimmerman's staff at John Hopkins University. Since 1991 he has been an advanced team scout for the Johns Hopkins lacrosse program, working with coaches Tony Seamon (1991-1998), John Haus (1999-2000), and Dave Pietramala (2001-present). England lives in Glen Burnie, Maryland.